Discoverability in Digital Repositories

T0386484

While most discoverability evaluation studies in the Library and Information Science field discuss the intersection of discovery layers and library systems, this book looks specifically at digital repositories, examining discoverability from the lenses of system structure, user searches, and external discovery avenues.

Discoverability, the ease with which information can be found by a user, is the cornerstone of all successful digital information platforms. Yet, most digital repository practitioners and researchers lack a holistic and comprehensive understanding of how and where discoverability happens. This book brings together current understandings of user needs and behaviors and poses them alongside a deeper examination of digital repositories around the theme of discoverability. It examines discoverability in digital repositories from both user and system perspectives by exploring how users access content (including their search patterns and habits, need for digital content, effects of outreach, or integration with Wikipedia and other web-based tools) and how systems support or prevent discoverability through the structure or quality of metadata, system interfaces, exposure to search engines or lack thereof, and integration with library discovery tools.

Discoverability in Digital Repositories will be particularly useful to digital repository managers, practitioners, and researchers, metadata librarians, systems librarians, and user studies, usability, and user experience librarians. Additionally, and perhaps most prominently, this book is composed with the emerging practitioner in mind. Instructors and students in Library and Information Science and Information Management programs will benefit from this book that specifically addresses discoverability in digital repository systems and services.

Liz Woolcott is Associate Dean for research collections at Utah State University Libraries in Logan, Utah, USA, and Co-Founder of the Library Workflow Exchange.

Ali Shiri is Professor in the School of Library and Information Studies at the University of Alberta, Edmonton, Alberta, Canada. He teaches courses in the areas of digital libraries and information organization and retrieval, and he conducts research on digital libraries and repositories, search user interfaces, user interaction with digital information, learning and data analytics, and more recently artificial intelligence and ethics.

Routledge Guides to Practice in Libraries, Archives and Information Science

This series provides essential practical guides for those working in libraries, archives, and a variety of other information science professions around the globe.

Including authored and edited volumes, the series will help to enhance practitioners' and students' professional knowledge and will also encourage sharing of best practices between different countries, as well as between different types and sizes of organisations.

For more information about this series, please visit: www.routledge.com/Routledge-Guides-to-Practice-in-Libraries-Archives-and-Information-Science/book-series/RGPLAIS

Discoverability in Digital Repositories

Systems, Perspectives, and User Studies

Edited by
Liz Woolcott and Ali Shiri

Routledge
Taylor & Francis Group

LONDON AND NEW YORK

Cover image: Thanakorn Lappattaranan/Getty Images

First published 2023
by Routledge
4 Park Square, Milton Park, Abingdon, Oxon OX14 4RN

and by Routledge
605 Third Avenue, New York, NY 10158

Routledge is an imprint of the Taylor & Francis Group, an informa business

British Library Cataloguing-in-Publication Data
A catalogue record for this book is available from the British Library

Library of Congress Cataloging-in-Publication Data
Names: Woolcott, Liz, editor. | Shiri, Ali, 1968- editor.
Title: Discoverability in digital repositories : systems, perspectives, and user studies / edited by Liz Woolcott, Ali Shiri.
Description: Milton Park, Abingdon, Oxon ; New York, NY : Routledge, 2023. | Series: Routledge guides to practice in libraries, archives and information science | Includes bibliographical references and index.
Identifiers: LCCN 2022059151 (print) | LCCN 2022059152 (ebook) | ISBN 9781032106595 (hardback) | ISBN 9781032106588 (paperback) | ISBN 9781003216438 (ebook)
Subjects: LCSH: Institutional repositories. | Digital libraries. | Electronic information resource searching.
Classification: LCC ZA4081.86 .D57 2023 (print) | LCC ZA4081.86 (ebook) | DDC 027—dc23/eng/20230113
LC record available at https://lccn.loc.gov/2022059151
LC ebook record available at https://lccn.loc.gov/2022059152

ISBN: 978-1-032-10659-5 (hbk)
ISBN: 978-1-032-10658-8 (pbk)
ISBN: 978-1-003-21643-8 (ebk)

DOI: 10.4324/9781003216438

Typeset in Times New Roman
by Apex CoVantage

To digital repository practitioners everywhere –
your work is visible, impactful, and important

Contents

Figures

Tables

Contributors

Mary Burke is a Ph.D. candidate in the University of North Texas' Interdisciplinary Information Science PhD program with a concentration in Linguistics. She serves as Curator for the Computational Resource for South Asian Languages (CoRSAL), a language archive hosted by the UNT Digital Library. Her work focuses on developing infrastructure for archiving endangered languages and promoting cross-disciplinary collaboration in fields like linguistics, information technologies, and education.

Danping Dong is Research Services Librarian at Singapore Management University and has seven years of experience working in scholarly communication. Her interests lie in repositories and CRIS systems, bibliometrics, and research data management.

Sharon Farnel (MLIS, PhD) is Head, Metadata Strategies at the University of Alberta Library, and Sessional Instructor in the University's Master of Library and Information Studies program. Her research interests are in critical knowledge organization, community-driven descriptive practices, and linked data for enhancing the discovery and use of cultural heritage resources. She is collaborating with colleagues at the Inuvialuit Cultural Centre in Inuvik to implement a culturally responsive metadata framework for the Inuvialuit Digital Library and to incorporate real-time digital storytelling features within it.

Teresa K. Hebron is Program Director for Mountain West Digital Library at the University of Utah's J. Willard Marriott Library. Her current research and work focus on large-scale metadata aggregation, metadata standards, and digital library administration. Her past work includes integrated library systems support, installation, and migration with an emphasis on public-facing web catalogs and discovery systems. Hebron is an alumna of the University of Michigan's School of Information.

Sara Hoover, MLIS, is Metadata and Scholarly Publishing Librarian at the Himmelfarb Health Sciences Library, The George Washington University. At Himmelfarb, she oversees their institutional repository, Health Sciences Research Commons, and chairs the library's Scholarly Communications committee. Prior to becoming a librarian, she worked in academic publishing.

Elizabeth Joan Kelly is Library Web and Applications Development Administrator at LOUIS: The Louisiana Library Network. Her primary responsibilities include managing the consortia's web presence, customizing user interfaces and search tools, analyzing usage data, and creating data visualizations to communicate assessment results and inform evidence-based decision-making. Kelly publishes and presents on archives, digital library assessment, and library pedagogy, and co-founded the DLF Digital Library Pedagogy group.

George Macgregor is a repository manager and technologist based at the University of Strathclyde, Glasgow (Scotland, UK). He works on repository and digital library developments, while also supporting institutional activities within Open Science, research discovery, and digital scholarship. George has a PhD in Computer and Information Sciences from the iSchool at the University of Strathclyde, specializing in topics surrounding resource discovery in digital content environments.

Anna Neatrour is Digital Initiatives Librarian at the University of Utah Marriott Library. She received her MLIS from the University of Illinois, Urbana-Champaign. Her research interests include metadata best practices, collaborative digitization, and collections as data.

Jenn Riley is Associate Dean, Digital Initiatives at McGill University Library in Montréal, where she leads library technology efforts including scholarly communication, digital scholarship, application development and management, resource discovery systems, and library web content. Jenn is interested in how technology is expanding and changing scholarship, advancing the preservation and discovery of digital content, and expanding access to research. She holds an MLS from Indiana University, an MA in Musicology from Indiana University, and a BM in Music Education from the University of Miami (FL).

Ali Shiri is Professor in the School of Library and Information Studies at the University of Alberta, Edmonton, Alberta, Canada, and is currently serving as Vice Dean of the Faculty of Graduate Studies and Research. He received his PhD in Information Science from the University of Strathclyde Department of Computer and Information Sciences in Glasgow, Scotland, in 2004. Ali has been teaching, researching, and writing about digital libraries and digital information interaction, knowledge organization, and data and learning analytics for the past two decades. In his current research, funded by the Social Sciences and Humanities Research Council of Canada, he is developing cultural heritage digital libraries and digital storytelling systems for the Inuit communities in Canada's Western Arctic.

Chee Hsien Aaron Tay is Lead, Data Services, at Singapore Management University Libraries. An academic librarian with over 15 years of experience, he has served in two academic libraries in Singapore in a variety of functions, including reference, cataloging, liaison, and analytics. He has interests in library discovery, bibliometrics, analytics, and more. He has been blogging his thoughts on librarianship at the award-winning blog *Aaron Tay's Musings about Librarianship* – https://musingsaboutlibrarianship.blogspot.com/ – since 2009 and tweets at @aarontay.

JoLinda Thompson, MLS, AHIP, is Systems Librarian at Himmelfarb Health Sciences Library, The George Washington University. She is the author of *Implementing Web-Scale Discovery Services: A Practical Guide for Librarians*, Rowman & Littlefield, 2014, and a number of peer-reviewed articles and presentations on discovery services in health sciences libraries. She has managed and developed discovery services at Himmelfarb Library since 2013.

Liz Woolcott is Associate Dean for research collections, formerly the Head of Cataloging and Metadata Services, for Utah State University Libraries. In the latter capacity she directed both the MAchine Readable Cataloging (MARC) and non-MARC metadata creation for the University Libraries. She is the co-founder of the Library Workflow Exchange and publishes and presents on workflow and assessment strategies for library technical services, digital content reuse, the impact of organizational structures on library work, and assessing the impact of metadata structures on user search behavior.

Oksana L. Zavalina is Professor at the University of North Texas College of Information (Department of Information Science). She studies user interactions with digital repositories: most recently, user needs for information organization in language archives, how these needs are currently met, and how they could be addressed better. Her research interests include metadata management, descriptive and authority metadata evaluation in brick-and-mortar and digital libraries and archives, with a focus on subject representation, collection-level description, Linked Data applications, and so on.

Acknowledgments or Credits List

We would like to acknowledge the contributions of many individuals who helped with the development of this book. Our deepest thanks and admiration first go to the talented chapter authors who lent their time and expertise to this manuscript (noted here in the order of their chapters): George Macgregor, Sharon Farnel, Jenn Riley, Anna Neatrour, Teresa K. Hebron, Oksana L. Zavalina, Mary Burke, JoLinda Thompson, Sara Hoover, Elizabeth Joan Kelly, Danping Dong, and Chee Hsien Aaron Tay. In light of the many hats you all wear and the high demand for your time and daily commitments, we truly appreciate that you agreed to collaborate on this project with us. It could not have happened without your collective expertise.

We would also like to express our most profound thanks and gratitude to Tanvi Mohile, whose copyediting and indexing skills made this book consistent and more readable. Thank you for your time, incredible attention to detail, and impressive organizational chops.

Thank you to our home institutions University of Alberta and Utah State University for their support during the two years this book took shape.

And most importantly, we would like to express our gratitude to our families for their encouragement and support. To Farzaneh Salehi, Kimia Shiri, and Bella Shiri, thank you so much for your love and support. To John Woolcott, Thomas Woolcott, Mary Alice Woolcott, and Henry Woolcott, thank you for putting up with the long hours and providing so much love, laughter, and comic relief. You make life grand. And to Gary Bradshaw and Cheryl Bradshaw, thank you for the lifelong love, support, and encouragement you unfailingly give.

Introduction

Discoverability

With the emergence of large-scale digital libraries and archives and institutional, research, and data repositories, the need for discoverability has become increasingly urgent. To ensure the effective management, accessibility, and discoverability of data, information, and digital objects in digital repositories, it is particularly important to develop a foundational and coherent understanding of the nature, types, functions, and user experiences of digital repositories, and of the factors affecting their discoverability.

Discoverability, the ease with which a user can find information, is the cornerstone of all successful digital information platforms. From search engines to Wikipedia to digital libraries, the ability of the platform to sift through millions of information objects and select the most relevant content is crucial in this age of digital information overload. As the gold standard for searchability has shifted from a simple focus on uploading material online to a greater understanding of the role of metadata, levels of description, and exposure to search engines, the digital repository manager/practitioner needs to develop a holistic and comprehensive understanding of how and where discoverability occurs. Furthermore, they need to be equipped with an understanding and knowledge of the ways in which they can evaluate the platforms they sustain and how their time and effort to present digital content online could be used most effectively.

Over the past two decades, various terms have been used to refer to systems that support the effective and efficient discovery of information, data, and items in libraries, archives, and repositories, including federated search systems, discovery systems, discovery tools, discovery layers, web-scale discovery systems, broadcast search, and meta search systems. With the unprecedented growth of digital data and information, discoverability of scholarly and credible information has become an area of research and development. In the context of libraries and archives, discoverability aims to ensure the full-scale findability and retrievability of various types of content, including books, journal articles, images, digitized collections, theses and dissertations, research data, software, code, and animation. Dempsey (2017) provides a proactive and compelling argument about the differences between discovery and discoverability, noting that the former aims to

DOI: 10.4324/9781003216438-1

make library resources known to its users, whereas the latter indicates a broader community perspective, allowing created materials to be shared institutionally and beyond via effective disclosure through search engine optimization and syndication of metadata to network hubs or specialist network-level resources. Such a conceptualization of discoverability provides a new perspective for digital information managers and enables them to view content in digital libraries, archives, and repositories as a dynamic and interconnected construct that could be shared, disseminated, used, and reused. Nonetheless, discoverability in the digital environment also poses new challenges and offers new opportunities to be innovative. How do we design discovery platforms that are web-scale, interoperable, and linked data enabled, that support the creation of knowledge graphs, that benefit from search engine optimization, and that provide positive user experiences? This is a multifaceted question that addresses the various themes and topics informing and impacting how we conceptualize, implement, and operationalize discovery platforms. In an attempt to answer this question, the chapters in this book are designed to provide a comprehensive understanding of discoverability by including topics such as metadata, linked data, search and browsing functionalities, user search behavior and system and metadata interoperability, search engine optimization, Wiki data integration, and visibility in scholarly search engines.

The proliferation of commercial as well as open-source discovery systems has resulted in the adoption, evaluation, and improvement of these systems. Various aspects of discovery systems have therefore been studied in academic digital libraries (Eun Oh & Colón-Aguirre, 2019; Guajardo et al., 2017), public digital libraries (Shiri & Oliphant, 2017; Wells, 2020; Heaton & Woolcott, 2021), and institutional repositories (IRs; Spezi et al., 2015). Recent research on the discoverability of health data in digital data repositories has focused on such topics as searching, browsing, and navigation functionalities, the richness of metadata description practices, and metadata-based filtering mechanisms (Thornton & Shiri, 2021). Macgregor (2019) argues that

> Whilst many of the prominent repository platforms (e.g., EPrints, DSpace, Digital Commons, OJS, etc.) now provide basic out-of-the-box support for discovery and interoperability with key academic tools, including meeting Google Scholar inclusion guidelines, wide variation still remains in the relative visibility and discoverability of repository content.
>
> (p. 2)

Digital Repositories

The terms *digital repositories*, *digital libraries*, and *digital archives* have been widely, and sometimes interchangeably, used in the literature of digital library research and development and digital preservation. Many libraries, archives, museums, and galleries, as well as numerous scholarly and academic institutions, use the term *digital repository* to refer to a digital platform that sustainably supports the collection, organization, preservation, and dissemination of digital data/

information/object/artifact and that supports and meets the information needs of a diverse range of user communities. The Open Archival Information System (OAIS) Reference Model provides a broad and abstract framework that describes the functions of a repository as follows: "An OAIS is an archive, consisting of an organization, which may be part of a larger organization, of people and systems that has accepted the responsibility to preserve information and make it available for a designated community" (Lee, 2010, p. 4024). Although this is a broad definition, it nonetheless covers the key functions of a repository, which remain common among the various types of digital repositories. Digital repositories may vary by content type, coverage, primary functionality, or target user group (Heery & Anderson, 2005). A detailed typology of digital repositories is presented in Chapter 1.

Over the past 25 years, a growing number of digital repositories have been developed, evaluated, and evolved. One of the most well-known examples of digital repositories is IRs. Crow (2002) notes that IRs are characterized by the fact that they are digital, institutionally defined, scholarly, cumulative and perpetual, open access, and interoperable. The proliferation of institutional and other types of digital repositories has resulted in the development of criteria and attributes for trusted digital repositories, whose mission is to provide their designated communities with reliable, long-term access to managed digital resources in the present and the future (RLG-OCLC, 2002). More recently, the digital repository community developed a set of guiding principles to demonstrate digital repository trustworthiness. These principles include Transparency, Responsibility, User focus, Sustainability, and Technology, long-term and reliable preservation, and access to digital data and repositories (Lin et al., 2020).

The Purpose of This Book

This book addresses an evolving field of research and development: discoverability of digital repositories. One of the primary gaps in the area of discoverability is the lack of a holistic approach for the evaluation of discoverability in digital repositories from the perspective of both the user and the system. Most evaluations of discoverability discuss digital repositories as a small piece in a larger digital information ecosystem, with greater emphasis placed on discovery layers and library systems, or more frequently, how the two intersect. Discovery layers and library systems provide discoverability for a different type of information resource than digital repositories. Library systems often reflect purchased material typically composed of published or produced information sources such as books, articles, videos, and so on, that are usually described with a specific metadata schema such as MAchine Readable Cataloging.

This book, however, will focus particularly on the digital repository. Digital repository material differs from traditional library material in content, description, and life cycle. It often includes primary resources, such as digitized archival objects, data sets, or article pre-prints. These materials are housed in platforms separate from purchased or produced information. They are represented and described by different metadata schemas (typically Dublin Core or Metadata Object Description Standard [MODS]) and are managed by practitioners with a different skill set and responsibilities than those that manage traditional library material.

The purpose of this book, therefore, is to provide a multifaceted examination of how discoverability occurs in digital repositories, specifically focusing on the perspectives of both systems and users alongside a robust discussion of the current scholarship on user search experience. This approach will be particularly useful to digital repository managers and practitioners, who often have to sift through monographs and articles about discovery layers and library systems to find the specific area of interest that is related to their work. The key characteristics of this collection include the following:

1. Particular focus on digital repositories and detailed treatment of their unique structure, content, and the lifecycle that impacts discoverability
2. Coverage of both introductory explanations and deeper analysis of user studies, system design, metadata architecture, and integration with web-based resources, making the book useful and applicable to both emerging and experienced professionals
3. Case studies that examine how repository structures, metadata, and user search habits integrate with the larger discovery ecosystem
4. Recommended methods, approaches, tools, resources, and services to support and enhance the discoverability and visibility of digital content

While developing this collection, we have paid particular attention to its structure and content to ensure that the key and current issues surrounding discoverability in digital repositories are covered. More importantly, we specifically invited authors that have a well-established research record and relevant professional experience to contribute to the collection in order to address both the theoretical and technical aspects of discoverability.

Fourteen authors, from the United States, Canada, UK, and Singapore, have contributed to this collection. In order to create an engaging, collegial, and inclusive experience for all the contributing authors, we held two rounds of Zoom meetings with them in June and September of 2021. During these meetings, we provided an overview of the book chapters, discussed chapter guidelines and formatting, reviewed the timeline for completing the first and second drafts of each chapter, and introduced the process of receiving feedback. All authors were provided access to a shared Google Drive that offered them the opportunity to view each other's chapters, which helped them structure and format their individual chapters. This approach was particularly useful to ensure consistency, coherence, and clarity of content.

This book will appeal to a broad range of audiences. It will serve as a useful and informative resource to digital and IR managers, digital librarians, metadata librarians, systems and usability librarians, and those interested in linked data and search engine optimization for digital collections in libraries and archives. Additionally, and perhaps most prominently, this book will serve as a valuable source for emerging practitioners who are new to the concept of discoverability and digital repositories. Finally, we believe that educators and students in Library and Information Science, Information and Data Management, and Data Science programs will benefit from this book as it covers a wide array of topics, techniques, resources, and recommended practices related to the discoverability of digital data, information, objects, and artifacts.

Chapter Summaries

Discoverability in Digital Repositories: Systems, Perspectives, and User Studies is divided into two parts, consisting of a total of eight chapters. The chapters present international, diverse, and current perspectives of discoverability in digital repositories. Part 1 focuses on the operation of digital repositories, considering both systems and metadata perspectives. The chapters in this part explore common repositories used by libraries and their similarities and differences in terms of system design and functionalities, metadata schemas in common digital repository platforms, and the structure and key components of repositories and introduce linked data and their role in the discoverability of digital material. Part 2 provides a foundational understanding of how users conduct searches and discover digital content. It addresses the ways in which digital repository managers identify user communities and solicit feedback. It also examines emerging scholarship on the use and reuse of digital content by communities to further understand the discoverability needs and expectations of user groups.

Chapter 1 by George Macgregor, titled "Digital Repositories and Discoverability: Definitions and Typology", provides a coherent introduction and background to digital repositories, their emergence, and their typical characteristics. It offers a useful typology of digital repositories and their content. Furthermore, it explores the concept of discoverability as a central construct for our understanding of repositories and the principal attributes of repository discoverability, including consideration of the most significant digital repository discoverability technologies and users' typical routes to repository content discovery.

In Chapter 2, titled "Understanding Repository Functionality and Structure", Sharon Farnel explores discoverability in the context of digital repositories and the ease with which users can find and access resources. She provides an insight into the ways in which discoverability from within the repository is impacted by metadata and knowledge organization; searching, faceting, and relevance ranking; and multilingual functionality and usability across devices. This chapter also includes a brief discussion of the shared characteristics of common digital repository platforms and the features or functionalities that influence their discoverability.

Jenn Riley's Chapter 3, titled "Understanding the Role of Metadata in a Digital Repository", takes a holistic approach to metadata in the cultural heritage sector and provides an overarching scope of the metadata universe. It covers different types of standards and guidance, including conceptual models, structure standards, content standards, controlled vocabularies, authority files, classification schemes, and markup languages. The chapter also provides a useful historical overview of metadata and how the associated standards and technologies have evolved over the years. The actual and potential value and application of metadata in digital repositories are discussed in this chapter.

In Chapter 4, "Understanding Linked Data and the Potential for Enhanced Discoverability", Anna Neatrour and Teresa K. Hebron provide an engaging overview of linked data, the benefits of its use in digital repositories and discovery systems, practical approaches to getting started, and real-world examples of linked data projects undertaken by Galleries, Libraries, Archives, Museums & Repositories (GLAMR) institutions. In particular, the chapter offers useful examples of linked data and semantic relationships, and how digital repositories represent and conceptualize linked data. It also offers examples of tools used by digital repository managers to create and manage linked data to support discoverability.

In Chapter 5, titled "User Search Behavior in Digital Repositories", Oksana L. Zavalina and Mary Burke examine user search behavior and needs in digital repositories. This chapter provides a well-referenced review and analysis of relevant research on user interaction with digital repositories, audience types, and user needs and expectations. It examines various search strategies and techniques that users may adopt during their interaction with digital repositories, including basic and advanced search modes, subject searching, and browsing. The chapter offers a particularly useful account of system and user interface features within digital repository systems and the ways in which controlled vocabularies may support and enhance discoverability.

In Chapter 6, titled "Discoverability Within the Library: Integrated Systems and Discovery Layers (Case Study)", JoLinda Thompson and Sara Hoover explore the technical and metadata interoperability of a digital repository platform with other library discovery systems such as the integrated library system, the discovery platform, and the library webpage. This chapter provides a real-world example of integrating IR content into a commercial discovery system to support the specific purpose of digital archiving for a nursing practice community. It also offers a particularly effective and pragmatic approach to metadata harvesting, mapping, and editing to support interoperability and discoverability.

Elizabeth Joan Kelly's Chapter 7, titled "Discoverability Beyond the Library: Wikipedia", provides a case study about the impact of popular digital information resources, such as Wikipedia or Wikidata, on the discoverability of digital repositories. It provides practical tips and techniques for practitioners to ensure the successful integration of their digital content with Wikipedia/Wikidata. The real-world examples of Wiki projects in this chapter offer a useful approach for enhancing visibility, search optimization, and discoverability, resulting in the increased use of digital content in repositories. This chapter provides a set of useful and practical factors for digital repository practitioners to consider when planning to use wikis for enhancing the discoverability of their digital content.

Finally, in Chapter 8, titled "Discoverability and Search Engine Visibility of Repository Platforms", Chee Hsien Aaron Tay and Danping Dong examine the ways in which digital repository content becomes discoverable by search engines. In particular, they explore how content is exposed to search engines and why the structure and design of a digital repository impact visibility and utility through search engines. This chapter provides a useful review of research on discoverability in IRs and the metrics used for measuring this discoverability and introduces several practical resources to assess discoverability. The case study reported in this chapter provides a methodological framework and a randomized controlled experiment to assess visibility and discoverability within an IR.

References

Crow, R. (2002). *The case for institutional repositories: A SPARC position paper, vol. 4.* The Scholarly Publishing and Academic Resources Coalition, Washington, DC. https://rc.library.uta.edu/utair/bitstream/handle/10106/24350/Case%20for%20IRs_SPARC.pdf

Dempsey, L. (2017). Library collections in the life of the user: Two directions. *LIBER Quarterly: The Journal of the Association of European Research Libraries*, *26*(4), 338–359.

Eun Oh, K., & Colón-Aguirre, M. (2019). A comparative study of perceptions and use of Google scholar and academic library discovery systems. *College & Research Libraries*, *80*(6), 876–891.

Guajardo, R., Brett, K., & Young, F. (2017). The evolution of discovery systems in academic libraries: A case study at the University of Houston libraries. *Journal of Electronic Resources Librarianship*, *29*(1), 16–23.

Heaton, R., & Woolcott, L. (2021). Unraveling the (search) string: Assessing library discovery layers using patron queries. *Library assessment conference*. www.libraryassessment.org/wp-content/uploads/2021/01/261-Heaton-Unraveling-the-search-string.pdf

Heery, R., & Anderson, S. (2005). *Digital repositories review*. UKOLN and Arts and Humanities Data Service. www.ukoln.ac.uk/metadata/publications/repositories/digital-repositories-review-2005.pdf

Lee, C. A. (2010). Open archival information system (OAIS) reference model. In M. J. Bates & M. N. Maack (Eds.), *Encyclopedia of library and information Sciences* (3rd ed., pp. 4020–4030). CRC Press.

Lin, D., Crabtree, J., Dillo, I., Downs, R. R., Edmunds, R., Giaretta, D., De Giusti, M., L'Hours, H., Hugo, W., Jenkyns, R., Khodiyar, V., Martone, M. E., Mokrane, M., Navale, V., Petters, J., Sierman, B., Sokolova, D. V., Stockhause, M., & Westbrook, J. (2020). The TRUST principles for digital repositories. *Scientific Data*, *7*(1), 1–5.

Macgregor, G. (2019). Improving the discoverability and web impact of open repositories: Techniques and evaluation. *Code4Lib Journal*, *43*.

RLG-OCLC. (2002). *Trusted digital repositories: Attributes and responsibilities*. Research Libraries Group. www.oclc.org/content/dam/research/activities/trustedrep/repositories.pdf

Shiri, A., & Oliphant, T. (2017). Temporal patterns of searching in a public library discovery system. *Canadian Journal of Information and Library Science*, *41*(1–2), 1–17.

Spezi, V., Creaser, C., & Conyers, A. (2015). The impact of RDS on usage of electronic content in UK academic libraries: Selected results from a UKSG-funded project. *Serials Review*, *41*(2), 85–99.

Thornton, G. M., & Shiri, A. (2021). Challenges with organization, discoverability and access in Canadian open health data repositories. *Journal of the Canadian Health Libraries Association/Journal de l'Association des bibliothèques de la santé du Canada*, *42*(1).

Wells, D. (2020). Online public access catalogues and library discovery systems. In B. Hjørland & C. Gnoli (Eds.), *ISKO encyclopedia of knowledge organization*. www.isko.org/cyclo/opac

Part 1

Digital Repository Functionality

1 Digital Repositories and Discoverability

Definitions and Typology

George Macgregor

Introduction

Digital repositories have established themselves as a key enabling technology of Galleries, Libraries, Archives, Museums, and Repositories (GLAMR) institutions over the past two decades, with a particular acceleration in their adoption and development in the 2010s (Gupta & Sharma, 2018). Within some communities of practice, such as research libraries, repository technology has come to dominate digital library strategy and has become a key enabler of emerging visions of so-called "Library 3.0" (Kwanya et al., 2013), including an increased emphasis on externally facing digital services focused on open scholarly publishing (Adema et al., 2017). By typically supporting established and open technical protocols, as well as rich interoperable metadata models, digital repositories have become the principal focus of digital object collection, storage, and reuse in many organizations. They present convenient platforms for the parallel management, curation, and preservation of digital objects, and – within the context of this volume – they include opportunities for better exposing digital content to search agents, thereby facilitating superior levels of discoverability.

As repositories have evolved technically, their scope and functions have also diversified to the extent that several distinct types have emerged. This chapter will seek to explore the concept of digital repositories and define them, including their purpose and characteristics. It will then present a typology of the varying repository systems and investigate the notion of discoverability within repository contexts.

Defining Digital Repositories

The "digital repository" concept could be said to have originated from computer software development. Digital software repositories are used to provide a location for the deposit of software packages or code libraries where software is stored, maintained, and reused, with metadata attached to support discovery. Such repositories became popular in software development methodologies in the 1980s (Boisvert et al., 1996) and are central to programming approaches today. Notable present-day software repositories include the Ruby Application Archive or the

DOI: 10.4324/9781003216438-3

Comprehensive Perl Archive Network. The digital repositories to be discussed in this chapter, and the wider monograph, are an extension of this software repository concept. They merge the concept with critical digital library innovations and functions, such as digital archiving and discovery.

Precise definitions of digital repositories vary in the literature (Bicknese, 2003; Björk, 2014; Lynch, 2006). This is partly because there has been rapid and significant diversification of the concept within GLAMR organizations since the early 2000s. This diversification will be addressed in a later section; however, in their most general form, digital repositories are information systems or platforms that support the ingest, storage, management, and exposure of digital content (Lynch, 2006). Their capacity for content storage and long-term content management means that they often support aspects of digital preservation (Xie & Matusiak, 2016), making them suitable systems for digital archiving.

Typical features of a digital repository include the following:

- A digital location, with front and backend functionality supporting the deposit and ingest of digital content (Clobridge, 2010). The nature and heterogeneity of this content depend on the type of digital repository but could include open scholarly articles, research datasets, digitized collections, multimedia assets, learning objects, complex digital objects, and so forth. Rich and extensible metadata schema will typically support the description and management of digital content (Mering & Wintermute, 2020), some of which may be exposed through the following repository discovery protocols or through complementary semantically aware approaches, such as linked open data (Candela et al., 2019).
- Support for the exposure, visibility, and discovery of digital content – often open – thereby generating (re)use and impact, especially of open scholarly research content (Arlitsch et al., 2014). Repository systems therefore typically support several established technical standards and protocols, all designed to ensure interoperability with discovery agents and enable participation in the wider, distributed global repository network. Though many repositories will vary in their observation of "discovery" standards, almost all will at least support the keystone protocols of the Open Archives Initiative Protocol for Metadata Harvesting (OAI-PMH) and Simple Web-Service Offering Repository Deposit (SWORD). Increasingly, repositories support emerging protocols associated with the Confederation of Open Access Repositories (COAR) Next Generation Repository initiative, such as ResourceSync (a successor to OAI-PMH) and Signposting (Rodrigues et al., 2017), and more recently, Notify, based on Linked Data Notifications (Shearer et al., 2021).
- Support for the management of digital content (or "assets") over time, normally using open-source technologies, thereby obviating software obsolesce. This is undertaken to ensure access, identification, and persistence of digital content. In some repositories, this also extends to the digital preservation and curation of digital content. Such management is especially important to the maintenance of unique digital collections held in trusted locations (Bak,

2016; Corrado, 2019); but it is also an increasingly important instrument in maintaining the "digital scholarly record", an issue being debated in scholarship where less stable academic publishing technologies have been employed (Klein et al., 2014).

The number of digital repositories has grown considerably since the mid-2000s as GLAMR organizations have sought convenient information systems with which to manage their growing digital content collections. According to the global Directory of Open Access Repositories (OpenDOAR), there are nearly 6,000 active digital repositories (Jisc, 2021). However, this figure is likely far higher since OpenDOAR is not exhaustive and does not necessarily record all repository types (Ali et al., 2018).

Discoverability: Resource Discovery Within Digital Repository Contexts

Our ability to communicate knowledge is what gives information, and information resources, their value, and their ability to satisfy users' information needs (Smucker, 2011). "Resource discovery" has been variously defined but most definitions are unified in their recognition that the concept entails the systematization of information resources in order to provide users with an intuitive, organized view of resources (Bowman et al., 1993). Seminal informatician Clifford Lynch has noted that the identification of potentially relevant information resources is the principal task in discovery, with resources intuitively organized and ranked, and their subsequent browsing made possible via results expansion or filtering tools. Though predating the emergence of digital repositories by many years, Lynch cites the "searching of various types of directories, catalogs or other descriptive databases" as typical examples of resource discovery, all of which have obvious parallels to our current era of digital repositories (Lynch, 1995, p. 1506). The concept of resource discovery is therefore central both to our understanding of how users explore, navigate, locate, and retrieve information resources and to the way in which our information technologies facilitate that discovery, i.e., *discoverability* (Beyene, 2016). We can be even more specific by suggesting that *discoverability* is a measure of the extent to which information systems or technologies purporting to be discoverable – in our case, digital repositories – are technically optimized to ensure it, for example, eliminating all possible discoverability barriers or optimizing technologies to interoperate with specific discovery tools or search agents, thereby ensuring maximum ease in discovery.

The mechanisms that facilitate discoverability are the focus of numerous chapters throughout this book. It is nevertheless worth considering discoverability within the context of digital repositories by providing a conceptual overview. Figure 1.1 provides a conceptual diagram of users' routes to digital repository content discovery. There are multiple routes, and they are contained within the ellipse and ultimately link to the digital repository, the content origin. Users are situated outside the ellipse and are presented with a multiplicity of discovery routes, which

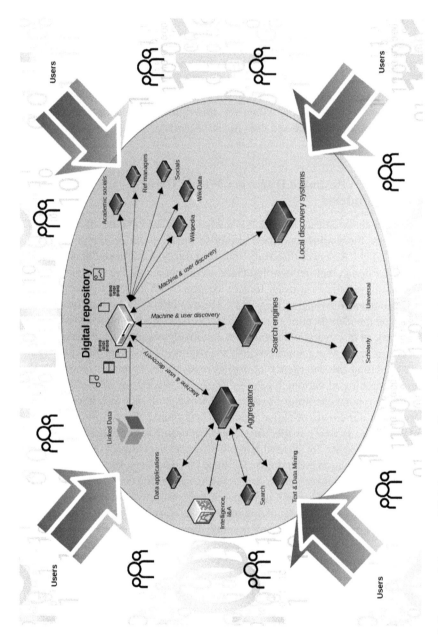

Figure 1.1 Conceptual diagram of digital repository discoverability and users' routes to content discovery

they may use knowingly or unknowingly. Such a multiplicity of discovery routes demonstrates the high levels of discoverability that digital repositories generally display – much of which is made possible through repository observance of discovery standards and protocols. But it also emphasizes the importance of identifying and eliminating discoverability barriers, since users' routes to repository discovery can be difficult to anticipate.

Using Figure 1.1 as a reference, we can observe that the discoverability of digital repository content will be achieved via the following routes:

- **Native**: Users may elect to use the digital repository directly. This route will typically be employed in known-item queries, particularly in repositories with a large corpus of rich, digital content or content that is less exposed via the alternative routes mentioned in the following. These alternatives are generally more conducive to unknown-item queries as they enable de facto federated searching of multiple digital repositories simultaneously.
- **Local discovery systems**: Digital repositories will often feature within local discovery tools as possible search targets. For example, the search layer of a university library management system (e.g., Ex Libris Primo) or an archival description platform (e.g., AtoM) may enable the discovery of content within the university's other digital repository solutions, normally through repository support for OAI-PMH.
- **Search engines**: It is increasingly necessary for digital repositories to optimize their discoverability in third-party search tools, especially given their ubiquity in users' search behavior (Pulikowski & Matysek, 2021). "Universal" search tools (e.g., Google, Bing, DuckDuckGo) contribute significant user traffic to repository content discovery; however, depending on the type of repository, an increasing proportion may also arrive via "scholarly" search engines, such as Google Scholar (Macgregor, 2020), powered by repository support for structured data.
- **Aggregators**: Although aggregators will be described in more detail in a later section of this chapter, we can note that such tools routinely harvest content from multiple digital repositories, aggregating content and data in a single location. This single aggregated collection can then be searched by users. However, such large aggregations enable other discovery routes, such as intelligence and indexing/abstracting tools, Text and Data Mining (TDM) applications, or discovery applications such as CORE Discovery or Unpaywall, providing single-click access to Open Access (OA) versions of research papers whenever users encounter paywall restrictions (Hoy, 2019).
- **Linked data**: Repositories contributing linked data to the "web of data" promote alternative forms of aggregation (Freire et al., 2019). Such reuse of linked repository data promotes its integration within new or novel services, often outside the traditional domains of GLAMR organizations, and can consequently drive the discovery and usage of repository content (Pennington & Cagnazzo, 2019). Linked data is a growth area in repository discovery and will be given more detailed attention in Chapter 4.

- **Social**: The importance of social networking services ("socials") as a route to discovering digital repository content is now well established (Moham-madi et al., 2018). However, these routes have diversified to include both academic social networks (e.g., ResearchGate, Academia.edu) and reference management software applications (e.g., Mendeley, ReadCube), many of which provide repository discovery functionality and the ability to share or search reference collections curated by other users, thereby presenting a more informal means of resource discovery. We may also include Wikimedia community projects, such as Wikipedia and WikiData (to be discussed in Chapter 7), both of which increasingly depend on open repository content to populate services but from which repositories often maximize the value and discovery impact of their services (Lubbock, 2018).

The above is merely a conceptual overview of digital repository discoverability and will be interrogated further in subsequent chapters. However, we should note that the nature of repository discoverability can also be associated with repository type. As digital repositories have evolved in their functionality, there has also been a diversification in the varieties of repository. Specific digital repositories have therefore emerged, each corresponding with specific use cases, organizational affiliations, or communities of practice. The following sections will summarize some of these before going on to propose a typology of repositories to aid understanding of the domain.

Digital Repository Types

Institutional Repositories: Scholarly Communications and Government

Institutional repositories (IRs) are digital repositories that have been established by an institution or organization, typically a higher education institution or research institute. Their purposes can be multifarious, but there is typically a focus on delivering a repository service supporting the management and dissemination of digital content created by the institution and the community it serves (Lynch, 2003). IRs therefore represent an institutional commitment to both the stewardship of the digital content gathered by the repository and its dissemination. For this reason, IRs are principally concerned with supporting open scholarly communication, serving textual content such as OA academic research articles, conference papers, research theses, and so forth. IRs are uniquely designed to promote the discovery and ergo impact of such scholarly content; the software they use (e.g., DSpace, EPrints, Islandora, and Invenio) demonstrates this and will be discussed in Chapter 2. However, they also function as a counterbalance to the costs associated with the "legacy" scholarly publishing industry by providing access to scholarly content that might otherwise reside behind a paywall (Björk et al., 2014; Tennant et al., 2016). Owing to their focus on literature, and the limited filetype scope that this infers, IRs tend to display only low to moderate levels of content heterogeneity, with generally low levels of object complexity.

A critical mass of this open scholarly content has emerged in recent years as IRs have grown to accommodate the requirements of national and funder-specific OA policies. IRs are therefore ubiquitous within the global digital repository landscape, accounting for 90 percent of all known digital repositories (Jisc, 2021). The increase in IRs is driven by policy compliance and the corresponding number of institutions that stand to benefit from their creation. Furthermore, some institutions have evolved to support several IRs in parallel, thereby better accommodating massive growth in collections and/or simplifying management of digital content: for example, separate IRs for academic articles, research theses, gray literature, and so on. This is particularly notable in the UK, where a mature policy framework promotes research openness and where the deposit of peer-reviewed manuscripts is mandated by both research funders and the UK's national research assessment exercise. The impact of these policy instruments is visible in OA data reported by the Centre for Science and Technology Studies (CTWS) Leiden Rankings, in which UK institutions report OA levels of more than 80 percent, and some in excess of 90 percent (de Castro, 2021).

Research libraries have been exploring alternative scholarly publishing models, especially those enabling organizational ownership over publishing infrastructure. In an extension of the scholarly communication aim, IRs – alongside subject-based repositories (discussed in the next section) – are increasingly used in the publication of so-called "overlay journals" (Marušić et al., 2019; Whitehead et al., 2019). Though not entirely a new concept, overlay journals are nevertheless an innovation in the institutional publishing space because they harness repository functionality and discovery potential to provide an alternative model of scholarly communication. In such a scenario, an editorial board of an overlay journal may accept deposits to a journal through the IR. Peer review is then undertaken within or outside the repository, and revised manuscripts are approved for deposit and inclusion in issues of the journal, to which a journal website might then hyperlink. Notable examples include the Journal of Data Mining and Digital Humanities and ST-OPEN, both of which are overlays of IRs (Thornton & Kroeker, 2021). However, the growth of overlay titles using subject-based repositories, especially those that enjoy a global user base such as arXiv, has been far greater in recent years, particularly within physical science domains (Marra, 2017).

While IRs are typically a declaration of a commitment to the stewardship of institutionally created digital content, they have historically been less concerned with the digital curation and preservation of that content (Li & Banach, 2011; Xie & Matusiak, 2016). As we shall see in the following sections of this chapter, other repository types have emerged that specialize in these aspects of digital content management, especially at larger GLAMR institutions. Nevertheless, as time has progressed and the fragility of digital content has become more apparent, most repository types have conceded that some digital curation of content is necessary. In IRs, the need to prioritize persistence in the scholarly record has motivated more recent attempts to improve digital curation (Macgregor & Neugebauer, 2020; Neugebauer et al., 2018; Xie & Matusiak, 2016), along with the increased deployment of persistent identifiers (PIDs) to describe and link to that content

(Ananthakrishnan et al., 2020; Bunakov & Madden, 2020; Klump & Huber, 2017). Unfortunately, recent systematic reviews of current approaches continue to suggest that IRs continue to see insufficient digital curatorial activity and that repository managers are avoiding their responsibilities to "assure the long-term access to the assets they store" (Barrueco & Termens, 2021, p. 170).

It has been convention to distinguish between IRs and so-called "governmental" digital repositories (Xie & Matusiak, 2016), but it is apposite to note that many governmental digital repositories are themselves IRs, established under the auspices of government organizations, that is, a repository service supporting the management and dissemination of digital content created by the institution and the community it serves. The Fiskeridirektoratets Digitalarkiv (Norwegian Directorate of Fisheries: https://fdir.brage.unit.no/) and the Irish Health Publications Archive (https://hselibrary.ie/), both of which discharge the digital archiving and dissemination responsibilities of their respective Norwegian and Irish government departments, are prototypical examples. Fewer than 3 percent of digital repositories listed on OpenDOAR are described as governmental, although many of these are government or nationally sponsored GLAMR repositories. It can be argued that such government-focused IRs are more receptive to the needs of digital curatorial action, especially in instances in which IRs are disseminating government records or supporting aspects of e-government (Aas et al., 2014; Kulovits et al., 2012). Nevertheless, while we maintain the repository distinction for the typology presented in the following section, it is increasingly becoming redundant.

Subject-Based and Preprint Repositories

Subject-based repositories – also known as "disciplinary repositories" – are those which coalesce around a specific subject or disciplinary area instead of a specific institution or organization (Björk, 2014). Their principal function is almost identical to that of IRs insofar as they provide a mechanism for the dissemination of open research content, thereby supporting the goals of OA, including providing infrastructure for the creation of overlay journal titles. Notable examples include arXiv (https://arxiv.org/), AgEcon (https://agecosearch.umn.edu/), RePEc (https://econpapers.repec.org/), and E-LIS (http://eprints.rclis.org/). Subject-based repositories enable content creators to engage with their knowledge community (i.e., peers) when sharing their work and to reach users who seek to discover new content within that knowledge community (e.g., Kuperberg, 2020); but they also provide access to repository infrastructure for those creators who are either unable or unwilling to use an IR alternative (Emery, 2018). As well as being well indexed by a wide variety of discovery tools, some subject-based repositories are so large that they are the principal source of literature for scholars (Clement et al., 2019).

The governance of subject-based repositories is an additional point of difference with IRs. Owing to their community focus, most subject-based repositories operate transparently through advisory boards, elected steering groups, and other models of community participation (Adamick & Reznik-Zellen, 2010). These governance mechanisms are used to determine questions surrounding repository collection policies, funding, development paths, and so forth; however, they also help guard against private interests in the management of open repository content, as has historically been the case with some privately operated platforms (e.g., Li, 2019).

There is an increasing crossover between subject and preprint repositories. The essential concept of preprints is not new, with progenitors existing for many decades within some disciplines (Brown, 2001; Cobb, 2017). A preprint can be described as a "precursor" to a research article that may ultimately find publication in a peer-reviewed journal (Brown, 2001). Preprints are therefore open research papers that have not undergone peer review but which enjoy rapid dissemination of results and the possibility of community feedback. Preprints have increasing acceptance within scholarly communities despite the criticism that they lack certification via peer review (Johansson et al., 2018). For example, it is now widely acknowledged that those preprints documenting science surrounding COVID-19, or severe acute respiratory syndrome coronavirus 2 (SARS-CoV-2), were critical to the global public health response to the COVID-19 pandemic. By circumventing conventional research publication routes, research results could be disseminated rapidly, thereby accelerating clinicians' understanding of the virus and its impact on humans (Fraser et al., 2021). Notable repositories in this instance of preprint dissemination included medRxiv (www.medrxiv.org/) and bioRxiv (www.biorxiv.org/), both of which took inspiration in their naming from perhaps the oldest and most well-known subject-based repository, arXiv.

Data Repositories

Opportunities for the digital archiving of data and datasets are almost as old as the web itself (Hahnel & Valen, 2020). In more recent times, mature repository solutions – data repositories – have emerged to support the management of often complex, multi-object research datasets. Since a dataset can be as simple as a single 30kb .csv data file but as sophisticated as, say, a complex 100TB dataset comprising millions of related data components, these repositories are optimized for data. They can harness rich metadata schema to capture sufficient descriptive, administrative, structural, and technical metadata about the data being managed. Such metadata is necessary not only to facilitate the discovery and reuse of datasets but also to ensure that datasets remain intelligible to users and machines, and that they can be subject to digital preservation actions. Typically, data repositories will attract deposits of structured quantitative or qualitative data; although we should acknowledge that definitions of "data" can vary across communities of practice such that, depending on the academic context, objects such as software, media, or research instruments may constitute data or a dataset. Furthermore, the heterogeneity of content within data repositories and the sophistication of the associated digital objects is far more expansive than in literature repositories. Open file standards may be managed alongside lesser known, proprietary data formats associated with, say, microscope software, like .opju.

Research data management, as well as open data more generally, has become a key focus at both research-intensive organizations and GLAMR institutions with a research support purview. The culture surrounding research integrity and public accountability has demanded improved data openness and transparency to support the goals of research verification and reproducibility, all largely delivered via data repositories. As in the case of IRs, the need to ensure persistence in the scholarly record means that research datasets are increasingly subject to digital curation requirements. Researchers may also have the opportunity of reusing an existing dataset, resulting in research and knowledge efficiency as duplication is avoided. This, in turn, has resulted in greater linkage between research literature and its underlying data, with research bodies and academic peers insisting on explicit linking between the two, or the inclusion of data availability statements (Colavizza et al., 2020). Linkage is an important dataset discovery path for users since dataset search tools remain experimental (Mannheimer et al., 2021; Sansone et al., 2017) and awareness of the existence of data may only arise through reading an associated research article (Singhal & Srivastava, 2017).

Like literature repositories (institutional, subject, preprint), data repositories have diversified to encompass both institutional and subject-based varieties, with latter examples often better fulfilling disciplinary metadata expectations. Popular open-source platforms used within the literature repository space (e.g., DSpace, EPrints) are available in data-centric releases, but there is an increasing preference for optimized solutions, such as Dataverse, CKAN, and Samvera. Although commercial solutions, such as Figshare and Mendeley Data, demonstrate some popularity, they are often deemed inconsistent with the requirements of open infrastructure (Bilder et al., 2020). Variability in the implementation of data repositories has resulted in a notional global agreement that such repositories should be FAIR, demonstrating defined levels of "findability, accessibility, interoperability, and reusability" (Wilkinson et al., 2016). Thus, the so-called "FAIRness" of data repositories, and the data they store, is now expected of data manager practitioners and research funders (Bahim et al., 2020).

Mega-Repositories

Mega-repositories are large-scale repositories that have few discernible restrictions on the type of material deposited, its format, size, peer review status, or discipline. Such repositories tend to be generalist in their scope, allowing participation from a wide variety of academic users. For our purposes, we can define a mega-repository as one containing more than two million heterogeneous objects, submitted by creators originating from multiple, geographically distributed organizations and disciplines. As this definition might suggest, there are few repositories falling into this category or having the resources to sustain their operation; however, those that do are among the most significant repositories of any type in the world. A good example of a mega-repository would be The European Organization for Nuclear Research (CERN) repository, Zenodo (https://zenodo.org/), which accommodates heterogenous objects of varying complexity, from simple preprints to more complex objects like software and learning objects (Peters et al., 2017). Built on CERN's own open-source repository platform, Invenio, Zenodo can also function as a publication platform for overlay journal titles and conference proceedings. Repositories like Zenodo are of such significance that they assist in the governance and development of core repository infrastructure, such as DataCite and ORCID. However, the generalist approach of mega-repositories can mean that suboptimal metadata modeling occurs where specificity might be sought for object types. For example, the earth and planetary science data repository, PANGAEA (www. pangaea.de/), could better satisfy the metadata requirements of an environmental science dataset than Zenodo, which necessarily takes a one-size-fits-all approach.

Trusted Digital Repositories

The digital curatorial focus at GLAMR institutions has typically been on items of artistic or cultural value rather than on traditional outcomes of scholarly research (e.g., academic manuscripts). This reflects their longer tradition of collecting, conserving, and ensuring long-term access to materials (Bak, 2016). The emergence of the trusted digital repository (TDR) concept (sometimes termed "trustworthy digital repository") emerged in recognition of these GLAMR traditions and was an acknowledgment that such institutions would increasingly accumulate potentially fragile digital collections, many of which would require dedicated curatorial attention (e.g., Research Library Group/OCLC Working Group on Digital Archive Attributes et al., 2002). Most repository types are set out to be reliable locations for the management of digital content; however, a TDR – often managed under the auspices of a much larger GLAMR or national memory institution – extends the commitment of reliability to one of trust. A TDR is therefore one "whose mission is to provide reliable, long-term access to managed digital resources to its designated community, now and in the future" (RLG/OCLC Working Group on Digital Archive Attributes et al., 2002, p. 5).

Early work by the RLG and OCLC (2002) established the expected attributes of a TDR. Resource discovery is a component of the TDR context; nonetheless, the priority of TDR management processes is to steward digital content over time and in accordance with recognized standards. This entails compliance with the Reference Model for an Open Archival Information System (OAIS), thereby guaranteeing a basis for long-term maintenance and access (Consultative Committee for Space Data Systems [CCSDS], 2012), as well as demonstrable evidence of "organization viability", "financial stability", "administrative responsibility", "technological suitability and procedural accountability", and "system security", the latter emphasizing the importance of disaster preparedness, digital content recovery procedures, data integrity actions, and so forth. Despite TDR adherence to recognized "trustworthy frameworks", there have been concerns recently that such approaches are technocratic or do not set sufficiently objective measures of trust (Bak, 2016). Therefore, certification of the trustworthiness of TDRs is increasingly sought through mechanisms such as the "CoreTrustSeal" or "DIN 31644", awarded to repositories satisfying rigorous trustworthy requirements (Corrado, 2019). Owing to the large digital corpora that TDR-hosting institutions tend to curate, it is not uncommon for TDRs to serve highly heterogeneous collections and for objects to be highly complex, particularly as many will be multipart and require preservation metadata.

Learning Object Repositories

Open learning object repositories (LORs) particularly demonstrate potential complexity in the digital objects managed by repositories. Sometimes known as "open educational resource repositories", LORs are typically used to share learning objects with others, normally teaching communities (Ochoa & Duval, 2009). A "learning object" is a digital object, or a collection of digital objects, which can be reused to support learning. Such learning objects may be as simple as a PDF document detailing a lesson plan for a teacher to reuse in an online course or as complex as a multipart digital learning object containing multiple related objects of various formats (e.g., textual documents, multimedia, assessments, interactive tests) designed for delivering an entire postgraduate module. By openly sharing learning objects via an LOR, learning materials can be reused and improved, thereby avoiding duplication of effort. These objects may then be re-shared for digitally supported teaching and learning purposes. As digital learning pioneer Stephen Downes noted in 2001: "the world does not need thousands of similar descriptions of sine wave functions available online. Rather, what the world needs is one, or maybe a dozen at most" (p. 1).

LORs provide a convenient technology for describing, organizing, presenting, and sharing learning objects. Prominent LORs are often established by higher education institutions (HEIs) where – notwithstanding a desire to share objects openly – there exists a concern about capturing the valuable knowledge assets created by staff in the delivery of curricula. Capturing them enables potential local teaching efficiencies to accrue as content is reused and for HEIs to be more responsive to students' real-time learning requirements (Sampson & Zervas, 2013). Although large global LORs exist, such as OER Commons, it is not uncommon for LORs to use optimized versions of IR software (Cervone, 2012). For example, EdShare at the University of Glasgow (https://edshare.gla.ac.uk/) and OpenEd@UCL at University College London (https://open-education-repository.ucl.ac.uk/) both use the EPrints "EdShare" repository "flavor".

It is important to note that managing learning objects within an LOR typically requires considerably extending LOR metadata models to facilitate the specialized organization and discovery requirements of LORs. In addition to typical descriptive, administrative, and technical metadata elements, LORs must capture adequate descriptive metadata concerning the teaching or learning context of the object as this is an important discovery avenue for potential reuse (Palavitsinis et al., 2014). This may include metadata pertaining to the intended learning outcomes of the learning object, intended audience and their education level, prerequisite study requirements, client software requirements, and so forth. In this context, there is some commonality between LORs and data repositories insofar as both have breached traditional digital description boundaries, although the complexity of LOR metadata – often expressed using Learning Object Metadata schema (Learning Technology Standards Committee [LTSC], 2020) – is frequently cited as one reason for metadata quality issues arising within LORs (Palavitsinis et al., 2014). A typology of repository types will be presented in the next section of this chapter, but it is noteworthy that LORs are now of such diversity that separate LOR typologies have been posited in the literature (e.g., McGreal, 2008).

Aggregating Repositories

Aggregating repositories are the final repository type to be considered as part of this chapter. We can identify two principal subtypes: "machine-aggregated" and "user-aggregated". Machine-aggregated repositories will typically harness repository technical protocols, such as OAI-PMH and/or ResourceSync, to harvest metadata and digital content from distributed repositories to aggregate it centrally. CORE (https://core.ac.uk/) and BASE (www.base-search.net/) are two prominent examples of this model. Both routinely harvest and aggregate as much content as possible from thousands of repositories, irrespective of their subject scope, affiliation, content heterogeneity, and object complexity (Knoth & Zdrahal, 2013). It is therefore apposite to note that smaller, more selective aggregations can and do occur, for example, based on a subject or topic. Public Health Scotland, for example, created a Covid-19 aggregating repository to unify Scottish Covid-19-related research made available through IRs or subject repositories (www.publichealthscotland.scot/). User-aggregated approaches perform a similar function to machine-aggregated ones but rely on user action to build the aggregation, normally by providing content to deposit. DataverseNL (https://dataverse.nl/) in the Netherlands provides a user-aggregated data repository, for example, with DataverseNL aggregating all data content from Dutch consortia member universities.

Whichever the subtype, aggregating repositories seek to "aggregate" content in a single digital location – with the location being a digital repository. The aggregating repository approach is cognate to the more established union catalog approaches that have been prevalent in digital libraries for decades (Dunsire, 2008), and even those examples emerging prior to the advent of the Web, such as WorldCat (Salmon, 1982). The benefits of providing these digital aggregations are obvious to users in their potential size, diversity, and the way in which they can support users' resource discovery needs (Hudson-Vitale, 2017). In addition, such aggregations of digital content and metadata present unique opportunities for large-scale computational TDM and also provide the foundation for countless novel applications, including recommendation engines (CORE, 2019; Knoth et al., 2017).

Proposing a Typology of Digital Repository Systems

In this section, we formalize the aforementioned "repository types" by placing each of them within a typology of digital repository systems. We also use several of the previously highlighted repository characteristics as typology facets, which are described in the following. Such a typology provides a useful conceptual aid to understand the repository landscape and how specific repository types differ

Table 1.1 Typology of digital repositories

Type	Volume	Object Complexity	Content Heterogeneity	Metadata Curation	Typical Governance
Preprint	Large	Low	Low	User	Community
Institutional	Variable	Low	Moderate	Mixed	Organizational
Subject	Large	Low	Moderate	User	Community
Data	Moderate	High	Moderate	Mixed	Community/ organizational
Mega	Large	High	High	User	Community
Trusted	Large	High	High	Organizational	Organizational
Learning object	Moderate	High	Moderate	Organizational	Organizational
Governmental	Moderate	Low	Low	Organizational	Organizational
Aggregating	Large	Moderate	Moderate	Mixed	Community

(or not). It will help to contextualize subsequent chapters as well. The typology is presented in Table 1.1.

- **Type** refers to the repository type, whether this is an IR or TDR or some other repository type. A total of nine repository types were outlined in previous sections.
- **Volume** refers to the typical size of the digital corpus served by the repository type. This is not a reference to digital storage size but denotes the volume of digital objects typically held by a specific repository type. For example, in our discussion of mega-repositories, we noted that they are characterized by serving a *large* digital corpus, normally more than two million digital objects. By contrast – and owing to the nature of the digital content they manage – data repositories are *moderate* and typically enjoy a slower rate of growth.
- **Object complexity** is an indicator of the complexity of the digital objects typically deposited in the repository type. Repositories that manage predominantly textual content, such as IRs and subject repositories, can be said to have *low* object complexity. The objects are similar in nature and their intellectual content is typically self-contained, for example, within a PDF file or similar. This is unlike, for example, data repositories in which a single dataset may comprise millions of data files, organized according to a specific structure. Such datasets are highly complex, multipart objects and may also have similarly complex metadata describing the complete data object to facilitate data interpretation or reproducibility (Soiland-Reyes & Goble, 2021). Their object complexity could therefore be considered *high*.
- **Content heterogeneity** attempts to characterize the extent of variety in the digital objects managed by an archetypal repository type and defines whether a repository typically manages a digital collection that exemplifies low or high levels of heterogeneity. If we consider, for example, preprint repositories, we

can observe that such repositories serve relatively homogenous textual content, suggesting a *low* level of content heterogeneity. Mega-repositories are almost the inverse in this respect, serving digital content of all varieties, file formats, and sizes – this can include everything from preprints to datasets to learning objects. Mega-repositories therefore typify *high* levels of content heterogeneity. As might be expected, repositories can demonstrate close alignment on content heterogeneity and object complexity such that a direct variation relationship can be said to occur. This is because as digital repositories accommodate the content of ever-increasing heterogeneity, the complexity of the digital objects managed will also tend to increase (Figure 1.2). As examples of generalist repositories, mega-repositories demonstrate this principle clearly. Similarly, as content becomes more homogeneous, object complexity correspondingly declines.

- **Metadata curation** helps to define the typical approaches adopted by repository types in their description, organization, and management of metadata associated with digital objects. Repositories' approach to metadata curation greatly varies, with some relying almost exclusively on *user*-generated metadata (e.g., preprint, subject, mega) and accepting the limitations posed by this. Those repositories with higher object complexity and content heterogeneity (e.g., trusted) demand *organizational* approaches in which metadata are managed by skilled professionals. Other repository types adopt a mixed approach.
- **Typical governance** denotes the way the repository type is usually governed. As we noted in previous sections, some repository types demonstrate strict adherence to forms of *community* governance to ensure transparency and guarantee openness. Others are founded, managed, and maintained by *organizational* entities, whether this is a library, university, or some form of national memory institution.

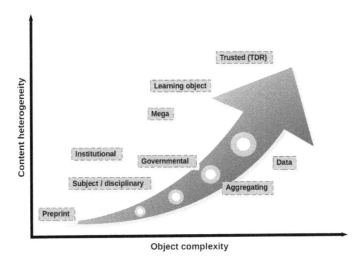

Figure 1.2 Illustration of the relationship between content heterogeneity and object complexity in digital repositories

Conclusion

In this chapter, we have attempted to define and characterize the nature of digital repositories, and we have explored the multifarious ways in which repositories can support digital content discovery. The extent to which digital repositories are discoverable is of core concern to GLAMR organizations. Furthermore, although repository software tends to demonstrate satisfactory levels of discoverability, it is always necessary for repositories to optimize discoverability. The typology presented formalizes our understanding of the digital repository types to be discussed in subsequent chapters. All typologies are subject to change, and it is apposite to highlight that the COAR Next Generation Repository initiative (Rodrigues et al., 2017) may, over time, modify repository behaviors in unanticipated ways, thereby necessitating future revisions to the typology. In the meantime, we can report that the typology is a useful conceptual tool to aid an understanding of the current and near-future repository landscape. Many of the themes and topics raised in previous sections will be explored in more detail in subsequent chapters. Chapters 2, 3, and 4 will continue the discussion of repository functionality, metadata schema, and discoverability optimization approaches via linked data.

References

Aas, K., Delve, J., Vieira, R., & King, R. (2014, December). Integrating e-government systems with digital archives: Paper – iPES 2014 – Melbourne. *Proceedings of the 11th international conference on digital preservation.* https://hdl.handle.net/11353/10.378127

Adamick, J., & Reznik-Zellen, R. (2010). Trends in large-scale subject repositories. *D-Lib Magazine, 16*(11/12). https://doi.org/10.1045/november2010-adamick

Adema, J., Stone, G., & Keene, C. (2017). *Changing publishing ecologies: A landscape study of new university presses and academic-led publishing.* Jisc. https://digitalcommons.unl.edu/scholcom/80

Ali, M., Loan, F. A., & Mushatq, R. (2018). Open access scientific digital repositories: An analytical study of the Open DOAR. *2018 5th international symposium on emerging trends and technologies in libraries and information services (ETTLIS)* (pp. 213–216). IEEE. https://doi.org/10.1109/ETTLIS.2018.8485265

Ananthakrishnan, R., Chard, K., D'Arcy, M., Foster, I., Kesselman, C., McCollam, B., Pruyne, J., Rocca-Serra, P., Schuler, R., & Wagner, R. (2020). An open ecosystem for pervasive use of persistent identifiers. *Practice and Experience in Advanced Research Computing,* 99–105. https://doi.org/10.1145/3311790.3396660

Arlitsch, K., OBrien, P., Kyrillidou, M., Clark, J. A., Young, S. W. H., Mixter, J., Chao, Z., Freels-Stendel, B., & Stewart, C. (2014). *Measuring up: Assessing accuracy of reported use and impact of digital repositories* (pp. 1–10). Montana State University. https://scholarworks.montana.edu/xmlui/handle/1/8924

Bahim, C., Casorrán-Amilburu, C., Dekkers, M., Herczog, E., Loozen, N., Repanas, K., Russell, K., & Stall, S. (2020). The FAIR data maturity model: An approach to harmonise FAIR assessments. *Data Science Journal, 19*(1), 41. https://doi.org/10.5334/dsj-2020-041

Bak, G. (2016). Trusted by whom? TDRs, standards culture and the nature of trust. *Archival Science, 16*(4), 373–402. https://doi.org/10.1007/s10502-015-9257-1

Barrueco, J. M., & Termens, M. (2021). Digital preservation in institutional repositories: A systematic literature review. *Digital Library Perspectives, 38*(2), 161–174. https://doi.org/10.1108/DLP-02-2021-0011

Beyene, W. M. (2016). Resource discovery and universal access: Understanding enablers and barriers from the user perspective. *Studies in Health Technology and Informatics, 229*, 556–566.

Bicknese, D. (2003). Institutional repositories and the institution's repository: What is the role of university archives with an institution's on-line digital repository? *Archival Issues, 28*(2), 81–93.

Bilder, G., Lin, J., & Neylon, C. (2020). The principles of open scholarly infrastructure. *Science in the open.* https://doi.org/10.24343/C34W2H

Björk, B.-C. (2014). Open access subject repositories: An overview. *Journal of the Association for Information Science and Technology, 65*(4), 698–706. https://doi.org/10.1002/asi.23021

Björk, B.-C., Laakso, M., Welling, P., & Paetau, P. (2014). Anatomy of green open access. *Journal of the Association for Information Science and Technology, 65*(2), 237–250. https://doi.org/10.1002/asi.22963

Boisvert, R., Browne, S., Dongarra, J., & Grosse, E. (1996). Digital software and data repositories for support of scientific computing. In N. R. Adam, B. K. Bhargava, M. Halem, & Y. Yesha (Eds.), *Digital libraries research and technology advances* (pp. 103–114). Springer. https://doi.org/10.1007/BFb0024606

Bowman, M., Danzig, P. B., Manber, U., & Schwartz, M. F. (1993). *Scalable internet resource discovery: Research problems and approaches; CU-CS-679-93* [Technical Report]. University of Colorado Boulder. https://scholar.colorado.edu/concern/reports/rx913q821

Brown, C. (2001). The E-volution of preprints in the scholarly communication of physicists and astronomers. *Journal of the American Society for Information Science and Technology, 52*(3), 187–200. https://doi.org/10.1002/1097-4571(2000)9999:9999<::AID-ASI1586>3.0.CO;2-D

Bunakov, V., & Madden, F. (2020). Integration of a national e-theses online service with institutional repositories. *Publications, 8*(2), 20. https://doi.org/10.3390/publications8020020

Candela, G., Escobar, P., Carrasco, R. C., & Marco-Such, M. (2019). A linked open data framework to enhance the discoverability and impact of culture heritage. *Journal of Information Science, 45*(6), 756–766. https://doi.org/10.1177/0165551518812658

Cervone, H. F. (2012). Digital learning object repositories. *OCLC Systems & Services: International Digital Library Perspectives, 28*(1), 14–16. https://doi.org/10.1108/10650751211197031

Clement, C. B., Bierbaum, M., O'Keeffe, K. P., & Alemi, A. A. (2019). On the use of ArXiv as a dataset. *arXiv.org.* http://arxiv.org/abs/1905.00075

Clobridge, A. (2010). Introduction. In *Building a digital repository program with limited resources* (pp. 3–11). Chandos Publishing. https://doi.org/10.1016/B978-1-84334-596-1.50001-8

Cobb, M. (2017). The prehistory of biology preprints: A forgotten experiment from the 1960s. *PLOS Biology, 15*(11), e2003995. https://doi.org/10.1371/journal.pbio.2003995

Colavizza, G., Hrynaszkiewicz, I., Staden, I., Whitaker, K., & McGillivray, B. (2020). The citation advantage of linking publications to research data. *PLoS ONE, 15*(4), e0230416. https://doi.org/10.1371/journal.pone.0230416

Consultative Committee for Space Data Systems (CCSDS). (2012). *Reference model for an open archival information system (OAIS) [ISO 14721:2012].* CCSDS Secretariat/ISO. https://public.ccsds.org/pubs/650x0m2.pdf

CORE. (2019, May 31). *CORE content and discovery.* www.youtube.com/watch?v=kp4cvk7aJjs

Corrado, E. M. (2019). Repositories, trust, and the CoreTrustSeal. *Technical Services Quarterly, 36*(1), 61–72. https://doi.org/10.1080/07317131.2018.1532055

de Castro, P. (2021, January 25). *Recent developments in open access: An overview* [Other]. International Federation of Catholic Universities (IFCU/FIUC). https://strathprints.strath.ac.uk/75158/

Downes, S. (2001). Learning objects: Resources for distance education worldwide. *The International Review of Research in Open and Distributed Learning, 2*(1). https://doi.org/10.19173/irrodl.v2i1.32

Dunsire, G. (2008). Collecting metadata from institutional repositories. *OCLC Systems and Services, 24*, 51–58.

Emery, J. (2018). How green is our valley?: Five-year study of selected LIS journals from Taylor & Francis for green deposit of articles. *Insights, 31*, 23. https://doi.org/10.1629/uksg.406

Fraser, N., Brierley, L., Dey, G., Polka, J. K., Pálfy, M., Nanni, F., & Coates, J. A. (2021). The evolving role of preprints in the dissemination of COVID-19 research and their impact on the science communication landscape. *PLoS Biology, 19*(4), e3000959. https://doi.org/10.1371/journal.pbio.3000959

Freire, N., Voorburg, R., Cornelissen, R., de Valk, S., Meijers, E., & Isaac, A. (2019). Aggregation of linked data in the cultural heritage domain: A case study in the Europeana network. *Information, 10*(8), 252. https://doi.org/10.3390/info10080252

Gupta, D. K., & Sharma, V. (2018). Analytical study of crowdsourced GLAM digital repositories. *Library Hi Tech News, 35*(1), 11–17. https://doi.org/10.1108/LHTN-07-2017-0055

Hahnel, M., & Valen, D. (2020). How to (easily) extend the FAIRness of existing repositories. *Data Intelligence, 2*(1–2), 192–198. https://doi.org/10.1162/dint_a_00041

Hoy, M. B. (2019). New tools for finding full-text articles faster: Kopernio, Nomad, Unpaywall, and More. *Medical Reference Services Quarterly, 38*(3), 287–292. https://doi.org/10.1080/02763869.2019.1629215

Hudson-Vitale, C. (2017). The current state of meta-repositories for data. In L. R. Johnston (Ed.), *Curating research data. Volume one: Practical strategies for your digital repository* (pp. 251–261). Association of Research Libraries. https://openscholarship.wustl.edu/lib_papers/19

Jisc. (2021). *OpenDOAR.* https://v2.sherpa.ac.uk/opendoar/

Johansson, M. A., Reich, N. G., Meyers, L. A., & Lipsitch, M. (2018). Preprints: An underutilized mechanism to accelerate outbreak science. *PLoS Medicine, 15*(4), e1002549. https://doi.org/10.1371/journal.pmed.1002549

Klein, M., Van de Sompel, H., Sanderson, R., Shankar, H., Balakireva, L., Zhou, K., & Tobin, R. (2014). Scholarly context not found: One in five articles suffers from reference rot. *PLoS ONE, 9*(12), e115253. https://doi.org/10.1371/journal.pone.0115253

Klump, J., & Huber, R. (2017). 20 years of persistent identifiers – Which systems are here to stay? *Data Science Journal, 16*, 9. https://doi.org/10.5334/dsj-2017-009

Knoth, P., Anastasiou, L., Charalampous, A., Cancellieri, M., Pearce, S., Pontika, N., & Bayer, V. (2017, June). *Towards effective research recommender systems for repositories.* Open repositories 2017. Brisbane, Australia. http://oro.open.ac.uk/49366/

Knoth, P., & Zdrahal, Z. (2013). CORE: Aggregation use cases for open access. *Proceedings of the 13th ACM/IEEE-CS joint conference on digital libraries* (pp. 441–442). IEEE. https://doi.org/10.1145/2467696.2467787

Kulovits, H., Rauber, A., Gamito, R., Barateiro, J., Borbinha, J. L., Mazive, M., & João, D. (2012, May). Archives and digital repositories in an eGovernment context: When the subsequent bird catches the worm. *IST-Africa 2012*. http://repositorio.lnec.pt:8080/jspui/handle/123456789/1003522

Kuperberg, G. (2020). Using the arXiv. *Notices of the American Mathematical Society*, *67*(2), 1. https://doi.org/10.1090/noti2022

Kwanya, T., Stilwell, C., & Underwood, P. G. (2013). Intelligent libraries and apomediators: Distinguishing between Library 3.0 and Library 2.0. *Journal of Librarianship and Information Science*, *45*(3), 187–197. https://doi.org/10.1177/0961000611435256

Learning Technology Standards Committee (LTSC). (2020). *IEEE 1484.12.1–2002 – IEEE standard for learning object metadata.* https://standards.ieee.org/standard/1484_12_1-2002.html

Li, T. (2019). SSRN and open access for non-institutional scholars [Preprint]. *LawArXiv*. https://doi.org/10.31228/osf.io/dq57y

Li, Y., & Banach, M. (2011). Institutional repositories and digital preservation: Assessing current practices at research libraries. *D-Lib Magazine*, *17*(5/6). https://doi.org/10.1045/may2011-yuanli

Lubbock, J. (2018). Wikipedia and libraries. *Alexandria*, *28*(1), 55–68. https://doi.org/10.1177/0955749018794968

Lynch, C. A. (1995). Networked information resource discovery: An overview of current issues. *IEEE Journal on Selected Areas in Communications*, *13*(8), 1505–1522. https://doi.org/10.1109/49.464719

Lynch, C. A. (2003). Institutional repositories: Essential infrastructure for scholarship in the digital age. *Portal: Libraries and the Academy*, *3*(2), 327–336. https://doi.org/10.1353/pla.2003.0039

Lynch, C. A. (2006). *Digital repositories*. Digital Curation Centre (DCC). www.dcc.ac.uk/sites/default/files/documents/resource/briefing-papers/digital-repositories.pdf

Macgregor, G. (2020). Enhancing content discovery of open repositories: An analytics-based evaluation of repository optimizations. *Publications*, *8*(1), 8. https://doi.org/10.3390/publications8010008

Macgregor, G., & Neugebauer, T. (2020). Preserving digital content through improved EPrints repository integration with Archivematica. *UK Archivematica User Group*, 1–10. https://strathprints.strath.ac.uk/73978/

Mannheimer, S., Clark, J., Hagerman, K., Schultz, J., & Espeland, J. (2021). Dataset search: A lightweight, community-built tool to support research data discovery. *Journal of EScience Librarianship*, *10*(1), 1189. https://doi.org/10.7191/jeslib.2021.1189

Marra, M. (2017). Astrophysicists and physicists as creators of ArXiv-based commenting resources for their research communities. An initial survey. *Information Services & Use*, *37*(4), 371–387. https://doi.org/10.3233/ISU-170856

Marušić, M., Tomić, V., Gudelj, D., Wager, E., & Marušić, A. (2019). University repository overlay journal – Increasing the quality and visibility of student research at the University of Split, Croatia. *European Science Editing*, *45*(2). https://doi.org/10.20316/ESE.2019.45.19007

McGreal, R. (2008). A typology of learning object repositories. In H. H. Adelsberger, P. Kinshuk, J. M. Pawlowski, & D. G. Sampson (Eds.), *Handbook on information technologies for education and training* (pp. 5–28). Springer. https://doi.org/10.1007/978-3-540-74155-8_1

Mering, M., & Wintermute, H. E. (2020). MAPping metadata. *Journal of Digital Media Management*, *9*(1), 71–85.

Mohammadi, E., Thelwall, M., Kwasny, M., & Holmes, K. L. (2018). Academic informa-tion on Twitter: A user survey. *PLoS ONE, 13*(5), e0197265. https://doi.org/10.1371/journal.pone.0197265

Neugebauer, T., Simpson, J., & Bradley, J. (2018, June 5). Digital preservation through EPrints-Archivematica integration. *International conference on open repositories*. Boze-man, Montana, USA. https://spectrum.library.concordia.ca/983933/

Ochoa, X., & Duval, E. (2009). Quantitative analysis of learning object repositories. *IEEE Transactions on Learning Technologies, 2*(3), 226–238. https://doi.org/10.1109/TLT.2009.28

Palavitsinis, N., Manouselis, N., & Sanchez-Alonso, S. (2014). Metadata quality in learn-ing object repositories: A case study. *The Electronic Library, 32*(1), 62–82. https://doi.org/10.1108/EL-12-2011-0175

Pennington, D., & Cagnazzo, L. (2019). Connecting the silos: Implementations and percep-tions of linked data across European libraries. *Journal of Documentation, 75*(3), 643–666. https://doi.org/10.1108/JD-07-2018-0117

Peters, I., Kraker, P., Lex, E., Gumpenberger, C., & Gorraiz, J. I. (2017). Zenodo in the spotlight of traditional and new metrics. *Frontiers in Research Metrics and Analytics, 2*, 13. https://doi.org/10.3389/frma.2017.00013

Pulikowski, A., & Matysek, A. (2021). Searching for LIS scholarly publications: A com-parison of search results from Google, Google Scholar, EDS, and LISA. *The Journal of Academic Librarianship, 47*(5), 102417. https://doi.org/10.1016/j.acalib.2021.102417

RLG/OCLC Working Group on Digital Archive Attributes, Research Libraries Group, & OCLC. (2002). *Trusted digital repositories: Attributes and responsibilities: An RLG-OCLC report*. RLG. www.oclc.org/content/dam/research/activities/trustedrep/reposito-ries.pdf

Rodrigues, E., Bollini, A., Cabezas, A., Castelli, D., Carr, L., Chan, L., Humphrey, C., Johnson, R., Knoth, P., Manghi, P., Matizirofa, L., Perakakis, P., Schirrwagen, J., Selematsela, D., Shearer, K., Walk, P., Wilcox, D., & Yamaji, K. (2017). *Next generation repositories: Behaviours and technical recommendations of the COAR next generation repositories working group*. Confederation of Open Access Repositories (COAR). https://doi.org/10.5281/zenodo.1215014

Salmon, S. R. (1982). The union catalogue: Functions, objectives and techniques. *Catalog-ing & Classification Quarterly, 2*(1/2). https://doi.org/10.1300/J104v02n01_03

Sampson, D. G., & Zervas, P. (2013). Learning object repositories as knowledge management systems. *Knowledge Management & E-Learning: An International Journal, 5*(2), 117–136.

Sansone, S.-A., Gonzalez-Beltran, A., Rocca-Serra, P., Alter, G., Grethe, J. S., Xu, H., Fore, I. M., Lyle, J., Gururaj, A. E., Chen, X., Kim, H., Zong, N., Li, Y., Liu, R., Ozyurt, I. B., & Ohno-Machado, L. (2017). DATS, the data tag suite to enable discoverability of datasets. *Scientific Data, 4*(1), 170059. https://doi.org/10.1038/sdata.2017.59

Shearer, K., Klein, M., & Walk, P. (2021, March 22). *Notify: The repository and services interoperability project*. https://vimeo.com/527538892

Singhal, A., & Srivastava, J. (2017). Research dataset discovery from research publications using web context. *Web Intelligence, 15*(2), 81–99. https://doi.org/10.3233/WEB-170354

Smucker, M. D. (2011). Information representation. In I. Ruthven & D. Kelly (Eds.), *Inter-active information seeking, behaviour and retrieval* (pp. 77–93). Facet.

Soiland-Reyes, S., & Goble, C. (2021, March 18). *RO-Crate: Describing and packaging FAIR research objects*. Scottish Covid-19 Response Consortium (SCRC). https://doi.org/10.5281/zenodo.4633655

Tennant, J. P., Waldner, F., Jacques, D. C., Masuzzo, P., Collister, L. B., & Hartgerink, C. H. J. (2016). The academic, economic and societal impacts of Open Access: An evidence-based review. *F1000Research*, *5*, 632. https://doi.org/10.12688/f1000research.8460.3

Thornton, G., & Kroeker, E. (2021). Overlay journals: Overlooked or emergent? *Proceedings of the annual conference of CAIS/Actes Du Congrès Annuel de l'ACSI*. CAIS. https://doi.org/10.29173/cais1199

Whitehead, M., Shearer, K., Matthews, C., & Rieger, O. (2019, November 26). Adding value to repositories through overlay journals. *The 14th international conference on open repositories (or2019)*. Hamburg, Germany. https://doi.org/10.5281/zenodo.3554328

Wilkinson, M. D., Dumontier, M., Aalbersberg, I. J., Appleton, G., Axton, M., Baak, A., Blomberg, N., Boiten, J.-W., da Silva Santos, L. B., Bourne, P. E., Bouwman, J., Brookes, A. J., Clark, T., Crosas, M., Dillo, I., Dumon, O., Edmunds, S., Evelo, C. T., Finkers, R., . . . Mons, B. (2016). The FAIR guiding principles for scientific data management and stewardship. *Scientific Data*, *3*(1), 160018. https://doi.org/10.1038/sdata.2016.18

Xie, I., & Matusiak, K. K. (2016). Digital preservation. In I. Xie & K. K. Matusiak (Eds.), *Discover digital libraries* (pp. 255–279). Elsevier. https://doi.org/10.1016/B978-0-12-417112-1.00009-0

2 Understanding Repository Functionality and Structure

Sharon Farnel

Introduction

A digital repository is a system that "ingest[s], store[s], manage[s], preserve[s], and provide[s] access to digital content" (Xie & Matusiak, 2016, p. 272). While it is a technical platform, it is also much more, including content and metadata, services, policies and procedures, workflows, and people to support it (Allan, 2009). The specific functions of a digital repository will differ depending on the users and its uses in a given context; however, its overarching goal is to collect and showcase digital resources and make them findable, accessible, interoperable, and reusable (GO FAIR Initiative, 2016).

Design and Functionality

Regardless of the underlying platform or software, digital repositories are generally structured in a similar fashion. They include a relational database (a storage system that enables access to data points that are related to each other) for managing metadata; software for retrieving data from the database and presenting it to users through a user interface; an approach for storing objects and metadata; and tools for managing user accounts and permissions, ingesting objects and metadata, and creating and configuring collections (Clobridge, 2010).

Presentation in digital repositories is designed around individual objects and sets of objects gathered together into collections based on various characteristics. These collections may also have metadata associated with them. An object is generally presented alongside metadata describing that object. Platforms differ in terms of the specific metadata standard(s) followed, the amount of metadata captured, and how that metadata is displayed; nonetheless, metadata is most often focused on characteristics or properties deemed most useful for finding, accessing, and understanding the objects presented on the platforms.

Digital repository platforms support interoperability in various ways. They generally follow one or more recognized metadata standards and often include functionality for exposing the metadata and their corresponding objects to external services. Some also allow downloading of objects and metadata and serialization of metadata in multiple formats.

DOI: 10.4324/9781003216438-4

Furthermore, most digital repository platforms allow for customizations. Defining additional metadata properties, tweaking the look and feel of the user interface, and defining access scenarios and user roles are common areas for local customizations. The level of customization possible, and how easy or difficult it is, differs depending on the platform being used. While customizations can be beneficial in terms of meeting local needs, they also come with challenges, including additional resource requirements and potential incompatibility with future core platform updates.

Common Digital Repository Platforms

The number and variety of available digital repository platforms are extensive, and scholars and practitioners characterize or type digital repositories in a variety of ways. One such detailed typology can be found in Chapter 1 of this text. Detailed inventories from the Registry of Open Access Repositories (2021), OpenDOAR (2021), the CARL Next Generation Repository Task Group (2020), the Collection Management System Collection (Blewer, 2017), the Open Access Directory (2021), the United States Electronic Thesis and Dissertation Association (2021), the University of Sheffield (n.d.), and Wikipedia (2018) can be referenced when searching for a potential digital repository platform. These lists contain varying levels of detail and are arranged in different ways. They are excellent resources for understanding the digital repository platform landscape.

Based on these lists as well as a scan of scholarly and practitioner literature, a subset of the most common platforms will be examined in this chapter. These are DSpace, EPrints, Digital Commons, Samvera, CONTENTdm, Omeka, Mukurtu, and Dataverse.

DSpace

DSpace is a freely available, open-source software designed to work with all types of digital objects including text, images, and datasets. DSpace organizes and presents content in a hierarchical tree structure of communities and collections. Individual objects in the repository have their own page, which includes the metadata for the item as well as links to download the associated file(s). DSpace supports interoperability by incorporating numerous standards and protocols for import, export, access, and use of digital objects, such as Open Archives Initiative Protocol for Metadata Harvesting (OAI-PMH) and Application Programming Interfaces (APIs). It is designed to be usable out of the box but has also been made customizable to meet local needs. Extensive customization requires either in-house technical expertise or contracting with a third-party service provider (Lyrasis, 2021a, 2021b).

EPrints

EPrints is a freely available and open-source software. Although most commonly used for text resources, it can also house other object types, such as images, audio, and datasets. EPrints organizes and presents content in hierarchical structures that reflect the structure of the host institution. Individual objects in the repository have their own page, which includes the metadata for that item as well as links to download the associated file(s). EPrints supports interoperability by incorporating numerous standards and protocols for import, export, access, and use of digital objects, such as OAI-PMH and APIs. It is designed to be easy to install and operate but has also been made customizable to meet local needs and interests. The EPrints Bazaar contains functional packages developed by the community that can be added to an instance to enhance functionality. Extensive customization requires either in-house technical expertise or contracting with a third-party service provider (EPrints Services, 2021).

Digital Commons

Digital Commons is a proprietary platform that can be used as a digital repository for a range of object types, including text, data, archives, and audio/video. It organizes and presents content using the concept of communities, which gather and display publications to create nested, hierarchical structures. Communities are often created for units within an organization, types of resources, and so on. Individual digital objects have their own page, tailored to their specific publication type. The page includes the metadata for that item as well as links to download the associated file(s). Digital Commons supports interoperability by incorporating numerous standards and protocols for import, export, access, and use of digital objects, such as OAI-PMH and APIs. It is a fully hosted platform that is customizable to meet local needs and interests. As a proprietary platform, customizations need to be negotiated with the service provider (bepress, 2021).

Samvera

Samvera is an open-source and freely available software that incorporates other open components or building blocks, including Fedora and Blacklight, allowing institutions to create the repository system that best fits their needs. It organizes and presents content using the concept of collections. Individual repository objects, which include metadata and associated files, are known as works. Pages for works contain both metadata and associated file(s) and can be tailored to specific work types. Samvera supports interoperability by incorporating numerous standards and protocols for import, export, access, and use of digital objects, such as OAI-PMH and APIs. There is an out-of-the-box version (Hyku) that incorporates the most commonly desired repository functionalities, but its underlying framework allows for customization. Incorporating community-developed extensions provides a means of customization that goes beyond what is available in the core code base. Extensive customization requires either in-house technical expertise or contracting with a third-party service provider (Samvera, 2021).

CONTENTdm

CONTENTdm is a proprietary platform developed and maintained by OCLC (since 2006). It can be used as a digital repository for a range of object types including text, images, and audio/video. CONTENTdm organizes and presents content based on the concepts of collections and items. Items, which are individual repository objects, are accessed on pages that contain both metadata and associated file(s). The metadata for these pages can be tailored on the basis of item type. The platform supports interoperability by incorporating numerous standards and protocols for import, export, access, and use of digital objects, such as OAI-PMH and APIs. It is a fully hosted platform that is customizable to meet local needs and interests. Since it is a proprietary platform, customizations beyond what is available in the base product have to be negotiated and resourced (OCLC, 2021).

Omeka

Omeka is an open-source and freely available digital repository software that can host objects of various types, including text, audio/video, and images. Organization and presentation of content in Omeka are built on the concept of items, the basic building blocks of a repository. Each item page consists of metadata and associated file(s) or media, and each item is grouped under collections or item sets. Pages for repository objects contain both metadata and associated file(s) and can be tailored to specific item types. The platform supports interoperability by incorporating numerous standards and protocols for import, export, access, and use of digital objects, such as OAI-PMH and APIs. Omeka is designed to be not only usable out of the box but also customizable to meet local needs. Incorporating community-developed plugins provides a means of customization that goes beyond what is available in the core code base. However, extensive customization requires either in-house technical expertise or contracting with a third-party service provider (Digital Scholar, 2021).

Mukurtu

Mukurtu is a freely available and open-source platform that can host objects of various types, including text, audio/video, and images. It includes options for using community cultural protocols to define access and use of the platform and enables multiple object descriptions. Mukurtu organizes and presents content based on the concepts of communities, cultural protocols, and categories. Individual repository objects, called heritage items, consist of metadata and associated file(s) or media. Pages for heritage items contain the associated file(s), protocols for access and use, basic metadata for the item, and one or more community metadata records for the object. Mukurtu is specifically designed to meet the unique needs of individual communities. Therefore, interoperability is enabled more so through the use of common base software components. Mukurtu is designed to be usable out of the box, but it does require configuration based on local context. This configuration work is designed to be undertaken in collaboration with the community that the repository is meant to serve. Extensive customization that goes beyond what is accounted for in the core code base requires either in-house technical expertise or contracting with a third-party service provider (Mukurtu, 2021).

Dataverse

Dataverse is a freely available, open-source digital repository platform designed specifically for research data. It can host objects of various types, including text, images, and audio/video, as well as tabular and geospatial files. Dataverse organizes and presents content using the concept of datasets, which can then be gathered into collections and individual dataverses (containers for datasets that share some relationship) within an institutional Dataverse installation. Dataverse supports interoperability by incorporating numerous standards and protocols for import, export, access, and use of digital objects. It not only is designed to be functional out of the box but can also be customized to meet local needs. Customization is possible by adding specialized metadata blocks or integrating tools developed by the community (Table 2.1). Extensive customization that goes beyond what is accounted for in the core code base requires either in-house technical expertise or contracting with a third-party service provider (Dataverse Project, 2021).

Digital Repository Platforms and Discoverability

Digital repositories are more than simply holding containers for content; they are destinations in and of themselves. According to Khan (2019), "searching and browsing [are] the major requirements" in any digital repository system (Khan, 2019, p. 48). Walton (2018) concurs, noting that discoverability is a critical aspect of interaction with digital repositories, and describes how "multiple ways to search", "useful metadata for each resource", and browsing a "diversity of content in meaningful ways" (p. 25) impact usability and the overall user experience. Therefore, addressing the discoverability of content "from within" a repository platform is a critical component of any service program.

Table 2.1 Overview of common digital repository platforms

	Open-Source	Supports Different Object Types	Customizable Metadata	Multilingual Versions	OAI-PMH
DSpace	Yes	Yes	Yes	Yes	Yes
EPrints	Yes	Yes (primarily text)	Yes	No	Yes
Digital Commons	No	Yes	Yes	No	Yes
Samvera	Yes	Yes	Yes	Yes	Yes
CONTENTdm	No	Yes	Yes	Yes	Yes
Omeka	Yes	Yes	Yes	Yes	Yes (via plugin)
Mukurtu	Yes	Yes	Yes	No	No
Dataverse	Yes	Yes (primarily tabular data)	Yes	Yes	Yes

Numerous features and functionalities affect this discoverability, such as metadata, which is critical to discoverability. How much metadata about a repository object can be captured? Does that metadata follow community standards? Can the metadata be tailored to specific object types? Are there options for enabling controlled vocabularies, or other means of ensuring that metadata is consistently applied across objects and collections? Is enough metadata displayed to the user so that they can understand, access, and use an object? Can that display be customized for different object types, collections, or communities? (NISO, 2007).

Knowledge organization, or the way in which content is organized for and presented to the end user, as well as navigation also impacts discoverability. How are objects organized within the repository? Is this structure intuitive and easy to browse? Can it be customized on the basis of a repository's content and its users? How easy is it to navigate between items and collections in the repository? Are there ways of easily navigating between related content (objects or collections)? Are repository objects or collections assigned persistent identifiers (or PID), like a Handle or a digital object identifier (DOI), for easy navigation back to that resource? (Bankier & Gleason, 2014).

Search, faceting, and relevance ranking also impact the discoverability of repository content (Khan, 2019). But what gets searched: metadata only or metadata and objects? Are there advanced search capabilities? Can either of these be customized on the basis of the nature of the content, or the repository's users and uses? How are search results ranked? Can you sort search results according to different facets (e.g., date or title)? Are there ways of faceting or limiting a search after an initial result set has been returned? If so, can these options also be tailored based on a given context?

There are two additional features that can impact discoverability from within the repository. One is multilingual functionality, which includes options for multilingual content and metadata, as well as for multilingual repository interfaces. While this may not be needed or desired in all contexts, users' ability to interact with both the platform and the content in their language of choice can greatly impact their discovery experience. A second additional feature that can impact discoverability is how well the platform operates on different devices, such as smartphones or tablets. The ability to effectively search and browse no matter the device is important to the digital repository experience (Duran, 2018).

While discoverability from within the repository is critical, discoverability of repository content elsewhere is also important as digital repositories are "used as modern ways of promotion and dissemination" (Formanek, 2021, p. 3). As Macgregor (2020) notes, "more than ever, users of repository content expect to discover open content easily, normally via search, and for their own content (typically scholarly content deposited in an open repository) to be equally discoverable" (p. 2). Walton (2018) confirms this, citing digital repository usability studies which show that the overall lack of visibility of a repository's content on the wider web is an important factor in users' assessment of the usability and relevance of that repository. Arlitsch et al. (2021) show that "data are confirming years of speculation that many IR suffer from low use and one significant causal factor is likely to be low indexing ratios in search engines" (p. 331). Therefore, understanding how the design and functionality of repository platforms impact their discovery "from without" is important for any service program.

Several features and functionalities affect the discoverability of content from outside of the repository platform. As we have seen, metadata is critical to discoverability from within a repository, and this is no less the case when we look at discoverability from without. In addition to the questions asked about metadata when considering discovery within a repository, it is also important to ask whether or not the repository platform includes support for individual item metadata export/ download in one or more formats, as well as support for individual item citation export/download.

An important aspect of discoverability without is the inclusion of repository metadata and/or objects in federated databases or aggregator platforms and its use by external services. To enable this, it is important to know if the repository platform supports harvesting standards and protocols such as OAI-PMH, OAI-ORE (Open Archives Initiative Object Exchange and Reuse), or ResourceSync, or includes APIs to support additional user interactions.

A final critical aspect of discoverability from without relates to optimizing a digital repository and its content for search engines. In addition to including metadata that can help search engines determine how relevant an item is to a user query (Arlitsch et al., 2021), does the repository platform meet Google Scholar inclusion guidelines, such as including structured item metadata in the <head> tag of repository object HTML pages (Macgregor, 2019)? Does it include options for implementing microdata such as Schema.org or enable the inclusion of sitemaps (COAR, 2017; Ratcliff, 2016)?

Discoverability Features and Common Digital Repository Platforms

Now that we have introduced some of the most common digital repository platforms and outlined the features and functionalities that impact discoverability both from within and without, we can compare and contrast these across the platforms.

DSpace

The default metadata schema in DSpace is Dublin Core (DC), with Qualified Dublin Core (QDC) also being supported. Currently, it can support other flat metadata structures. Furthermore, support for hierarchical metadata schemas is on the development roadmap. The metadata captured can be customized for different types and/or collections. Incorporating controlled vocabularies and using authority control for enhancing metadata consistency and quality is also supported. The labels used for metadata elements can be customized, as can the display of object and collection pages. DSpace incorporates the Handle PID system and provides the functionality to configure the repository to use DOIs as well.

DSpace structures content into collections and communities. These can be configured to represent organizational departments, thematic or object type groupings, or other characteristics. It also allows for browsing by both community and collection, as well as by any number of metadata elements, with author, title, date, or subject being the defaults. From within a community or collection, or while on an individual object page, a user can navigate up or down the hierarchy, and to individual items. Moreover, additional browse options (e.g., by title or subject) can be configured when within a community or collection. DSpace can also be configured to allow for additional browsing through related objects based on metadata, such as author or keyword(s). Furthermore, recent submissions as well as item suggestions ("more like this") based on specific characteristics can also be configured to provide additional browse opportunities.

DSpace puts search front and center in its functionality. Search works across all metadata fields and is configurable. It also includes full-text searching of numerous common file types. Rather than employing advanced search, it incorporates faceted searching and browsing, which can be customized to specific metadata fields. It also includes a spell check for searching. Search results can be configured to include different types of content. The sort order of search results, as well as how many results are returned per page, is configurable. While there is little detail in the DSpace documentation about relevance ranking, because it comes with the configurable Apache Solr search platform, there will be opportunities to address relevance ranking within its configuration.

DSpace is available in numerous languages, and additional translations can be added. It also supports multilingual metadata by being Unicode (UTF-8) compliant. DSpace interface design supports discovery and access across a variety of device types and screen sizes.

DSpace includes support for metadata and object harvesting through both OAI-PMH and OAI-ORE, and it also supports emerging best practices for exposing and sharing resources. DSpace also includes APIs to enable interaction with repository content and services. In support of search engine optimization (SEO), DSpace allows for the creation of sitemaps. It also enables the use of microdata by incorporating both DC and Google Scholar-specific metadata fields on the HTML page of every repository item. The mapping of metadata elements to these two formats can be tailored on the basis of the extent to which a repository's metadata schema has been customized. However, it does not currently support individual item metadata or citation download.

EPrints

The default metadata supported in EPrints is DC. The captured metadata can be customized for different types of objects. Furthermore, incorporating controlled vocabularies for enhancing metadata consistency and quality is supported. The labels used for metadata elements can be customized, as can the display of item pages. EPrints includes a locally unique Uniform Resource Identifier (URI) for each repository object and also incorporates DOIs.

EPrints organizes its content according to organizational structure (e.g., department, division) and allows rich browsing accordingly. In addition, it allows for browsing by subject (which is based on the Library of Congress Classification [LCC]) and year by default. Additional browsing options are configurable. From anywhere within a hierarchy, a user can navigate up or down and to individual items. Browsing through related objects based on metadata elements, such as author or object type, is also possible. Recent submissions can be configured to provide additional browsing opportunities. Based on the search and/or browse criteria, users can also set up a feed to be notified of new relevant repository items. Moreover, it provides options for visualizing search and browse results, including word clouds and author collaboration graphs. An additional new feature allows for curating lists of objects based on certain criteria, such as subject, and making those available for browsing.

EPrints incorporates both simple and advanced searches, which can be applied across metadata fields as well as the full text of repository files. Fields available for both simple and advanced searches are customizable based on local needs. However, faceting is unavailable after an initial search. A spell check is available when searching, and the sort order of search results is configurable. There is little detail in the EPrints documentation about relevance ranking.

EPrints supports multilingual metadata by being Unicode (UTF-8) compliant. While not currently available in multiple languages out of the box, EPrints can be made available in other languages if the necessary translation and configuration work is completed. EPrints interface design supports discovery and access across a variety of device types and screen sizes.

EPrints enables the use of microdata by incorporating DC metadata fields on the HTML page of every repository item. The mapping of metadata elements to this format can be tailored based on the extent to which a repository's metadata schema has been customized. It also includes EPrints microdata. EPrints includes support for metadata and object harvesting through OAI-PMH and also includes APIs to enable interaction with repository content and services. In support of SEO, EPrints allows for the creation of sitemaps as required by Google and other search engines. It also includes a formatted citation for each repository object and allows for metadata and citation download/export in an extensive list of formats. Furthermore, it allows for easy sharing using social media platforms as well as email.

Digital Commons

Digital Commons has DC and QDC as its default metadata support. The captured metadata can be customized for different object types and/or collections. The incorporation of controlled vocabularies, including the Digital Commons taxonomy of academic disciplines and authority control on author names, is supported. The labels used for metadata elements and the display of item and collection pages can be customized. Furthermore, Digital Commons includes a locally unique URI for each repository object and also incorporates DOIs.

Digital Commons organizes its content according to collections, as well as academic disciplines, and allows rich browsing through both. Additional browsing options are configurable. From anywhere within a hierarchy, a user can navigate up or down and to individual items. Although browsing through related objects based on author name is possible, other metadata elements are not configured to support this. Furthermore, recent submissions, top downloads, and paper of the day provide additional browsing options. The platform also enables the configuration of various visualizations such as a map or discipline wheel to provide additional pathways into the repository's content. Exhibits and galleries can also be configured. Users can save searches for future use and can set up feeds to be notified of new content based on browse criteria.

Digital Commons incorporates both simple and advanced searches, which can be applied across metadata fields as well as the full text of repository files. Fields available for both simple and advanced searches are customizable based on local needs. Digital Commons also supports faceted searching, allowing a result set to be further narrowed according to discipline, subject, date, and several other properties. By default, the sort order is according to relevance, but this can be changed to publication date. The results of an advanced search can be returned as a list of links to further explore or can be exported as a set of bibliographic citations. Because Digital Commons is a community of platforms shared through a single service provider, the ability to search across all repositories is an additional option available to users. There is little detail in the Digital Commons documentation about relevance ranking.

Digital Commons supports multilingual metadata by being Unicode (UTF-8) compliant. It is not currently available in multiple languages. Its interface design supports discovery and access across a variety of device types and screen sizes.

Digital Commons includes support for metadata and object harvesting through OAI-PMH. It also includes APIs to enable interaction with repository content and services. In support of SEO, Digital Commons allows for the creation of sitemaps and enables the use of microdata by incorporating metadata fields on the HTML page of every repository item. Metadata element mapping can be tailored on the basis of the extent to which a repository's metadata schema has been customized. Digital Commons includes a formatted citation for each repository object, but it does not have functionality for metadata or citation download/export. It also allows for easy sharing using social media platforms and email.

Samvera

The basic metadata profile within Samvera incorporates properties from several standards, including DC and QDC. Customization enables the incorporation of properties from additional standards. The captured metadata can be customized for different object types and/or collections, and support for controlled vocabularies can be programmed. The labels used for metadata elements and the display of item and collection pages can both be customized. Samvera incorporates local PIDs and can be customized to work with the Handle, DOI, or other PID systems.

Samvera organizes its content by object (called Works) and collections and allows for browsing by collection as well as other properties such as creator or subject. Additional properties can be configured to enable browsing. From within a collection or from a repository object page, the means of navigating up and down the hierarchy can be customized to suit local needs. Browsing through related objects based on metadata elements is also possible. Visual browsing, such as through thumbnails or a map, can be custom programmed, and other means of showcasing or highlighting objects or collections can also be defined and programmed.

Samvera allows for both simple and advanced searches, which can be applied across metadata fields as well as the full text of repository files, if configured. Fields available for both simple and advanced searches are customizable based on local needs. Samvera also supports faceted searching, allowing a result set to be further narrowed. By default, the sort order is according to relevance, but this can be changed to date or other properties as desired. The number of results returned per page can also be configured. There is little detail in the Samvera documentation about relevance ranking. However, because it comes with the configurable Apache Solr search platform, there will be opportunities to address relevance ranking within its configuration.

Samvera supports multilingual metadata by being Unicode (UTF-8) compliant. The Hyku (repository in a box version) application is currently available in Chinese and Spanish as well as English and can be made available in other languages if the necessary translation and configuration work is completed. Samvera interface design provides some support for discovery and access across a variety of device types and screen sizes.

Samvera supports metadata harvesting via OAI-PMH through the services available as part of Fedora and Blacklight, as well as through add-ons developed as part of the Advancing Hyku project, which concluded in 2022. In support of SEO, Samvera allows for the creation of sitemaps and enables the use of microdata by incorporating metadata fields on the HTML page of every repository item. Metadata element mapping can be tailored based on the extent to which a repository's metadata schema has been customized. Samvera can be configured to show a citation for each repository object, and to make that citation downloadable/exportable. However, it does not currently support metadata export/download. It can be configured to allow for easy sharing using social media or email.

CONTENTdm

Default metadata in CONTENTdm is QDC. While the metadata captured for object types and/or collections can be customized, a maximum of 125 metadata elements exist for a given collection. Numerous controlled vocabularies, including many of those most commonly used in libraries, such as Medical Subject Headings (MeSH), Art & Architecture Thesaurus (AAT), and Thesaurus for Graphic Materials (TGM), are supported. The labels used for metadata elements, as well as the item and collection pages display, can be customized. CONTENTdm includes a locally unique URI for each repository object but does not assign PIDs such as DOIs or Handles.

CONTENTdm organizes its content into collections and allows rich browsing accordingly. Additional forms of browsing are configurable. From anywhere within a hierarchy, a user can navigate up or down and to individual items. Browsing through related objects based on a variety of metadata fields, such as subject or date, is configurable. Various visual approaches to browsing and navigation, such as through image thumbnails or maps, can be configured.

CONTENTdm incorporates both simple and advanced searches, which can be applied across metadata fields as well as the full text of repository files. Fields available for both simple and advanced searches are customizable based on local needs. CONTENTdm also supports faceted searching, allowing a result set to be further narrowed according to any number of metadata properties. The default sort order is by relevance, but this can be changed to title, date, or other properties. The number of search results per page can also be customized. Users can set up an account and save searches for future access or share them with a custom link. There is little detail in the CONTENTdm documentation about relevance ranking.

CONTENTdm supports multilingual metadata by being Unicode (UTF-8) compliant. It currently has localizations in numerous languages. Additional localizations can be configured by creating a Translation Memory eXchange (TMX) XML file. CONTENTdm incorporates principles of responsive design and supports discovery and access across a variety of device types and screen sizes.

CONTENTdm includes support for metadata harvesting through OAI-PMH. It also includes APIs to enable interaction with repository content and services. In support of SEO, CONTENTdm allows for the creation of sitemaps and enables the use of microdata by incorporating metadata fields on the HTML page of every repository item. Metadata element mapping can be tailored on the basis of the extent to which a repository's metadata schema has been customized. In addition, CONTENTdm is integrated with OCLC's Digital Collections Gateway which allows for streamlined inclusion in WorldCat. CONTENTdm can be configured to allow for easy sharing through social media platforms and email, but it does not allow for the download or export of individual object metadata.

Omeka

The default metadata standard for Omeka Classic is DC. Additional custom elements can be defined, and other metadata schemas can be included through plugins. Based on the Dublin Core Metadata Initiative (DCMI) guidelines, using controlled vocabularies is recommended for certain fields. There are plugins to incorporate lookup functionality for particular vocabularies, such as Library of Congress Subject Headings (LCSH), and also to create local controlled vocabularies. Tags, which are keywords that describe repository items, are also available. Although Omeka Classic comes with DC item types, new item types can be created and defined. Each item can be described with both standard DC elements and with custom elements created for specific item types. Labels for the DC elements cannot be easily changed, but custom elements can be given desired labels. The item and collection page display can be customized. Omeka includes a locally unique URI for each repository object, but it does not assign PIDs such as DOIs or Handles.

Omeka organizes its content into collections and allows for the creation of exhibits from the digital objects in the repository through a plugin. Browsing through items, collections, and tags is available by default, and additional navigational links can be defined. Additional browsing options, such as by exhibits or maps, can be made available through plugins. Browsing through related objects based on a variety of metadata fields is also possible through plugins. From within a collection or exhibit, a user can browse to different items. From an item page, a user can browse to the next and the previous items in the collection or exhibit or up a level to the collection or exhibit page. Browse pages allow for reordering of items by title, creator, date, or other properties.

Omeka incorporates both simple and advanced searches, which can be applied across metadata fields for all item types, including the text on the repository's descriptive pages. A user can adjust the settings for the basic search to indicate whether the search is based on keyword, Boolean, or exact match and can also limit the items they wish to search. Only items can be searched using the advanced search option, and it allows for a search across specific elements. The number of results per page for browse and search can be customized. Faceted searching can be incorporated through a plugin. The default sort order is by relevance. Through a social bookmarking plugin, users can share items through email and social networking sites. There is little detail in the Omeka documentation about relevance ranking.

Omeka supports multilingual metadata by being Unicode (UTF-8) compliant. It manages translation through transifex.com, which is centered around a community-based approach to creating multilingual versions. Fully functional translations include Chinese, Spanish, and Italian, and other languages are in process. Additional languages can be proposed and started at any time. Functionality is enabled through a plugin with the appropriately translated files. Discovery and access of Omeka repositories generally work fairly well across a variety of device types and screen sizes.

Omeka is equipped with a basic API to enable interaction with repository content and services. OAI-PMH is available through a plugin. The mappings from local metadata into a variety of OAI-PMH metadata formats can be configured based on local usage. Omeka does not have extensive support for SEO, such as built-in support for sitemaps or inclusion of microdata. Each item in Omeka has an autogenerated citation from the item metadata, and metadata for items can be made downloadable in several formats such as JSON or XML.

Mukurtu

Metadata in Mukurtu is based on DC but is expanded to include additional properties that can capture community-specific information, such as access protocols and cultural narrative(s) about an item. The specific elements used and the method of their usage can be customized based on community needs. Mukurtu supports the use of controlled vocabularies in various fields such as subject, license, and Traditional Knowledge labels. Categories, which are high-level descriptive terms that enable discovery through search and browse, are unique to each site. The item and collection page display can be customized. Mukurtu includes a locally unique URI for each repository object, but it does not assign PIDs such as DOIs or Handles.

Mukurtu organizes its content by communities, collections, and categories and allows browsing by these groupings. Nonetheless, other browse options can be configured. Browsing through related objects based on a variety of metadata fields is possible. A metadata field for specifying related items based on other characteristics such as creator or subject is available by default. From within a collection, category, or community, a user can browse to different items, and from an item page, a user can go back to the appropriate collection, community, or category page. Browsing all items allows the user to view an entire repository in list or grid form, as well as by location on a map. Items can be ordered not only by relevance by default but also by date or title. When browsing all items, they can also be filtered by community, category, media type, and other properties.

Mukurtu provides a basic search functionality that searches across all metadata. There are currently no options for easy sharing of content through social media or email. There is little information in the Mukurtu documentation about relevance ranking.

Mukurtu supports multilingual metadata by being Unicode (UTF-8) compliant. It does not appear to have extensive support for multilingual instances at this time. However, it is built on Drupal, which has capabilities for localizing interfaces. Therefore, implementing a multilingual Mukurtu repository should be possible. Discovery and access of Mukurtu repositories generally work fairly well across a variety of device types and screen sizes. It has also recently developed and made available Mukurtu Mobile, a companion application that allows interaction with a Mukurtu repository.

Mukurtu comes with a basic API to enable interaction with repository content and services. It does not currently support metadata harvesting through protocols such as OAI-PMH. Although indexed by search engines such as Google, Mukurtu does not have extensive support for SEO, such as built-in support for sitemaps or inclusion of microdata. However, this is largely due to conscious decisions to exclude these functions because Mukurtu has been created for the specific purpose of enabling Indigenous communities' control over their own content, and how it is organized and described, who has access to it, and what they can do with it. Citations can be added to individual item pages, but there is currently no option for downloading individual item metadata.

Dataverse

Dataverse is equipped with a rich set of supported metadata. Three levels of metadata are available for a dataset: citation metadata, domain-specific metadata, and file-level metadata. Each of these is compliant with internationally recognized standards such as the Data Documentation Initiative (DDI), DC, and Datacite, among others. Metadata is configured through metadata blocks, and custom blocks can be created to meet local needs. The use of controlled vocabularies is encouraged and supported. The display of metadata as well as the dataset and dataverse pages can be customized. Dataverse includes functions for enabling both Handle and DOI PID systems.

Dataverse organizes content by dataverses and datasets. Basic browsing categories are by dataverse, category, date, and other properties, which are configurable. From a dataverse page, a user can easily browse to datasets or files, which can be filtered by category, date, subject, or other configurable properties, and move up or down the hierarchy. From a dataset page, a user can navigate up the hierarchy, view citation- and domain-specific metadata, view terms of access and use, access files, and see versions of the dataset. Browsing all the content of the repository allows for faceting by type (i.e., dataverse, dataset, and files) as well as other customizable properties such as date and category. Items in the "browse all" list can be sorted by date or name.

Dataverse provides both a basic and an advanced search, which searches across metadata and files. However, the advanced search is normally displayed only after a basic search has been run. Search results are not only sorted according to relevance by default, but they can also be sorted by date or name. Results can be further refined by a set of customizable facets such as subject or date. They can be shared via a search URL that can be copied and pasted into email or other tools. Advanced search allows the user to specify fields for search, and this can be customized based on local needs. More granular search within a specific dataverse or dataset is also possible. Users can share individual datasets, files, or dataverses using a PID such as a DOI. Saved searches as a feature are currently being tested. There is little in the Dataverse documentation that describes relevance ranking.

Dataverse supports multilingual metadata by being Unicode (UTF-8) compliant. It is currently being translated into multiple languages by the community, and several multilingual instances are already functional. A multilingual site can be enabled through specific configurations. Discovery and access of Dataverse repositories generally work fairly well across a variety of device types and screen sizes.

Dataverse is equipped with an extensive set of APIs to enable interaction with repository content and services. It supports discovery from without the repository by including a Dataverse widget for embedding a dataverse on an external site. In addition, integration with Datacite is built into the application; when datasets are published, the metadata is sent to Datacite for inclusion in its discovery portal. Dataverse also supports harvesting through OAI-PMH, with mappings of local metadata being customizable to the required standard(s). Dataverse generates a citation for every dataset, which can be downloaded in several common formats, including RIS and BibTeX. Metadata for individual files and datasets can be exported in a variety of formats, including JSON, DDI, and Datacite. Dataverse promotes SEO by supporting sitemaps and robots.txt. It currently incorporates some microdata, including Schema.org and DC, in the meta tags of dataset pages.

Conclusion: Key Considerations in the Choice and Evaluation of a Repository System

As outlined in the previous sections, each repository platform addresses discoverability from within and from without in its own way. Some functionality, such as basic search and browse, is commonly available while other, such as multilingual capabilities or support for DOIs, is not as consistently available.

Evaluating platform options and making a decision on which to choose is a process that involves understanding and balancing multiple interests and needs. A thorough grasp of the types and formats of your resources is important in order to understand the capabilities of any given repository platform to handle them in terms of discoverability and access.

Understanding your community (or communities) of users is a crucial aspect of this decision. Recognizing who these groups are and what they expect in terms of discoverability, both through the repository and through external services such as search engines or aggregators, will assist in the assessment of the viability of various repository platforms (DeRidder, 2007; Walton, 2018).

In addition, the resources (human, financial, technological) available to support the repository need to be articulated and compared against what is needed to create, sustain, and grow a repository using each of the potential repository solutions. This includes factoring in variables such as funds available for hosted solutions or custom development, and in-house expertise to customize existing code or develop new code. Larger institutions or consortia with strong information technology and/or financial resources often work with a variety of systems and contribute to their development and enhancement as part of the broader open-source community. Smaller institutions that may not have the same level of resourcing may benefit from simpler, out-of-the-box solutions.

In terms of discoverability, there is no single platform that will work best for all organizations or institutions. The optimal choice will depend on the circumstances in any given context. A great strength of the increasing role and presence of digital repositories in the library domain is the richness and variety of resources that can be brought to bear to assist in this important organizational decision.

References

Allan, R. (2009). *Virtual research environments: From portals to science gateways.* Chandos Publishing.

Arlitsch, K., Wheeler, J., Pham, M. T. N., & Parulian, N. N. (2021). An analysis of use and performance data aggregated from 35 institutional repositories. *Online Information Review, 45*(2), 316–335.

Bankier, J.-G., & Gleason, K. (2014). *Institutional repository software comparison.* UNESCO. https://unesdoc.unesco.org/ark:/48223/pf0000227115

Bepress. (2021). *Digital commons.* https://bepress.com/products/digital-commons/

Blewer, A. (2017). The collection management system collection. *Ashley Blewer.* https://bits.ashleyblewer.com/blog/2017/08/09/collection-management-system-collection/

CARL Next Generation Repository Task Group. (2020). *Inventory of Canadian repository platforms.* http://bit.ly/CanadianRepositories

Clobridge, A. (2010). *Building a digital repository program with limited resources.* Chandos Publishing.

COAR. (2017). *Next generation repositories.* www.coar-repositories.org/files/NGR-Final-Formatted-Report-cc.pdf

Dataverse Project. (2021). *The Dataverse project: Open source research data repository Software*. https://dataverse.org/

DeRidder, J. L. (2007). Choosing software for a digital library. *Library Hi Tech News, 24*(9/10), 19–21.

Digital Scholar. (2021). *Omeka*. https://omeka.org/

Duran, A. F. (2018, September 12). Responsive web design: Our 5 proven principles. *Level*. https://level-level.com/blog/responsive-web-design-our-5-proven-principles/

EPrints Services. (2021). *EPrints*. www.eprints.org/uk/

Formanek, M. (2021). Solving SEO issues in DSpace-based digital repositories: A case study assessment of worldwide repositories. *Information Technology and Libraries, 40*(1). https://doi.org/10.6017/ital.v40i1.12529

GO FAIR Initiative. (2016). *FAIR principles*. www.go-fair.org/fair-principles/

Khan, S. (2019). Dspace or Fedora: Which is a better solution? *SRELS Journal of Information Management, 56*(1), 45–50.

Lyrasis. (2021a). *DSpace*. https://duraspace.org/dspace/

Lyrasis. (2021b). *Fedora*. https://duraspace.org/fedora/

Macgregor, G. (2019). Improving the discoverability and web impact of open repositories: Techniques and evaluation. *Code4Lib Journal, 43*. https://journal.code4lib.org/articles/14180

Macgregor, G. (2020). Enhancing content discovery of open repositories: An analytics-based evaluation of repository optimizations. *Publications, 8*(1). https://doi.org/10.3390/publications8010008

Mukurtu. (2021). *Mukurtu CMS*. https://mukurtu.org/

NISO. (2007). *A framework of guidance for building good digital collections*. www.niso.org/sites/default/files/2017-08/framework3.pdf

OCLC. (2021). *CONTENTdm*. www.oclc.org/en/contentdm.html

Open Access Directory. (2021). *Free and open-source repository software*. http://oad.simmons.edu/oadwiki/Free_and_open-source_repository_software

OpenDOAR. (2021). *OpenDOAR statistics*. https://v2.sherpa.ac.uk/view/repository_visualisations/1.html

Ratcliff, C. (2016, January 21). SEO basics: 22 essentials you need for optimizing your site. *Search Engine Watch*. www.searchenginewatch.com/2016/01/21/seo-basics-22-essentials-you-need-for-optimizing-your-site/

Registry of Open Access Repositories. (2021). *Browse by repository software*. http://roar.eprints.org/view/software/

Samvera. (2021). *Samvera: A vibrant and welcoming community*. https://samvera.org/

United States Electronic Thesis and Dissertation Association. (2021). *Institutional repository software/services/systems*. www.usetda.org/resources/institutional-repository-software/

University of Sheffield. (n.d.). *Repository platforms*. https://sites.google.com/a/sheffield.ac.uk/rdm_links/technical/platforms

Walton, R. (2018). Evaluating IR platforms: Usability criteria for end users and IR managers. *Against the Grain, 30*(1), 25–26. https://doi.org/10.7771/2380-176X.8000

Wikipedia. (2018). *Category: Free institutional repository software*. https://en.wikipedia.org/wiki/Category:Free_institutional_repository_software

Xie, I., & Matusiak, K. K. (2016). *Discovering digital libraries: Theory and practice*. Elsevier.

3 Understanding the Role of Metadata in a Digital Repository

Jenn Riley

Library Metadata: Some Concepts, Formats, and History

Foundations and Early Developments

In the cultural heritage sector, the term *metadata* is common parlance. Often it is understood to be *cataloging*, or (in North America) a description of a library holding in the MAchine Readable Cataloging (MARC) format using Library of Congress (LC) standards. Similarly, archives frequently conceptualize metadata as finding aids created in the archive, while museums define it as data describing objects in collection inventories. This is indeed metadata; yet, its full scope is much wider in the context of digital repositories.

The metadata universe encompasses many different types of standards and guidance. These include the following:

- **Conceptual models** that define entities and their relationships (e.g., IFLA's Library Reference Model and the International Council of Museums Committee on Documentation [CIDOC] Reference Model);
- **Structure standards** (aka data dictionaries; metadata formats) that define *fields* that should be populated by appropriate metadata, which may or may not be defined as a specific technical schema or data format (e.g., MARC, Dublin Core [DC], Visual Resources Association Core Categories [VRA Core], and Canadian Heritage Information Network [CHIN] Data Dictionaries);
- **Content standards** that provide instruction on how the values added in a given data element can be constructed (e.g., Resource Description and Access [RDA], Describing Archives: A Content Standard [DACS], and Rules for Archival Description [RAD]);
- **Controlled vocabularies** that provide lists of permissible values in a given metadata field and sometimes define relationships between vocabulary terms in a thesaurus or ontology (e.g., Library of Congress Subject Headings [LCSH], Medical Subject Headings [MeSH]), Faceted Access to Subject Headings [FAST], and Getty Art & Architecture Thesaurus [AAT]);

DOI: 10.4324/9781003216438-5

- **Authority files** that record information about an entity for the purpose of uniquely identifying it and defining a standard name for it (e.g., Union List of Artist Names [ULAN]);
- **Classification schemes** that categorize a resource by its primary topic and generate a call number to indicate where an item is physically placed in a collection (e.g., Library of Congress Classification [LCC], Dewey Decimal Classification [DDC], and Iconclass);
- **Markup languages** that encode the content of an information resource to mark structural or semantic features (e.g., Test Encoding Initiative [TEI] and Encoded Archival Description [EAD]).

There are a number of "introduction to metadata" resources that examine metadata formats and standards of the cultural heritage sector in detail and introduce key terms (Baca, 2016; Pomerantz, 2015; Riley, 2017). This chapter will refer to some of these metadata practices, but it will predominantly focus on the evolution of metadata structure standards and their use in digital repositories.

Most of the metadata that arises from the traditional cataloging process is *descriptive* in nature and therefore describes a thing or a concept within the repository. A descriptive metadata standard pre-selects a set of *fields* or *elements* that represent the features that the standard considers important about said thing or concept. For books, for example, traditional cataloging standards provide for recording elements such as the book's author, title, the number of pages, and topic. Descriptive metadata's primary purpose is to assist users in locating material of interest.

This concept of a catalog with descriptive information used to explore a collection is by no means new. Among cataloging's foundational concepts is Charles Cutter's late 19th-century list of objectives for a library catalog (1891, p. 8):

1. To enable a person to find a book of which either
   (A) the author
   (B) the title
   (C) the subject

   . . . is known.

2. To show what the library has
   (D) by a given author
   (E) on a given subject
   (F) in a given kind of literature

3. To assist in the choice of a book
   (G) as to its edition (bibliographically)
   (H) as to its character (literary or topical)

These traditional cataloging practices are well-established in libraries and form the foundation of modern metadata approaches. The evolution of these practices shows increasing complexity and possibility, with each step building on the last.

Early practices in libraries such as browsing physical items on the shelf and early handwritten registers inventorying library collections required simpler discovery methods than we see today. These are examples of David Weinberger's "first-order" organization, where there is only one dimension to the organization – the characteristic chosen by a library to order books on a shelf. Within such an organization, discovery is possible only via that one facet of a book's metadata, and finding a grouping of items through another form of similarity is difficult or impossible (Weinberger, 2007, pp. 17–18). Weinberger's "second-order" organization is exemplified by the catalog card model, which first emerged as a simple cataloging code shared, cleverly, on the back of playing cards in France in 1791 (Library of Congress, 2017, pp. 21–22). Registers and inventories slowly gave way to standardization on 7.5 cm × 12 cm cards under the guidance of the American Library Association over the next century (Library of Congress, 2017, p. 84). In such a "second-order" organization, multiple access points are presented, but the physical nature of the medium for conveying information (i.e., the size of the card and the drawers into which cards for the entire collection must fit) provides an inherent limitation to how many access points (or different metadata elements) can be used for discovery (Weinberger, 2007, pp. 17–19).

With the advent of machine-readable cataloging, a progression toward "third-order" organization began. In 1968, after several pilot projects, the U.S. LC released specifications for the MARC format for bibliographic data (specifically books) to the library community, and in 1969, it began a service to provide machine-readable catalog records on digital tape to interested libraries on a weekly basis (Avram, 1975, p. 9). Computerized library catalogs that were based on and shared the MARC record metadata between institutions evolved in parallel, with what was then called the Ohio College Library Center (now OCLC) first emerging in 1967 (Borgman, 1997, p. 220).

Computerized library catalogs advanced several generations during the next few decades, becoming part of integrated library systems that managed acquisitions, circulation, cataloging, and discovery while still using the MARC Bibliographic format at their core. Despite these advances, catalogs were not yet repositories – they did not host or provide direct access to digital content. It was the rise of the world wide web in the 1990s that enabled digital repositories to develop, and metadata practices along with them.

Rise of the World Wide Web

Moving collections on to the web presented many challenges to libraries. First, the metadata scheme the library community knew so well (MARC Bibliographic) utilized a data storage format designed to minimize the amount of space a record took up on digital tape, via which it was transmitted. This record structure, which used variable length fields and signifiers for when one field ended and the next began, was wholly incompatible with the relational databases underlying websites. Second, each individual item in a library collection that would go online could not feasibly receive expert MARC cataloging. The missing piece was technology that could make use of the robust, if quirky, metadata in the MARC record and also provide access to resources with minimal description, if any (Besser, 2004, p. 565).

To address this need, a metadata workshop was held in March 1995 in Dublin, Ohio, which included attendees from a wide variety of knowledge and cultural heritage fields. Participants quickly realized the impossibility of one metadata format being useful in all scenarios. They decided instead to focus on "the definition of a simple data element set that could be used by information providers to describe their own resources". This simple metadata format could be used with minimal instructions (Caplan & Guenther, 1996, pp. 45–46). Thus, the Dublin Core (DC) was born. The structure and features of DC are widely documented elsewhere (Waibel, 1997; Coleman, 2005). Here, suffice it to say that as a simple 15-element metadata set with most elements having descriptive English-language names ("Title", "Subject", "Date", etc.) with a flat structure that made it simple to store in a relational database, DC received wide adoption quickly.

The digital library community used DC as a lowest-common-denominator format for describing individual photographs, letters, posters, and other special collections items that had never before received any kind of item-level description. Systems used it for the exchange of metadata, assuming that the simplicity of the element set would allow for interoperability. Even the open web caught on – webpage authors inserted DC metadata into HTML <meta> tags designed to signal the topic of a page to search engines. This method was quickly abused by webpage authors, who added high-ranking terms of interest into spam webpages that had nothing to do with the tags used (Gyöngyi & Garcia-Molina, 2005, p. 3). In response, search engines moved toward the now ubiquitous approach of indexing the complete text of a webpage.

While proving useful in practice, DC was persistently criticized for its lack of nuance for resource description (Gorman, 1999, pp. 15–21; Huthwaite, 2003). In response, the Dublin Core Metadata Initiative created extensions to DC, leading to a slightly more robust metadata schema they called Qualified Dublin Core (QDC). QDC had three types of additions to DC: refinements to original elements (e.g., Date had qualifiers "created", "issued"); encoding schemes signifying what thesaurus or formatting standard the value of the element uses (e.g., Subject had qualifiers "LCSH", "DDC"); and additional elements (e.g., Audience, Provenance). The idea behind the qualifiers was that even if a system processing the metadata did not understand the semantics of the qualifier, it would still understand its value as the original unqualified element. Thus, the timing of the emergence of DC and QDC in the early web days, along with their relative simplicity, has contributed to the longevity of the two formats. Over 25 years later, DC and QDC are still in use in digital repository software, as seen in the analysis in Chapter 2 of this volume.

Another response to criticisms of DC/QDC in the library community was an attempt to find a middle ground between DC and MARC. LC designed the Metadata Object Description Schema (MODS) for this purpose. First released in 2002, the MODS element set largely matched with MARC. However, MODS elements were English-language words or abbreviations, as opposed to the numbered fields in MARC, and MODS was defined in the widely-used XML technology rather than the specialized binary format of MARC (Guenther & McCallum, 2003, p. 12). As such, it was significantly easier to use in a web application, though the deep hierarchy of the MODS XML model was still not directly transferable to a relational database. MODS was a major step forward in the design of metadata standards in the library community, although it has not found wide adoption elsewhere. Today, MODS is not commonly used for interchange, but it is still the underlying descriptive metadata language in some digital repository implementations.

Move to Linked Data

A more modern approach to a metadata schema that can be used for any type of resource is BIBFRAME (Bibliographic Framework). In contrast to MODS, which was designed to be an alternative to MARC for use in digital repositories, BIB-FRAME is intended as a replacement for the long-antiquated MARC technology. It goes far beyond being simply a new format, however. BIBFRAME is defined as a Resource Description Framework (RDF) ontology, which indicates that it can be used by anyone on the web as linked data. Many descriptions of the mechanics of RDF and linked data are available (Lampert & Southwick, 2013; Yoose & Perkins, 2013). For this context, suffice it to say that RDF is a method to unbundle metadata *records* of the past into a series of independent facts, with unique identifiers for the people, objects, and concepts pertaining to those facts, and machine-readable statements of the relationships between them. Linked data is the emerging *graph* of knowledge when RDF-encoded data is shared, allowing data sets from different sources to be merged. Through the graph, the software can understand the relationships stated and infer new conceptual relationships from the underlying knowledge represented. Linked data is covered in more depth in Chapter 4 of this volume.

The BIBFRAME model defines a Work (e.g., the text of a novel), an Instance (a specific edition), and an Item (a specific copy) as core concepts, each with their own attributes (e.g., author for a novel/Work, translator for an edition/Instance, and author autograph for an identifiable copy/Item). It further defines core entities that have relationships with the Work/Instance/Item: Agents (people, organizations, etc.), Subject (what works are *about*), and Events (things that happen). LC is leading the effort to develop BIBFRAME and is positioning itself as the worldwide authority on entities and relationships for information resources. The promise of its approach is that organizations could then use the entities and relationships defined in BIBFRAME to describe their own information resources. Relationships would then exist between data sets, and all of them together would contribute to a global cloud of knowledge. BIBFRAME can be considered an intentional step away from the existence of library metadata solely to describe the information resources a given library curates and a step toward contributing to computerized representations of knowledge at a higher level.

RDA developed roughly in parallel with BIBFRAME. It was originally conceived as the Anglo-American Cataloging Rules, third edition (AACR3), a successor to the long-standing second edition (AACR2), a content standard that gives instructions on how values in the metadata fields, defined in a separate standard, should be worded and formatted. RDA was designed to conform with a variety of international cataloging standards (Oliver, 2021, p. 22), and as of this writing, it has been translated into eight additional languages from the original English. It is used as a content standard by libraries around the world, which enter values according to RDA guidelines into MARC record fields and subfields. In addition, RDA can be seen as a "package of data elements" (Oliver, 2021, p. 20). Because of this, it has been expressed in the form of RDF classes and properties. RDF-encoded RDA descriptions can be released to the web and can integrate with knowledge from other sources in the same manner as BIBFRAME.

However, libraries do not have a monopoly on metadata for information resources. Search engines are also making the old new again, and the concept of a webpage using embedded metadata to more fully describe its contents has returned. To accomplish this, the search engine industry came together to define the Schema.org metadata vocabulary. Schema.org is "a broad, Web-scale, shared vocabulary focusing on popular concepts. It stakes a position as a 'middle' ontology that does not attempt to have the scope of an 'ontology of everything' or go into depth in any one area" (Ronallo, 2012). It is designed as a formal ontology that will contribute significantly to the linked data cloud. As such, the Schema.org metadata embedded in a webpage not only describes the webpage as an information resource but also encodes the information contained in the content of that page. Schema.org is pervasive in the technology and e-commerce industries, and anywhere high search engine rankings are vital to business. Its success is a reminder that despite libraries' first steps toward integrating their metadata into the open web, the metadata properties, entities, and relationships (the *schemas* or ontologies) defined by the library community are still primarily of internal use to the community and not to the web at large.

With the move to linked data environments, library metadata now embodies Weinberger's "third-order" organization (Weinberger, 2007, pp. 19–21). As described earlier, "first-order" organization allows only one access point – the order of tangible items in their physical space. The card catalog exemplifies "second-order" organization. Discovery occurs using cards as proxies for items in a collection, but limitations of physical space still restrict the number of access points provided. "Third-order" organization is achieved in the digital environment when metadata flows from many sources and links together. Knowledge is thus advanced beyond what is possible for any one or few sources. An unlimited number of RDF statements can be made about a resource, and there is no absolute limit to the number of resources that may be described. Discovery by any feature of a resource is not limited by the storage and presentation format of its metadata but rather only by human decisions regarding where their time and technical resources can be spent.

One Size Does Not Fit All

As seen with the development of MARC, BIBFRAME, and Schema.org, knowledge communities tend to develop metadata structures for their own use, with data elements that suit their community culture and goals. The idea that a metadata schema is inherently designed for a specific community goes back to early catalog standardization efforts within libraries. Charles Cutter opens his *Rules for a Dictionary Catalogue* with the caution "No code of cataloguing could be adopted in all points by everyone, because the libraries for study and the libraries for reading have different objects, and those which combine the two do so in different proportions" (Cutter, 1891, p. 7).

In the web era, the archives community has developed its own metadata formats, despite some overlap with libraries in the types of material being held. Archives' tradition of creating textual finding aids and inventories for collections or fonds grew into EAD. Since the finding aid describes the fonds, EAD operates at two levels – encoding the text of the finding aid itself (structuring lists of box numbers, providing standardized forms of names, delineating one paragraph from the next in a content or biographical note, etc.) and serving as descriptive metadata for the fonds. This practice led the archives community toward a more standardized collection description and a less narrative approach in favor of more structured metadata. Today, the vast majority of archival description is prepared in an archival management system such as AtoM or ArchiveSpace, and EAD is solely an export format for interchange.

A parallel development to community-specific formats is the rise of descriptive metadata formats that provide deeper, more specific descriptions for one type of information resource. Again, this concept is not new to the web era. While the first MARC format released was for books, even at that early stage, plans existed to add additional "content designators" (i.e., metadata elements) for other types of resources such as serials, maps, and music (Avram, 1975, p. 7). Cultural heritage institutions needed ways to make previously hidden material available with minimal description. Photographs, sheet music, glass lantern slides, postcards, posters, and much more were digitized. However, MARC cataloging for these resources was wholly impractical. A proliferation of alternative metadata standards thus appeared as the solution.

The museum community was particularly in need of this approach. Art museums invested heavily in metadata models to meet their community needs, with the Getty Research Institute leading metadata infrastructure development. Their Categories for the Description of Works of Art (CDWA) is, like RDA, on the border between a structure standard and a content standard. The Getty's thesauri and authority files for art collections are extensive and heavily used – the Art & Architecture Thesaurus (AAT), Cultural Objects Name Authority (CONA), Iconography Authority (IA), Thesaurus of Geographic Names (TGN), and Union List of Artist Names (ULAN) are all publicly and freely available through an Open Data Commons license. Natural history and science museums relied more heavily on metadata schemas developed in specialized research areas, such as the CIDOC Core Data Standard for Archeological Objects, Space Physics Archive Search and Extract Data Model, Access to Biological Collection Data, and Climate and Forecast Metadata Conventions. More generally, a few cross-museum metadata standards emerged, for example, the Canadian Heritage Information Network (CHIN)

Data Dictionaries and the International Council of Museums' Comité International pour la Documentation [International Committee for Documentation] Conceptual Reference Model (CIDOC CRM).

Other communities followed suit with metadata formats suited to their own disciplinary needs. Many adopted DC's principle of simplicity. These include the Visual Resources Association (VRA) Core Categories, which describe reproductions of artworks held by pedagogical collections supporting Art History; Public Broadcasting Core for audiovisual resources; and Darwin Core for biological organisms. The Software Metadata Recommended Format was developed for the software preservation community. The publishing industry (publishers, distributors, retailers, etc.) uses ONIX (ONline Information eXchange) for Books as descriptive information, as books flow through the supply chain to customers. NISO's E-Book Bibliographic Metadata Requirements in the Sale, Publication, Discovery, and Preservation Supply Chain provides guidance on the construction of titles, names, dates, identifiers, and subjects for e-books regardless of which metadata format is used. The Data Documentation Initiative (DDI) describes data in the social sciences, documenting project design (e.g., codebooks and survey instruments), data collected through research (e.g., survey responses), and data analysis techniques.

Specialized metadata formats are also needed for aspects other than discovery and for specific forms of information objects. Hundreds of these exist, all for different purposes. For example, a repository of digital content must store some technical information about its files and maintain a log of activities undertaken to manage files in order to effectively preserve the content into the future. The PREMIS Data Dictionary for Preservation Metadata is one standard created for this purpose. Another example is AES57–2011 (r2017), an Audio Engineering Society standard for technical features of digital audio files.

How Metadata Is Used by Digital Repositories (or Could Be!)

Indexing

Descriptive metadata, however, rules the roost. The vast majority of metadata activities in the cultural heritage sector are dedicated to descriptive metadata that is used for discovery. At its simplest, descriptive metadata provides search engines with words that are indexed and are then compared to words in a user's query. Controlled vocabularies, authority files, and content standards are methods that the cultural heritage sector has used since the card catalog era to standardize the construction of entries in a catalog. This practice makes the terms in the index more predictable and groups similar things together. Theoretically, then, a knowledgeable user is able to find everything that matches the need behind their query (known as "recall") and exclude everything irrelevant (known as "precision") (Zhou et al., 2006, n.p.).

A user's query compared to an index of important features of digital content forms the basis for discovery in digital repositories. However, a brute force approach of indexing everything and comparing the exact query to the index is not particularly effective, even with consistent use of standard terminology. To improve discovery, repositories must enhance the index, optimize the ranking of search results, and parse or expand the user's query. The technologies used to do this principally come from the research field of information retrieval, which has been developing and refining mathematical algorithms for searching for decades (Manning et al., 2008).

Repositories for cultural heritage objects frequently present users with the option to do a keyword search or an advanced search. The former is typically a single box, and queries entered are compared to a keyword index. The latter is designed to take advantage of metadata structure, allowing users to specify their interest in a certain word or phrase present in a given metadata element, such as a title or an author. A keyword index would include terms from multiple fields, whereas an advanced search index might derive its terms from only one or a few fields of metadata.

It is common in the cultural heritage sector to hear feedback from users that they "just want it to work like Google!" The success of modern Internet search engines is largely a result of the technologies they have built to improve the index behind their search. In environments such as library discovery systems where search logs show that basic searches far outweigh advanced searches (Zavalina & Vassilieva, 2014; Cohen & Pusnik, 2018), it is even more important that the keyword index be optimized. As such, repository designers must make decisions about what metadata will be included in the keyword index. For example, since users would not typically be looking for preservation, technical, or structural metadata in a keyword search, these formats are generally omitted from the index. Other descriptive metadata fields, such as language or a rights statement, might similarly flood keyword results with inappropriate terms. Some elements, such as language, publisher, or the format of a resource, are more effective as facets or limits on searches (described later) than in a keyword index.

A standard part of both the indexing process and the parsing of a query is stemming, which involves truncating words down to the root so that queries are less likely to be affected by grammatical differences between queries and indexed terms. The removal of stopwords, frequently appearing terms that add little or no value if matched to a search, is also common. Common stopwords include articles (a, an, the) pronouns (his, her, their), transition words (which, because, further), and qualifiers (must, should, some, very). Many openly licensed stopword lists are available, and they are generally already part of indexing modules used in software development.

A particularly effective way to expand an index for textual resources is to include the full text of those resources in it. The ability to use the full text to improve discovery is a major difference between discovery in the analog era (i.e., catalog cards) and in the digital era; however, not all commonly used repositories in the cultural heritage community support full-text indexing. Stemming and stopword removal are typically used when indexing full text. Additional features to index phrases rather than only individual words are also part of nearly every software module for indexing that a repository system designer might use. Including full text in an index requires additional enhancement techniques to provide high-quality results.

Enhanced Approaches to Text-Based Discovery

These enhancement techniques come from the information retrieval community and more recently from machine learning and artificial intelligence. Many of the algorithms for retrieval defined in these areas of research are based on a conceptual vector space with documents as points in the space. The placement of a point is a representation of its similarity to other documents, with texts on the same topic clustered closely together but farther away from groups of documents focusing on less and less closely connected themes. One commonly used algorithm that demonstrates how vector space models can improve retrieval is Term Frequency/ Inverse Document Frequency (TF/IDF), a method designed in 1972 by Karen Spärck Jones (2004). With TF/IDF, the frequency of the occurrence of a term in a document is compared to the frequency of its occurrence in the other indexed documents. If a term has a high number of occurrences in more than one document, then it suggests not only that those documents are similar but also that the term is quite common. In contrast, a high number of occurrences of a term in one document and a small number of occurrences in other documents suggest something potentially more useful – that the document with the high usage is distinctively about that topic and is a better match to a query on that term than the others (Zhou et al., 2006, n.p.).

Computing document similarity to identify and rank search results is fundamentally different from the Boolean searching that has been used in cultural heritage discovery systems since the advent of computers. Originally, Galleries, Libraries, Archives, Museums, and Repositories (GLAMRs) had come to expect that an item in the repository either will or will not match their query terms (a binary choice) and that the list of matching results will then be sorted by various means based on structured metadata. However, with full-text indexing, GLAMR institutions and their users are presented with a more Google-like model of results which is ranked by likely similarity to the query. This structure might seem more familiar and easier to use for those not steeped in the Boolean tradition.

While many algorithmic retrieval techniques are part of standard indexing software, others are still being studied and have not yet been implemented in the cultural heritage sector's repositories on a large scale. One example is Named Entity Recognition (NER), a method for identifying proper names, such as places and people, from a full text, and then using those names to improve the index entries or construct structured metadata for that text. NER may also be used to expand user queries on an unenhanced index. The use of "knowledge-based systems" which "rely on lexicon resources and domain specific knowledge" (e.g., thesauri, ontologies, authority files, or gazetteers) is a common approach to NER (Yadav & Bethard, 2018, p. 2147). However, more recent work applying neural network models that do not use domain-specific data has shown that these models are beginning to outperform earlier algorithms that do (Yadav & Bethard, 2018, pp. 2152–2153).

Another method for improving retrieval leveraging existing structured metadata in libraries is using facets to improve search results. Unlike NER, the use of facets is widespread in digital repositories of cultural heritage material. Facets can be present as fields on an advanced search screen to scope initial results, but they are more commonly used on results screens to limit results after the initial set is provided. Facets contain lists of possible values for a certain metadata element, which when clicked restrict the existing search result to only those that have that value. Controlled vocabularies and authority files are useful for this purpose and are easy to implement when the metadata in a repository has been created using those same vocabularies. The most effective facets are either those with small numbers of values (e.g., Resource Type would have image, text, audio, dataset) or those that can be represented hierarchically (e.g., Location). Facets with large numbers of possible values each with a relatively low number of matches (e.g., Author Name) are clumsier to interact with on a typical repository search results screen. It is also important to consider the percentage of items in the repository that have no values in their metadata for an important facet. Large numbers of search results would fall away entirely if a faceted value was selected for a field that is blank for the majority of the items in the repository.

The relationship between terms in library-controlled vocabularies can also be used to expand user queries. Consider a user seeking pictures of Boston Terriers in an online image repository. In keeping with the cataloging principle of assigning the most specific and relevant subject heading from a list, several appropriate records would indeed have the subject heading Boston Terriers. Yet there are many cases when records for images that feature Boston Terriers have the subject heading Dogs instead. There might be a number of dogs of different breeds in the image, or the cataloger may not have been able to identify the Boston Terrier breed. A Boston Terrier lover would likely want to see those adorable pups as well, perhaps with a lower relevance ranking. Or perhaps the user refers to these dogs by an older name, Boston Bull Terriers – they would certainly still want to see pictures labeled as Boston Terriers. Therefore, thesaurus-based query expansion processes have been the subject of research projects (Greenberg, 2001; Solomou & Papatheodorou, 2010) and experimental library digital collections (Dalmau et al., 2005). In library catalogs, the Summon discovery layer enabled query expansion to pull in additional potentially relevant results in their 2.0 release in 2013 (Breeding, 2003, n.p.). OCLC introduced a version of similar capabilities to its WorldCat Discovery catalog in 2020 (OCLC, 2020, n.p.). Despite these and similar implementations, thesaurus-based query expansion is not yet widely implemented in digital repository software.

One area of discovery is still a significant challenge for our global society – multi-language searching. Languages can differ between the query, the metadata, and the resource. Ideally, one could have any of these three in any language and it would all work seamlessly. But until we can reach that stage, online instant translation services are beginning to become commercially available, which could serve as a core part of multi-language support (Google Cloud, n.d., n.p.). Real-time translation of metadata and full text is not yet a reality, but it could be sooner than one might think.

Translation is just one area in which the technologies in use in the search industry are far beyond those commonly implemented for repositories in the cultural heritage sector. The vast data sources and computing power needed to run the technology used by Google and other major search engines are the primary challenges. Consider the massive data corpus of documents, language, queries, and user behavior available to Google: the text of the entire open web and the links between pages; the contents of closed databases when their administrators wish that content to be found; structured metadata from open databases (Wikipedia, library catalogs, open government data, etc.); scanned books; the contents of every Gmail account, Chat, and Hangout; text submitted for free translation; content created with Google Docs; blogs hosted with Google; user bookmarks; statistics on what users choose to click on when using Google services, including during ubiquitous experiments to determine which of the various available options is preferred, and the list goes on, seemingly forever. Google is using that data not only to improve its search services but also to encode knowledge as structured metadata. This metadata set with millions of entities, objects, concepts, and relationships between them is known as the Google Knowledge Graph (Singhal, 2012, n.p.). Google makes this information available through an API. Perhaps in the future, this immense amount of highly structured metadata will be available to the search tools that repositories in the cultural heritage sector use.

Looking Within: Bias in Descriptive Metadata

Impact of Metadata Decisions

As seen in Chapter 2, no single repository software tool is a good fit for every type of use. This chapter has discussed the ways in which no single metadata format is appropriate to describe every type of resource. Therefore, decisions must be made, which means that for THIS to be *in*, THAT has to be *out*. Metadata and system designers make intentional and conscious decisions during this design work; however, every human's unconscious cultural framework and implicit biases also affect metadata design and creation.

One's perspective defines what one considers the most important features of an information resource. Consider graphic novels. A public library would likely prioritize the age group targeted, series, and characters. Researchers might primarily be interested in the author of the text or the visual design and identity of the illustrator. Other groups might solely appreciate the cover art.

Metadata and systems choices have very real impacts. Internationalization is one area in which the results of these choices can be problematic. The language of the metadata record has a significant effect on who can use a discovery system. As digital repositories in the cultural heritage sector typically do not translate queries, these systems and the information they contain (the vast majority in English) are largely inaccessible to other language communities. In the Western world, libraries have gotten by for decades by almost solely focusing on English and the romance languages, drawing on an assumed model of the library user as an educated, white English-speaking colonizer who might also speak a Western European language. In the developing world and the Global South, communities have fought this exclusion by building their own repositories in their own languages. Yet these remain largely isolated from the English-language West, segregating knowledge among the communities that produce it. Therefore, a serious inequality that the cultural heritage sector must face is communities having access only to the art, literature, science, and technology produced by their own culture.

Cultural heritage sector repositories' treatment of languages in non-Latin scripts adds further barriers to access for the communities that speak those languages. Historically, non-Latin scripts were Romanized in Western catalogs due to technological issues. Yet, long after Unicode became the norm in computer systems, library cataloging rules and practices stuck with Romanization in their records, further alienating the cultures producing these works.

Critical Cataloging (#critcat)

Questioning who benefits and who is excluded from using a digital repository based on language and script use is one example of analysis using the Critical Librarianship model, also known as #critlib. Critical librarianship can trace its origins at least as far back as the founding of the American Library Association's Social Responsibilities Round Table in 1969 (Nicholson & Seale, 2018, p. 2). It became widely known within librarianship in 2010 (Nicholson & Seale, 2018, p. 6). Critical theory has also been applied to specific domains within librarianship, including "critical cataloging" (#critcat) and "critical information literacy" (Critical IL). Each of these explores different aspects of how the practice of librarianship reflects and upholds systemic inequities and sparks action toward dismantling them. Through the Critical IL lens, "librarians will cease to study the 'library-as-subject,' and will instead become specialists in coaching intellectual growth and critical development" (Elmborg, 2006, p. 198).

Critical cataloging primarily focuses on the terminology used in descriptive metadata and less on the selection and granularity of metadata elements. Within descriptive metadata, controlled vocabularies and classification schemes have been studied the most from a critical theory perspective as they inevitably show the biases and perspectives of their creators. They reflect reality as a certain (small) group of humans perceive it, as well as the context of a certain culture at a certain time. A critical cataloging lens prompts one to question both outdated and current terminology as potentially marginalizing a community or idea.

Reducing bias in subject headings and classification schemes is not a new endeavor; indeed, efforts to do so have been documented for decades. Many of these attempts faced resistance or lack of recognition, demonstrating the inherently political nature of categorization and classification and the intransigence of systemic racism and other forms of bias. The case of Dorothy Porter is a good example. Porter was a Black librarian at Howard University who, from the 1930s to the 1970s, heavily adapted the Dewey classification system due to its unusability for Black materials. Porter sent her proposed revisions to the publisher of the classification scheme and was met with a response that plainly displays the systemic reinforcement of traditional power structures and casts her as an outsider. The publisher informed her that adopting her revisions would "destroy all standardization" and that "the Dewey organization would likely accuse her of copyright infringement if she shared her classification with other curators who requested it" (Helton, 2019, p. 106).

As Porter reached the end of her career, another notable librarian-activist, Sandy Berman, published the book *Prejudices and antipathies: A tract on the LC subject heads concerning people* (1971), beginning his decades-long campaign to reduce bias in LCSH. His efforts were moderately successful but were not without controversy. Berman operated largely outside of the formal structures of power at his workplace and the broader library community and was devoted to the goal of increasing social responsibility in libraries. He is a divisive figure, championed by many and considered a nuisance by others. His supporters celebrate his persistent extra-system advocacy, believing "Sandy's ranting is his greatest contribution" (Eichenlaub, 2003, p. 20).

Even established groups have found the need to eschew formal processes in order to move forward expediently in reducing bias in library description. In early 2022, the Canadian Research Knowledge Network (CRKN) announced that they had begun decolonizing the metadata of the Canadiana online cultural heritage collections by "replacing the subject heading 'Indians of North America' with 'Indigenous peoples'". CRKN made this change preemptively, diverging from established cataloging practice, "outlining interim subject headings developed as a stop-gap measure while a national vocabulary is being established" (Canadian Research Knowledge Network, January 25, 2022). Other organizations or affinity groups are providing guidance on similar decolonization work, including Cambridge University (Skinner et al., 2021), the Archives for Black Lives in Philadelphia through its Anti-Racist Description Working Group (September 2020), and the National Library of Scotland (Chew, 2021).

The case of the term "illegal aliens" within the LCSH is an example of the depth to which systemic bias prevents change. The first few phases of this complex saga are documented in a 2016 Cataloging News column in *Cataloging & Classification Quarterly*. In summary, at Dartmouth University in 2014, student activists issued a set of demands. One demand was to replace cases of "illegal" (referring to people) with "undocumented" in the context of immigration. The Dartmouth Library consulted with student representatives and in December 2014 submitted a proposal to the LC through appropriate channels to make this change in five subject headings. At first, LC declined, citing the offensive term as used in the legal context and therefore appropriate (Baron et al., 2016, pp. 506–508). It was not until March 2016 that the LC approved and announced a similar change, including the removal of the term "illegal aliens" (Library of Congress, 2016, March 22). Immediately thereafter, Republicans in the U.S. Congress took notice

of the publicity raised and used legislative protocol to attempt to explicitly pro-
hibit LC from making the announced change. Despite support for the change from
several groups within the American Library Association, LC put their plans on
hold after a brief consultation period, giving into legislative pressure (Baron et al.,
2016, pp. 508–509). Finally, in November 2021, the change was made (American Library Association, November 12, 2021), seven years after the Dartmouth
proposal, and only after a flip in the majority party in Washington. Thus, even the
structural power of LC, often wielded against the vulnerable in the library community, was subject to structural racism from above.

Updating descriptive practices to reflect less biased terminology, such as changing
subject headings, could be interpreted as endorsing the neutrality of formal descriptive systems. Indeed, Dorothy Porter is described as one who "was as orthodox as she
was heretic", "never doubted the ideals of standardization and order", and "exhibited
full faith in classification", and stands as an important predecessor to critical cataloging praxis in libraries (Helton, 2019, p. 101). In fact, the entire critical cataloging
approach could be criticized as one with a misplaced faith in the system as able
to achieve a truly neutral descriptive practice, if one only makes enough changes.
Emily Drabinski takes this view in her landmark article "Queering the Catalog". She
applies the lens of queer theory to examine how identity interacts with categorization and naming and to argue for reference librarians teaching users the same critical
examination of the politics of naming that catalogers employ (Drabinski, 2013).

Trends toward social justice practices and increasing reliance on technology
in the cultural heritage sector are highlighting issues on equity, diversity, and
inclusion far more clearly than in the past. The stakes are higher than ever as
the GLAMR community moves toward critical access to knowledge rather than
simply discovery of items. It is incumbent on metadata and systems designers to
think critically about our protocols, continually and consciously work to reduce
bias in their systems, and take intentional steps toward global information inequity.

Metadata Formats and Guidelines Referenced

Conceptual Models

>CIDOC CRM (International Council of Museums' Comité International pour
>la Documentation [International Committee for Documentation] Concep-
>tual Reference Model) www.cidoc-crm.org/
>LRM   (Library   Reference   Model)   https://repository.ifla.org/
>handle/123456789/40

Structure Standards

>ABCD (Access to Biological Collection Data) https://abcd.tdwg.org/
>AES57–2011 (r2017): AES standard for audio metadata – Audio object
>structures for preservation and restoration www.aes.org/publications/stan-
>dards/search.cfm?docID=84

BIBFRAME (Bibliographic Framework) www.loc.gov/bibframe/

CDWA (Categories for the Description of Works of Art) www.getty.edu/ research/publications/electronic_publications/cdwa/

CF (Climate and Forecast) Metadata Conventions http://cfconventions. org/

CHIN Data Dictionaries https://app.pch.gc.ca/application/ddrcip-chindd/? lang=en

CIDOC Core Data Standard for Archaeological Objects www.arqueo-ecua-toriana.ec/en/methodological-standards/21-generalidades/233-cidoc-core-data-standard-for-archaeological-objects

Darwin Core https://dwc.tdwg.org/

DC (Dublin Core) [Classic version] www.dublincore.org/specifications/ dublin-core/dces/

DDI (Data Documentation Initiative) https://ddialliance.org/

E-Book Bibliographic Metadata Requirements in the Sale, Publication, Discovery, and Preservation Supply Chain www.niso.org/publications/ rp-29-2022-ebmd

MARC (MAchine Readable Cataloging) www.loc.gov/marc/bibliographic/

MODS (Metadata Object Description Schema) www.loc.gov/standards/ mods/

ONIX (ONline Information eXchange) https://bisg.org/page/onixforbooks

PB (Public Broadcasting) Core https://pbcore.org/

PREMIS Data Dictionary for Preservation Metadata www.loc.gov/standards/ premis/

QDC (Qualified Dublin Core) [Classic version] www.dublincore.org/speci-fications/dublin-core/dcmes-qualifiers/

RDA (Resource Description & Access) www.rdatoolkit.org

SMRF (Software Metadata Recommended Format) www.softwarepreserva-tionnetwork.org/smrf-guide/

SPASE (Space Physics Archive Search and Extract) Data Model https://spase-group.org/data/

VRA (Visual Resources Association) Core www.loc.gov/standards/vracore/

Content Standards

CDWA (Categories for the Description of Works of Art) www.getty.edu/ research/publications/electronic_publications/cdwa/

DACS (Describing Archives: A Content Standard) www2.archivists.org/ groups/technical-subcommittee-on-describing-archives-a-content-stan-dard-dacs/describing-archives-a-content-standard-dacs-second-

E-Book Bibliographic Metadata Requirements in the Sale, Publication, Discovery, and Preservation Supply Chain www.niso.org/publications/ rp-29-2022-ebmd

RAD (Rules for Archival Description) www.cdncouncilarchives.ca/archdes-rules.html

RDA (Resource Description & Access) www.rdatoolkit.org

Controlled Vocabularies

AAT (Art & Architecture Thesaurus) www.getty.edu/research/tools/vocabularies/aat/index.html

FAST (Faceted Access to Subject Headings) www.oclc.org/research/areas/data-science/fast.html

LCSH (Library of Congress Subject Headings) www.loc.gov/aba/cataloging/subject/

MeSH (Medical Subject Headings) www.nlm.nih.gov/mesh/meshhome.html

TGN (Thesaurus of Geographic Names) www.getty.edu/research/tools/vocabularies/tgn/index.html

Authority Files

CONA (Cultural Objects Name Authority) www.getty.edu/research/tools/vocabularies/cona/index.html

IA (Getty Iconography Authority; integrated with CONA) www.getty.edu/research/tools/vocabularies/cona/index.html

ULAN (Union List of Artist Names) www.getty.edu/research/tools/vocabularies/ulan/index.html

VIAF (Virtual International Authority File) http://viaf.org/

Classification Schemes

DDC (Dewey Decimal Classification) www.oclc.org/en/dewey.html

Iconclass www.iconclass.org

LCC (Library of Congress Classification) www.loc.gov/catdir/cpso/lcc.html

Markup Languages

EAD (Encoded Archival Description) www2.archivists.org/groups/technical-subcommittee-on-encoded-archival-standards-ts-eas/encoded-archival-description-ead

TEI (Text Encoding Initiative) https://tei-c.org/

References

American Library Association (2021, November 12). ALA welcomes removal of offensive "Illegal aliens" subject headings. *ALA Member News*. www.ala.org/news/member-news/2021/11/ala-welcomes-removal-offensive-illegal-aliens-subject-headings

Anti-Racist Description Working Group. (2020, September). Anti-racist description resources. *Archives for Black lives in Philadelphia*. https://github.com/a4blip/A4BLiP/tree/master/Resources

Avram, H. D. (1975). *MARC: Its history and implications*. Library of Congress. https://hdl.handle.net/2027/mdp.39015034388556

Baca, M. (Ed.). (2016). *Introduction to metadata* (3rd ed.). Getty Publications. www.getty.edu/publications/intrometadata

Baron, J., Gross, T., & Cornejo Cáseres, Ó. R. (2016). Cataloging news: Timeline of "illegal alien" subject heading change petition, January 2014–July 2016. *Cataloging & Classification Quarterly, 54*(7), 506–509. http://doi.org/10.1080/01639374.2016.1218707

Berman, S. (1971). *Prejudices and antipathies: A tract on the LC subject heads concerning people.* Scarecrow Press.

Besser, H. (2004). The past, present, and future of digital libraries. In S. Schreibman, R. Siemens, & J. Unsworth (Eds.), *A companion to digital humanities* (pp. 557–575). Blackwell.

Borgman, C. L. (1997). From acting locally to thinking globally: A brief history of library automation. *Library Quarterly, 67*(3), 215–249.

Breeding, M. (2003). Serials solutions to launch summon 2.0. *Smart Libraries Newsletter.* https://librarytechnology.org/document/18059

Canadian Research Knowledge Network. (2022, January 25). *Decolonizing Canadiana metadata: An overdue step in removing harmful subject headings.* www.crkn-rcdr.ca/en/decolonizing-canadiana-metadata-overdue-step-removing-harmful-subject-headings

Caplan, P., & Guenther, R. (1996). Metadata for internet resources: The Dublin Core metadata elements set and its mapping to USMARC. *Cataloging & Classification Quarterly, 22*(3–4), 43–58. https://doi.org/10.1300/J104v22n03_04

Chew, C. (2021). *Inclusive terminology: Guide & glossary for the cultural heritage sector.* https://drive.google.com/file/d/1C3fjqUi0nmAjhghzAO2FXxUbdbqX0fJo/view

Cohen, R. A., & Pusnik, A. T. (2018). Measuring query complexity in web-scale discovery: A comparison between two academic libraries. *Reference & User Services Quarterly, 57*(4), 274–284. https://doi.org/10.5860/rusq.57.4.6705

Coleman, A. (2005). From cataloging to metadata: Dublin Core records for the library catalog. *Cataloging & Classification Quarterly, 40*(3/4), 153–181. https://doi.org/10.1300/J104v40n03_08

Cutter, C. A. (1891). *Rules for a dictionary catalog* (3rd ed.). Government Printing Office. https://archive.org/details/rulesfordictiona00cuttrich

Dalmau, M., Floyd, R., Jiao, D., & Riley, J. (2005). Integrating thesaurus relationships into search and browse in an online photograph collection. *Library Hi Tech, 23*(3), 425–452. https://doi.org/10.1108/07378830510621829

Drabinski, E. (2013). Queering the catalog: Queer theory and the politics of correction. *The Library Quarterly: Information, Community, Policy, 83*(2), 94–111. https://doi.org/10.1086/669547

Eichenlaub, N. (2003). Silencing Sandy: The censoring of libraries' foremost activist. In K. Roberto & J. West (Eds.), *Revolting librarians redux: Radical librarians speak out* (pp. 120–128). McFarland & Co.

Elmborg, J. (2006). Critical information literacy: Implications for instructional practice. *The Journal of Academic Librarianship, 32*(2), 192–199.

Google Cloud. (n.d.). *Translation AI.* https://cloud.google.com/translate

Gorman, M. (1999). Metadata or cataloguing? A false choice. *Journal of Internet Cataloging, 2*(1), 5–22. https://doi.org/10.1300/J141v02n01_03

Greenberg, J. (2001). Optimal query expansion (QE) processing methods with semantically encoded structured thesauri terminology. *Journal of the American Society for Information Science and Technology, 52*(6), 487–498. https://doi.org/10.1002/asi.1093.abs

Guenther, R., & McCallum, S. (2003). New metadata standards for digital resources: MODS and METS. *Bulletin of the American Society for Information Science and Technology, 29*(2), 12–15. https://doi.org/10.1002/bult.268

Gyöngyi, Z., & Garcia-Molina, H. (2005). Web spam taxonomy. *First international workshop on adversarial information retrieval on the web (AIRWeb 2005).* http://ilpubs.stanford.edu:8090/771/1/2005-9.pdf

Helton, L. E. (2019). On decimals, catalogs, and racial imaginaries of reading. *PMLA (Journal of the Modern Language Association), 134*(1), 99–120. https://doi.org/10.1632/pmla.2019.134.1.99

Huthwaite, A. (2003). AACR2 and other metadata standards: The way forward. *Cataloging & Classification Quarterly, 36*(3/4), 87–100. https://doi.org/10.1300/J104v36n03_08

Lampert, C. K., & Southwick, S. B. (2013). Leading to linking: Introducing linked data to academic library digital collections. *Journal of Library Metadata, 13*(2/3), 230–253. https://doi.org/10.1080/19386389.2013.826095

Library of Congress. (2016, March 22). *Library of Congress to cancel the subject heading "illegal aliens".* www.loc.gov/catdir/cpso/illegal-aliens-decision.pdf

Library of Congress. (2017). *The card catalog: Books, cards, and literary treasures.* Chronicle Books.

Manning, C., Raghavan, R., & Schütze, H. (2008). *Introduction to information retrieval.* Cambridge University Press.

Nicholson, K. P., & Seale, M. (2018). Introduction. In K. P. Nicholson & M. Seale (Eds.), *The politics of theory and the practice of critical librarianship* (pp. 1–18). Litwin Books.

OCLC. (2020). *WorldCat discovery release notes*, April 2020. https://help.oclc.org/Discovery_and_Reference/WorldCat_Discovery/Release_notes/2020_WorldCat_Discovery_release_notes/075WorldCat_Discovery_release_notes_April_2020

Oliver, C. (2021). Why RDA? Organizing bibliographic information in the 21st century. *Proceedings of the 10th Eurasian academic libraries conference.* Nazarbayev University Library. https://nur.nu.edu.kz/handle/123456789/5840

Pomerantz, J. (2015). *Metadata.* MIT Press.

Riley, J. (2017). *Understanding metadata.* NISO Press. www.niso.org/publications/understanding-metadata-2017

Ronallo, J. (2012). HTML5 microdata and schema.org. *Code4Lib Journal, 16.* https://journal.code4lib.org/articles/6400

Singhal, A. (2012, May 16). *Introducing the knowledge graph: Things, not strings.* The Keyword (Google blog). https://blog.google/products/search/introducing-knowledge-graph-things-not/

Skinner, J., Zénere, C. P., Greenberg, C., Marsh, F., & Lacey, E. (2021). Cataloguing, classification, and critical librarianship at Cambridge University. In J. Crilly & R. Everitt (Eds.), *Narrative expansions: Interpreting decolonisation in academic libraries* (pp. 173–188). Facet Publishing. https://do.org/10.29085/9781783304998

Solomou, G., & Papatheodorou, T. (2010). The use of SKOS vocabularies in digital repositories: The DSpace case. *Proceedings – 2010 IEEE 4th international conference on semantic computing, ICSC 2010* (pp. 542–547). IEEE. https://doi.org/10.1109/ICSC.2010.83

Spärck Jones, K. (2004). A statistical interpretation of term specificity and its application in retrieval. *Journal of Documentation, 60*(5), 493–502. Reprinted from *Journal of Documentation, 28*(1), 1972.

Waibel, S. (1997). Discovering online resources. The Dublin Core: A simple content description model for electronic resources. *Bulletin of the American Society for Information Science, 24*(1), 9–11. http://doi.org/10.1002/bult.70

Weinberger, D. (2007). *Everything is miscellaneous: The power of the new digital disorder.* Times Books.

Yadav, V., & Bethard, S. (2018). A survey on recent advances in named entity recognition from deep learning models. *Proceedings of the 27th international conference on computational linguistics* (pp. 2145–2158). Association for Computational Linguistics. https://aclanthology.org/C18-1182

Yoose, B., & Perkins, P. (2013). The linked open data landscape in libraries and beyond. *Journal of Library Metadata, 13*(2/3), 197–211. https://doi.org/10.1080/19386389.2013.826075

Zavalina, O., & Vassilieva, E. V. (2014). Understanding the information needs of large-scale digital library users: Comparative analysis of user searching. *Library Resources & Technical Services, 58*(2), 84–99. https://doi.org/10.5860/lrts.58n2.84

Zhou, W., Smalheiser, N. R., & Yu, C. (2006). A tutorial on information retrieval: Basic terms and concepts. *Journal of Biomedical Discovery and Collaboration, 1*(Article 2). https://doi.org/10.1186/1747-5333-1-2

4 Understanding Linked Data and the Potential for Enhanced Discoverability

Anna Neatrour and Teresa K. Hebron

Introduction

In the 1977 film *Star Wars*, the character Obi-Wan Kenobi describes the Force as "an energy field [that] surrounds us and . . . binds the galaxy together" (IMDB, n.d.). You may have heard linked data described in similarly vague terms: it's been around for a while; it is something that *someone else* is doing, but that can't be precisely described; and you're not quite sure what it's good for. If this sounds familiar – you're not alone!

Chapter 3 discusses metadata in digital repositories in depth, and this chapter should be considered in tandem with that topic. Many metadata practitioners have written extensively about linked data, and therefore this chapter will by no means be exhaustive. Several of the sources used during our research for this chapter provide a more complete history and background on the development of linked data (Carlson et al., 2020; Riley, 2017). There are numerous case studies that illuminate linked data projects in GLAMR institutions in professional literature, and we recommend seeking out further specific examples.

Simply put, linked data is information stored as semantic relationships that form a graph, rather than the traditional tree structure seen in MARC, Dublin Core, or XML-based records. These relationships are expressed in *triples*, comprising a subject, predicate, and object. Any point can be a point of entry (discovery) from which other relationships can be derived. These principles first began to take practical shape in the late 1990s in the form of the Resource Description Framework (RDF), a standard for web-based metadata advanced by the World Wide Web Consortium. Tim Berners-Lee is credited with advancing the concept of linked data as a foundation for the so-called semantic web, based on four principles:

1) Use Uniform Resource Indicators (URIs) as names for things.
2) Use hypertext transfer protocol (HTTP) URIs so that people (and computers) can look up those names/things.
3) When someone looks up a URI, provide useful information.
4) Include links to other URIs, so they can learn more things.

(Riley, 2017)

DOI: 10.4324/9781003216438-6

If this doesn't sound like ancient ways and hokey religions, you're probably a Jedi! But a brief example from a galaxy not so far away might make things clearer.

The world of competitive figure skating is made up of a web of individuals related to one another in various ways. A skater may have multiple coaches over the course of their career, they may work with external specialty coaches or choreographers, and many skaters themselves go on to coaching careers after their competitive careers end. A simple triple about a skater could be as follows:

Jason Brown: is coached by: Brian Orser

From this relationship, we could derive the following reverse statement:

Brian Orser: coaches: Jason Brown

Brown previously worked with coach Kori Ade, leading to another possible statement:

Jason Brown: was coached by: Kori Ade

Brian Orser was himself also a competitive skater, so we could assert:

Brian Orser: was coached by: Doug Leigh

Or the reverse:

Doug Leigh: coached: Brian Orser

This could go on endlessly, building a web of relationships between related individuals all over the skating world. As seen in Figure 4.1, developing a graph database of relationships within figure skating and their corresponding events would enable someone who noticed Brian Orser constantly changing jackets to represent his various affiliations at the 2022 Winter Olympics to ask, "Which 2022 Olympic athletes were coached by Brian Orser?" They could then easily identify that he was working with Jason Brown, Cha Jun-hwan, and Yuzuru Hanyu. A traditional Library of Congress Name Authority File (LCNAF) record may have some useful facts about Orser, but it will not include the type of relationships between people that would support immediate discovery in the case of the example skating research question earlier. These relationships can be derived via linked data without them being explicitly stated, as users are accustomed to in traditional GLAMR description. For GLAMR institutions, these triples describe the relationships users are already familiar with, such as creator:work, item:collection, characteristics of works (topics, publication dates, language of publication), and so on.

Based on the four principles of linked data noted earlier, these names and relationships would be replaced with URIs from authoritative sources in practice. If we first represent a few statements about Jason Brown in a tabular format, it could look like Table 4.1.

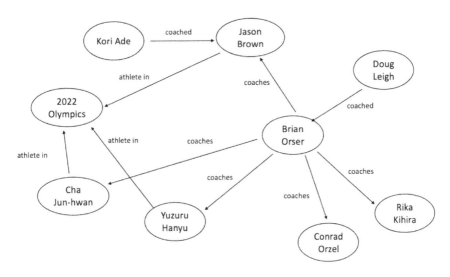

Figure 4.1 Representation of figure skating relationships

Table 4.1 Tabular triples about figure skater Jason Brown

Subject	Predicate	Object
Jason Brown	Is coached by	Brian Orser
Jason Brown	Was coached by	Kori Ade
Jason Brown	Represents	United States
Jason Brown	Is from	Highland Park

Table 4.2 Triples about figure skater Jason Brown replaced with example URIs

Subject	Predicate	Object
http://fs-facts.org/entity000	http://fs-facts.org/prop000	http://fs-facts.org/entity001
http://fs-facts.org/entity000	http://fs-facts.org/prop000	http://fs-facts.org/entity002
http://fs-facts.org/entity000	http://fs-facts.org/prop001	http://fs-facts.org/entity003
http://fs-facts.org/entity000	http://fs-facts.org/prop002	http://fs-facts.org/entity004

Since there is no single authoritative source describing figure skating entities and minting URIs, we will pretend these entities have URIs in a source called fs-facts.org. Swapping out these entities and properties with fake URIs, we have data that looks like Table 4.2.

Local RDF files that store these semantic statements are published to the web via serialization, a process that converts data from one format to another while retaining the original structure. Several serialization formats emerged:

- RDF/XML: an early attempt to combine eXtensible Markup Language (XML) with RDF that was ultimately abandoned due to poor legibility, cumbersome creation, and management issues;
- N-Triples: a slight improvement on RDF/XML that represents full triples on single lines;
- TURTLE: short for Terse RDF Language, TURTLE collapses predicates and objects that share a subject and allows for namespace declarations that help save space and reduce repetition;
- JSON-LD: the most recent serialization that combines Java Script Object Notation (JSON) and linked data to deliver triples via a widely-used data format.

(Carlson et al., 2020)

As RDF/XML is now obsolete, we will not provide an example of it in this chapter. Interested readers could refer to W3Schools[1] for more details.

We can represent our statements about Jason Brown as N-Triples as follows:

00   <http://fs-facts.org/entity000><http://fs-facts.org/prop000><http://fs-facts.org/entity001>.

01   <http://fs-facts.org/entity000><http://fs-facts.org/prop000><http://fs-facts.org/entity002>.

02   <http://fs-facts.org/entity000><http://fs-facts.org/prop001><http://fs-facts.org/entity003>.

03   <http://fs-facts.org/entity000><http://fs-facts.org/prop002><http://fs-facts.org/entity004>.

The drawbacks of N-Triples include repetition and the possibility of very long lines.

TURTLE groups predicates and objects with shared subjects and thus reduces the repetitive nature of N-Triples. Moreover, it allows for namespace declarations that reduce redundancy and save space.

A simple TURTLE file could look like this:

<http://fs-facts.org/entity000>
<http://fs-facts.org/prop000><http://fs-facts.org/entity001>;
<http://fs-facts.org/prop000><http://fs-facts.org/entity002>;
<http://fs-facts.org/prop001><http://fs-facts.org/entity003>;
<http://fs-facts.org/prop002><http://fs-facts.org/entity004>.

TURTLE represents data about a common subject in a run-on sentence of sorts: "Jason Brown is coached by Brian Orser; and was coached by Kori Ade; and represents the United States; and is from Highland Park". An improved TURTLE file using the namespace declaration for our pretend source (fs-facts.org) would change it as follows:

@prefix fsf: <http://fs-facts.org>.

fsf:entity000
   fsf:prop000 fsf:entity001;
   fsf:prop000 fsf:entity002;
   fsf:prop001 fsf:entity003;
   fsf:prop002 fsf:entity004.

The namespace declaration tells the user once, at the beginning, which source to refer to instead of repeating it with each use.

JSON merges the customizable, structured data format of XML with attribute–value pairs like a relational database, and JSON-LD combines JSON with RDF. Like TURTLE, JSON-LD uses namespace declarations to save space. Thus, our skating triples are transformed into JSON-LD results in the following manner:

```
{
   "@context": {
       "fsf": {
               "@id": "http://fs-facts.org", "@prefix": true
               },
       "fsf:prop000": {
               "@type": "@id"
       },
       "fsf:prop001": {
               "@type": "@id"
       },
       "fsf:prop002": {
               "@type": "@id"
       },
   },
   "@id": "fsf:entity000",
   "fsf:prop000": "fsf:entity001",
   "fsf:prop000": "fsf:entity002",
   "fsf:prop001": "fsf:entity003",
   "fsf:prop002": "fsf:entity004"
}
```

In this example, the @id attribute identifies Jason Brown (entity000) as the common subject for the block of attribute–value pairs. This is known as a node identifier. Since we know these predicates have URI objects (instead of literals, strings of text or numbers), we use the @context to state this before the block.

This serialized published linked data, known as triplestores, can be queried by humans and software using a specialized Structured Query Language (SQL) called SPARQL (a recursive acronym for SPARQL Protocol and RDF Query Language; pronounced *sparkle*). Linked data authorities offer SPARQL endpoints/application programming interfaces (APIs) for remote users (both human and machine) to retrieve data from them.

An effort that bridges traditional library cataloging practices and linked data is BIBFRAME (Bibliographic Framework Initiative), an initiative started by the Library of Congress that focuses on providing ways to migrate the MARC 21 format for bibliographic data into linked data (*BIBFRAME – Bibliographic Framework Initiative (Library of Congress)*, n.d.). BIBFRAME has gone through several phases of development, with the involvement of the Program for Cooperative Cataloging (PCC), OCLC, and the linked data for production (LD4P) collaborative project (Kim et al., 2021). Institutions such as the University of Illinois have experimented with the development of BIBFRAME editing tools and have tested the BIBFRAME model (Michael & Han, 2019). Zepheira, a company that consulted on the development of BIB-FRAME with the Library of Congress, has released the BIBFRAME Lite vocabulary (Zepheira, n.d.).

Riley summarizes the tension between traditional GLAMR description and linked data neatly:

> Whereas XML models information as a tree, RDF models it as a graph, with small bits of information each connected to other small bits of information. No one entity or piece of data has primary importance in a graph; the network of information can be accessed equally at any point. As such, the concept of a metadata record, the sum total of information known about a single entity or a defined set of data elements intended to travel together, as used in relational databases and XML, does not fit well in the RDF model.
>
> (Riley, 2017, p. 10)

Despite this apparent mismatch, GLAMR institutions (and their users) stand to benefit from linked data in several key ways.

Benefits

Metadata quality is a key component of discoverability, and linked data can help improve consistency and currency across collections and institutional boundaries. Seymore and Simic (2019) present a use case of developing a linked data-controlled vocabulary manager for authority work on Oregon Digital and describe the pitfalls of traditional authority sources (such as them being Western-centric, historical, and too broad to capture local personages often found in the archival source material). Using linked data-controlled vocabularies created and maintained by underrepresented or marginalized groups helps counteract systematic biases found in widely-used vocabularies such as the Library of Congress Subject Headings (LCSH; Hardesty & Nolan, 2021). Myntti and Cothran (2013) detail another administrative benefit to metadata practitioners that derives from linked authority data's web-accessible principle:

> Typically, data information has been stored as strings, which need to be periodically updated with the latest version of the textual strings. Linked data

obviates the need for replacing the data with other data by establishing a master record of the authorized data in a Web-accessible location.

(p. 96)

Interoperability has been considered another primary benefit of linked data as traditional descriptive standards and integrated library systems (ILS) do not expose library metadata well on the web. Projects such as the LD4 Wikidata Affinity Group bring librarians' expertise in metadata to the larger linked open data (LOD) community and serve as a template for interoperability in the wider world. For example, as is discussed in further detail in Chapter 7, libraries hold edit-a-thons to improve Wikidata, thus in turn improving their own data. Michigan State University's (MSU's) special collections is home to one of the largest comic art collections in North America; MSU has held Wikidata editing events to engage users and GLAMR professionals while improving their records by using Wikidata to disambiguate creators and artists previously misidentified in traditional authority sources (Topham & Huff, 2021). These efforts de-silo knowledge by creating interoperable metadata between previously-closed library systems and external information sources. Therefore, another way to look at interoperability might be by de-siloing knowledge. As linked data vocabularies and standards continue to proliferate, GLAMR institutions and professionals have a role to play in shaping the larger data community (Wearn, 2021).

Aggregation tools (such as discovery layers commonly used in libraries) gather metadata from disparate sources into a single presentation layer. For example, it is common to see metadata for physical holdings (monographs, archival collections), serial publications, digital library collections, institutional repositories, and more presented side by side in a single discovery layer. However, these may be described using different schema and descriptive standards. Using linked data in aggregation tools may help smooth out such differences and improve findability for end users. Imagine a campus discovery layer that contains records from the main library and the campus art museum. The library might use the Library of Congress Name Authority File (LCNAF) for artist names, while the museum might use Getty's Union List of Artist Names. Using a linked data authority to provide a single, common heading in the discovery layer will improve the faceting and discoverability of such entries for non-expert users while retaining each holding institution's preferred descriptive standard in their local systems. A related example can be found in Chapter 6, which presents a case study of integrating unique content into the discovery layer at Himmelfarb Health Sciences Library at George Washington University.

Toward Enhanced Discoverability

Anyone who uses a search engine can readily see the advantages of linked data. For example, the Google knowledge cards that provide additional context on topics began to be built with a semantic framework after Google acquired Freebase in

2010 (Chah, 2018). A promotional blog post from Google provides an overview of the technology:

> Google's Knowledge Graph isn't just rooted in public sources such as Freebase, Wikipedia and the CIA World Factbook. It's also augmented at a much larger scale – because we are focused on comprehensive breadth and depth. It currently contains more than 500 million objects, as well as more than 3.5 billion facts about and relationships between these different objects. And it's tuned based on what people search for, and what we find out on the web.
>
> (Singhal, 2012)

The following figure is an example of a semantic search providing more information about Brian Orser with structured data through the knowledge panel that gives information about him, such as when he was born and who his parents are (Figure 4.2).

Another widespread use of linked data on the Internet is in the application of Schema.org, a vocabulary used to embed structured data in web pages. It can be expressed in formats such as JSON-LD and RDFa. The representation of bibliographic formats in Schema.org[2] has been extended. Examples of markup for library-centric items can be referenced from documentation pages for Creative

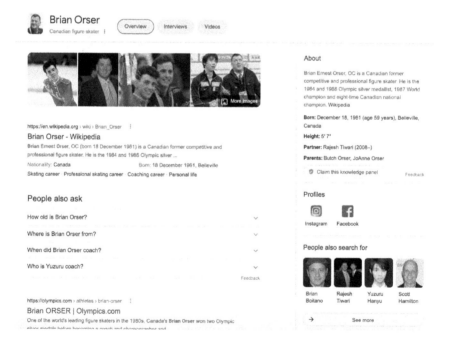

Figure 4.2 Search results for Brian Orser

Work[3] or Book.[4] Many libraries have conducted research projects and experiments expressing collections and holdings with Schema.org. For example, the University of Illinois explored the relationship between bibliographic holdings data, identifying issues with how information about item availability, borrowing terms, and borrowers is expressed (Han et al., 2015). OCLC and Montana State University have also conducted research to examine how metadata for theses and dissertations can be mapped to Schema.org for improved Search Engine Optimization (Mixter et al., 2014). For a period of time, OCLC incorporated Schema.org markup into WorldCat (OCLC, 2021a) as an experiment that concluded in early 2021. Europeana has developed recommendations for Schema.org markup to improve the representation of cultural heritage materials in search engines (Wallis et al., 2017).

Many institutions have been influenced by LOD principles and data models, even if their underlying technology might not be directly built on linked data technologies. The Digital Public Library of America's (DPLA's) metadata application profile leveraged the Europeana Metadata Model to describe best practices and requirements for metadata in an aggregated environment (Digital Public Library of America, 2017). In 2017, DPLA transitioned its ingestion system, which was storing data as native RDF, to an approach informed by big data and data science due to scalability issues (Altman et al., 2017). In archives, the approach to entity management articulated in the Encoded Archival Context for Corporate Bodies, Persons, and Families (EAC-CPF) standard and expressed in the successful collaborative Social Networks and Archival Context (SNAC) project shows new possibilities in research through browsing relationships between people as well as archival holdings information. SNAC aggregates information about people and organizations from various sources, showing the benefits of a decentralized approach combined with focused identity management. SNAC also incorporates information from linked data authorities' datasets such as the Virtual International Authority File (VIAF), LCNAF, and Wikidata. By allowing users to browse by exploring the connections between entities represented in the collections of multiple institutions, this project advances discovery for Special Collections and Archives (Larson et al., 2014).

When examining the history of aggregation for the Swedish Open Cultural Heritage (SOCH) project, Smith (2021) points out the benefits for under-resourced institutions:

> Making your data available in a way that can be harvested by an aggregator presents a lower threshold than operating your own Linked Data platform, both in terms of cost and required technical skill. Joining an aggregator shared by other similar CHIs also offers benefits in terms of networking and collaboration around shared problems and requirements.
>
> (p. 69)

However, while celebrating the success of the SOCH aggregation program, Smith (2021) also acknowledges the difficulties encountered in maintaining an aggregation platform that was arguably ahead of its time, with a unique data model and a low barrier for metadata quality for the contributed datasets.

Successful large-scale aggregated digital libraries with linked data support, such as Europeana, provide platforms for additional pilot projects and opportunities for further research. In addition to providing the extremely influential Europeana Metadata Model, further experiments from their partners showcase new ways of thinking about digital libraries. For example, the Polymath Virtual Library used linked data from Europeana to document and model spheres of influence for authors and their associated works (Charles, 2014). A case study from the Dutch Digital Heritage Network and the National Library of the Netherlands examined linked data aggregation workflows by using Schema.org to describe datasets for harvesting by Europeana, with additional tools, workflows, and mappings developed to support the project (Freire et al., 2019). This study was then broadened to examine linked data aggregation for additional partners in Europeana, demonstrating how using Schema.org instead of EDM expands the possibilities of aggregation beyond traditional protocols like Open Archives Initiative Protocol for Metadata Harvesting (OAI-PMH), although some partners found it challenging to provide information in the required formats (Freire et al., 2020). It will be interesting to see if additional use cases of data providers submitting aggregated metadata in linked data ready formats can improve processes for aggregators who are tasked with harvesting, normalizing, and in some cases, publishing their central index as LOD.

Examples in Discovery Systems

Support for linked data usage from commercial library systems vendors is another factor to be considered within the linked data landscape. More vendors are making efforts to include these supports, and consequently, an increasing number of libraries are requiring this support from their vendors.

The 2018 BIBFRAME Expectations for ILS Tenders specification document therefore asserts,

> Before defining the requirements for a new ILS compliant with BIBFRAME the Library needs to clearly establish who is the end user that will use the linked data: should the project to publish or produce data in BIBFRAME be designed to be read by machines (to allow for reasoning processes, semantic indexing and so on) or people?
>
> (*BIBFRAME Expectations for ILS Tenders*, 2018)

Any library pursuing linked data needs to align systems and strategies to achieve good outcomes, and this will be discussed in more depth in the Practical Approaches section of this chapter.

Discovery tools are often bundled with ILS or library service platforms (LSP) and "[f]ew academic libraries enter separate procurement projects for discovery services as was often the case a decade ago" (Breeding, 2021b). One outlier is Bibliocommons, which only offers BiblioCore as an independent discovery layer that can integrate with varying ILSs (Breeding, 2021b). Ex Libris also "continues to develop and support Primo as an independent discovery service that can be used with Alma or any other major resource management system" (Breeding, 2021b).

A few brief examples of linked data integration in commercial discovery systems are the following. Zepheira, previously an independent linked data service provider, was acquired by EBSCO in 2020 (Breeding, 2020). This builds on an earlier partnership to enhance the content in EBSCO's Novelist Select product and will presumably bring linked data capabilities to EBSCO's flagship discovery product, EBSCO Discovery Service (EDS). Meanwhile, OCLC announced developing "a persistent, shared, and centralized entity management infrastructure for library linked data work" (OCLC, 2021b). Ex Libris is working on the integration of linked data in its Alma and Primo products as well (Sanders, 2015; Sanders, 2017). Despite a series of acquisitions over the past decade, Innovative has announced a new LSP, Vega, that promises the integration of data sources including BIBFRAME versions of MARC records for its Vega Discover platform (Breeding, 2021a). There are many such linked data case study write-ups in the field, and reviewing these prior to embarking on a linked data project might be helpful as well.

Practical Approaches to Working With Linked Data

Developing a Linked Data Strategy

First, take a step back and consider how linked data work will fit in with your existing systems, workflows, and job responsibilities.

Why do you want to engage with linked data? Are you contemplating a system migration soon? Do you have digital collections that would be better expressed as linked data, for example, a collection of manuscripts or correspondence that would benefit from having the relationships between people mapped? Are you interested in developing a project that will meet some professional development goals and continuing education goals for you or your staff?

Libraries everywhere have been tasked with doing more with less for decades. An additional question that should be answered before you begin a linked data project is what the library staff will NOT do when embarking on a new project. You should not underestimate the data modeling, technical infrastructure, data cleaning, and learning curve for a linked data project. At the same time, how you have approached other projects in the past can inform your planning and development of a linked data strategy.

Very few institutions are fortunate enough to have reliably consistent descriptive metadata. How much staff time does your institution currently spend on cleaning and enhancing legacy metadata? As you begin to develop your strategy, it is essential to review and articulate your policies, procedures, and best practices for descriptive metadata. Have a clear model for your data in the form of an application profile or metadata dictionary. Consistency in the metadata elements that are likely to connect to the larger semantic web should be a priority. For many institutions, these metadata aspects will be focused on fields with information about personal or corporate names, subjects, or the genre of an item. These areas have data that will be easier to reconcile with larger linked data sources. Mapping out where you may be using controlled vocabularies that are already leveraging the benefits of linked data can give you ideas about where your local descriptive metadata may better utilize the Getty Art & Architecture Thesaurus, LCNAF, VIAF, or International Standard Name Identifier (ISNI) databases. Although relying on persistent resources from larger institutions as part of a local linked data strategy can be attractive, it is important to remember that even large, well-resourced institutions have difficulty in supporting long-term linked data projects. For example, the British Museum's SPARQL end point inspired the Twitter account "Is the British Museum's endpoint working?",[5] with replies detailing sustainability concerns as well as issues with relying too much on external URIs for local linked data strategies (Is the British Museum's Endpoint Working?, n.d.).

Furthermore, many institutions have digitized and made materials available online with little research into copyright issues. Therefore, living up to the idea of openness evoked by the phrase "Linked Open Data" can also lead to good and necessary work around rights management to ensure that you provide useful context for users who discover your digital assets. Transitioning to the use of standards like rightsstatements.org can provide essential information for users of your content, both in a local and in an aggregated context.

Moving Forward

An important step before developing a linked data strategy is completing an environmental scan of your current systems and your institution's capacity for technical support. For example, what type of software powers your library's online catalog? If you have digital collections or an institutional repository, which software is used for that infrastructure? Are you using any additional systems that might publish data as JSON-LD, such as OmekaS for digital exhibits? What external vocabularies and authority files do you use for your current projects, and are some of these built with LOD in mind? Can you test open-source software or do you have a sandbox area on a server for experimentation? Or is your institution mainly committed to using vendor-provided solutions? The answers to all these questions provide essential information about the environment you are working in, which will impact your approach to developing linked data projects and your overall plan.

Most importantly, consider the staff involved in linked data work. How many people might be participating in it, and how many hours would they be able to commit to it? Try to pick a project or exercise that is scoped appropriately for your bandwidth. For people just getting started, putting together a linked data reading group to familiarize them with the literature might be an important first step. For people who have been actively familiarizing themselves with linked data already, developing a small pilot project could be a productive way of mapping out workflows and exploring the tools and infrastructure needed for a broader linked data strategy at their institution.

Tools

No single tool or technology stack works for all possible linked data projects. The needs of a particular project will often dictate the tools required to support it. Defining the tasks that the tools need to perform and assessing the possibilities of which tool seems the most practical for a particular use case is helpful. In an article that reviewed linked data and digital libraries, Hallo et al. (2016) found that

> [t]here are problems to be solved for using linked data technologies in digital libraries, such as the need for support tools, mechanisms for data quality control and better querying interfaces, the lack of technical staff with knowledge of these new technologies and the difficulty of defining linked data rights. Furthermore, few data, most of them presented like statistics, about the use of linked data in library evaluation were found.
>
> (p. 125)

Using data journalists as a use case, Klímek et al. (2019) developed criteria and requirements for the evaluation of LOD tools for the consumption of linked data and concluded that there is a need for more tools that can be easily used by people who are not linked data experts:

> However, non-LD experts still cannot exploit many benefits of LD principles and technologies. This poses a problem for LD adoption, as consumers often still find consuming 3-star data such as CSV files more comfortable than working with LD. At the same time, the potential LD publishers have a hard time convincing their superiors to invest the additional effort into achieving LD publication, when there are no immediately appreciable benefits of doing so.
>
> (p. 36)

Most linked data projects will need to go through stages of data assessment, data cleaning, reconciliation, and publishing, and the tools needed to accomplish each of these stages will vary. In many cases, the steps required to prepare for linked data will have the additional benefit of improving metadata quality; as Mitchell (2016) argues,

> Another important area of work in LD is the application of existing tools to improve the quality of data. Although not necessarily focused on generating LD, the increase in use of these tools is important to the long-term viability of data cleanup and normalization.
>
> (p. 8)

We discuss a representative selection of tools and platforms here, although a combination of these tools or others with similar functionality will likely be needed for any successful library linked data project:

OpenRefine:[6] OpenRefine (previously GoogleRefine) provides excellent ways to visualize, cleanup, and reconcile data. There are many effective tutorials and recipes available for using OpenRefine to create linked data for libraries, for example from the Library Carpentries project.[7] OpenRefine can also be used with WikiData projects (www.wikidata.org/wiki/Wikidata:Tools/OpenRefine), which may be attractive for librarians wishing to get started with linked data.

MarcEdit:[8] Developed by Terry Reese, MarcEdit is the tool of choice for anyone wanting to work with MARC-based catalog records. It includes a linked data framework that supports reconciliation, as well as a variety of other useful data management and enhancement features. Linked data pilots with MARC records often involve adding URIs in subfields in preparation for the move to linked data (Shieh & Reese, 2016).

TemaTres:[9] For those who are engaged in developing and publishing vocabularies or ontologies, TemaTres is an open-source option that can run in a standard web development environment using Apache, PHP, and MySQL.

Apache Jena:[10] Apache Jena is an open-source software framework that provides methods for publishing data in triplestores and ontologies, and developing SPARQL endpoints.

Cmap Tools:[11] Developed and maintained by the Florida Institute for Human & Machine Cognition (IHMC), Cmap Tool is a free knowledge modeling tool that may be useful when working with graphical representations of library data. It has a robust user community to rely on for support.

Examples of Linked Data Work

Linked data in libraries has been addressed for years, but it has yet to reach widespread adoption. A pragmatic overview can be found in the accessible book *Linked Data for the Perplexed Librarian*:

> First, only a few in the GLAM community use (and evangelize) linked data, compared with the many who do not. Research and experiments in linked library data are costly, in terms of both technological support and staff time spent away from ongoing library work. Visit a GLAM conference's sessions on linked data and you will chiefly find attendees who have the institutional and financial support to play with linked data (not to mention the institutional and financial support to simply attend conferences). The result is a small assemblage of linked data enthusiasts that rarely grows or changes, which in turn stagnates the technical infrastructure that would welcome others into linked data Land.
>
> (Carlson et al., 2020 p. x)

According to the 2018 OCLC survey for linked data implementers, the datasets with the most use were provided by national libraries such as the Bibliotheque

National du France, Europeana, the Library of Congress linked data service, and nomisama, which supports numismatic research (Yoshimura, 2018).

Digital library repositories have advanced with the support of the Samvera community framework for linked data publishing, notably with Fedora as a repository layer that stores RDF. Furthermore, Oregon Digital provides a use case for Samvera, since the collaborative effort between the University of Oregon and Oregon State University has incorporated a variety of LOD principles and standards. These include the development and maintenance of local vocabularies such as Opaquenamespace[12] and local hosting of URIs representing predicates used in digital collections. The Portland Common Data Model[13] is also used to model linked data publishing best practices. Islandora 8 also supports linked data publishing through the usage of URIs and JSON-LD (Islandora Foundation, 2020).

Heng et al. (2021) comment on the landscape available for LOD to be implemented in authorities' work:

> The increasing reliability and availability of LOD sources can be seen as both a blessing and a curse. Needing to consider more sources when trying to definitively identify and formulate headings for people, corporate entities, and subjects is a complicating factor, but the additional information LOD sources bring to the process has the potential to facilitate authority work.
>
> (p. 2)

Engaging in local or regional authorities' work can be an important strategic step for organizations wishing to engage in linked data work. For example, NC State University maintains Organization Name linked data,[14] a dataset drawing upon vocabulary properties from Simple Knowledge Organization System (SKOS), RDF, Friend of a Friend (FOAF), and Web Ontology Language (OWL). The data is enhanced by linking to information in sources such as the VIAF, DBpedia, ISNI, and the Library of Congress.

Wikidata represents an attractive possibility for institutions wishing to engage in linked data work who might not have the resources to develop and implement an accompanying technical infrastructure. The PCC participated in a Wikidata pilot[15] with support for sharing use cases, training sessions, and regular meetings. OCLC recently completed a pilot project centered around CONTENTdm and linked data by developing data models and workflows utilizing Wikibase, which is the software foundation for Wikidata. Information about CONTENTdm entities was also mapped to Schema.org and embedded in web pages to improve Search Engine Optimization. OCLC also developed a number of software programs to support the type of entity management needed for the project as part of the pilot (Bahnemann et al., 2021). OCLC continues to develop programs around entity management with the support of the Mellon Foundation (OCLC, 2021a).

For further practical examples of linked data work and learning opportunities, attending or reviewing the offerings at conferences dedicated to library linked data such as Semantic Web in Libraries (SWIB) can be beneficial. As the landscape for linked data continues to develop, more library software systems are likely to offer native linked data support or provide serialization for metadata in linked data-friendly formats. Furthermore, authorities' work shifting to entity management practices and workflows that leverage existing large-scale linked data datasets will be the norm. Linked data work can be accomplished by institutions with varying levels of institutional investment and support, as long as the projects are well-scoped.

Conclusion

The landscape of linked data continues to evolve for GLAMR institutions. Although its potential has yet to be fully realized, as more vendors, open-source projects, and the larger community continue to grow and experiment with linked data technologies, it is clear that engaging with it can still provide opportunities for reimagining discovery systems, workflows, and philosophies. This chapter introduced the principles of linked data, its potential benefits, and approaches to developing a linked data strategy, and discussed practical examples and tools. As you move forward in your own work with linked data, pay attention to those areas that you can control, and look to institutions who have already done successful pilots to see what might resonate with you.

And may the Force be with you – always!

Notes

 1 www.w3schools.com/xml/xml_rdf.asp
 2 https://schema.org/docs/bib.home.html
 3 https://bib.schema.org/CreativeWork
 4 https://schema.org/Book
 5 https://twitter.com/bm_lod_status
 6 https://openrefine.org/
 7 https://librarycarpentry.org/lc-open-refine
 8 https://marcedit.reeset.net/
 9 www.vocabularyserver.com/
10 https://jena.apache.org/
11 https://cmap.ihmc.us/cmaptools/
12 http://opaquenamespace.org/
13 https://github.com/samvera/hyrax/wiki/Portland-Common-Data-Model-Resources
14 www.lib.ncsu.edu/ld/onld
15 www.wikidata.org/wiki/Wikidata:WikiProject_PCC_Wikidata_Pilot

References

Altman, A., Breedlove, M., Della Bitta, M., & Williams, S. (2017, March). *Changing course in a technology project*. DPLAfest 2017, Chicago, IL, United States. https://docs.google.com/presentation/d/1oKXfb6WlNnDi3V-WmG8Cj2aCJ9dID24DJqrblzDxZJo/pub?slide=id.p

Bahnemann, G., Carroll, M. J., Clough, P., Einaudi, M., Ewing, C., Mixter, J., Roy, J., Tomren, H., Washburn, B., & Williams, E. (2021). *Transforming metadata into linked* data to improve digital collection discoverability: *A CONTENTdm pilot project*. OCLC Research. https://doi.org/10.25333/FZCV-0851

BIBFRAME – Bibliographic Framework Initiative (Library of Congress). (n.d.). [Webpage]. Retrieved November 29, 2021, from www.loc.gov/bibframe/

BIBFRAME Expectations for ILS Tenders. (2018). *Organizer group 2018 European workshop BIBFRAME*. Florence, Italy. https://wiki.dnb.de/download/attachments/125433008/BIBFRAME_Expectations_for_ILS_Tenders.pdf?version=1&modificationDate=1517924536000&api=v2

Breeding, M. (2020). Smarter libraries through technology: Linked Data brings challenges and opportunities to libraries. *Smart Libraries Newsletter*, *40*(4), 1–2.

Breeding, M. (2021a). Innovative interfaces introduces Vega. *Smart Libraries Newsletter*, *41*(3), 2–5.

Breeding, M. (2021b, May 3). 2021 library systems report. *American Libraries Magazine*, *52*(5). https://americanlibrariesmagazine.org/?p=123094

Carlson, S., Lampert, C., & Melvin, D. (2020). *Linked data for the perplexed librarian*. ALA Editions; eBook Collection (EBSCOhost). https://search.ebscohost.com/login.aspx?direct=true&db=nlebk&AN=2433508&site=ehost-live

Chah, N. (2018). OK Google, what is your Ontology? Or: Exploring freebase classification to understand Google's knowledge graph. *ArXiv:1805.03885 [Cs]*. http://arxiv.org/abs/1805.03885

Charles, V. (2014, November 18). *The polymath virtual library and EDM*. https://pro.europeana.eu/page/polymath-edm

Digital Public Library of America. (2017). *Metadata application profile*. Digital Public Library of America. https://pro.dp.la/hubs/metadata-application-profile

Freire, N., Meijers, E., de Valk, S., Raemy, J. A., & Isaac, A. (2020). Metadata aggregation via linked data: Results of the Europeana Common Culture project. *Zenodo*. https://doi.org/10.5281/ZENODO.4062454

Freire, N., Voorburg, R., Cornelissen, R., de Valk, S., Meijers, E., & Isaac, A. (2019). Aggregation of linked data in the cultural heritage domain: A case study in the Europeana network. *Information*, *10*(8), 252. https://doi.org/10.3390/info10080252

Hallo, M., Luján-Mora, S., Maté, A., & Trujillo, J. (2016). Current state of linked data in digital libraries. *Journal of Information Science*, *42*(2), 117–127. https://doi.org/10.1177/0165551515594729

Han, M.-J. K., Cole, T. W., Lampron, P., & Sarol, M. J. (2015). Exposing library holdings metadata in RDF using Schema.org semantics. *International conference on dublin core and metadata applications*, 41–49. https://dcpapers.dublincore.org/pubs/article/view/3772.html

Hardesty, J. L., & Nolan, A. (2021). Mitigating bias in metadata: A use case using Homosaurus linked data. *Information Technology and Libraries*, *40*(3), 1–14. http://doi.org/10.6017/ital.v40i3.13053

Heng, G., Cole, T. W., Tian, T. (Cindy), & Han, M.-J. (2021). Rethinking authority reconciliation process. *Cataloging & Classification Quarterly*, *60*(1), 45–68. https://doi.org/10.1080/01639374.2021.1992554

IMDB. (n.d.). *Star Wars (1977), Quotes*. www.imdb.com/title/tt0076759/quotes/qt0440668

Is the British Museum's Endpoint Working? [@bm_lod_status] (n.d.) *Tweets* [Twitter profile]. https://twitter.com/bm_lod_status

Islandora Foundation. (2020). *Islandora 8 fact sheet*. https://islandora.ca/content/islandora-fact-sheet

Kim, M., Chen, M., & Montgomery, D. (2021). Moving toward BIBFRAME and a linked data environment. In S. Schmehl Hines (Ed.), *Technical services in the 21ˢᵗ century* (Vol. 42, pp. 131–154). Emerald. https://doi.org/10.1108/S0732-067120210000042011

Klímek, J., Škoda, P., & Nečaský, M. (2019). Survey of tools for linked data consumption. *Semantic Web, 10*(4), 665–720. https://doi.org/10.3233/SW-180316

Larson, R. R., Pitti, D., & Turner, A. (2014). SNAC: The social networks and archival context project: Towards an archival authority cooperative. *IEEE/ACM joint conference on digital libraries* (pp. 427–428). IEEE. https://doi.org/10.1109/JCDL.2014.6970208

Michael, B., & Han, M.-J. K. (2019). Assessing BIBFRAME 2.0: Exploratory implementation in metadata maker. *Proceedings of the 2019 international conference on Dublin Core and metadata applications* (pp. 26–31). https://dcpapers.dublincore.org/pubs/article/view/4229/2423.html

Mitchell, E. T. (2016). *Library linked data: Early activity and development.* ALA TechSource.

Mixter, J. K., OBrien, P., & Arlitsch, K. (2014). Describing theses and dissertations using Schema.org. *International conference on Dublin Core and metadata applications* (pp. 138–146). https://dcpapers.dublincore.org/pubs/article/view/3715.html

Myntti, J., & Cothran, N. (2013). Authority control in a digital repository: Preparing for linked data. *Journal of Library Metadata, 13*(2/3), 95–113. https://doi.org/10.1080/19386389.2013.826061

OCLC. (2021a, February 17). *What happened to the linked data that previously displayed on records in WorldCat.org?* OCLC Support. https://help.oclc.org/Discovery_and_Reference/WorldCat-org/Troubleshooting/What_happened_to_the_linked_data_that_previously_displayed_on_records_in_WorldCat.org

OCLC. (2021b, September 29). *WorldCat – Shared entity management infrastructure.* OCLC. www.oclc.org/en/worldcat/oclc-and-linked-data/shared-entity-management-infrastructure.html

Riley, J. (2017). *Understanding metadata: What is metadata, and what is it for?: A primer.* NISO. www.niso.org/publications/understanding-metadata-2017

Sanders, S. (2015, August 23). Library linked data: Making it happen. *Ex Libris Tech Blog.* https://developers.exlibrisgroup.com/blog/Linked-Library-Data/

Sanders, S. (2017, October 3). Linked library data: It's happening. *Ex Libris.* https://exlibrisgroup.com/ko/blog/linked-library-data-its-happening/

Seymore, S. E., & Simic, J. (2019). Enhancing Opaquenamespace.org: Refinement of local name authority files and workflows. *Journal of Library Metadata, 19*(1/2), 99–115. https://doi.org/10.1080/19386389.2019.1589704

Shieh, J., & Reese, T. (2016). The importance of identifiers in the new web environment and using the uniform resource identifier (URI) in subfield zero ($0): A small step that is actually a big step. *Journal of Library Metadata, 15*(3–4), 208–226. https://doi.org/10.1080/19386389.2015.1099981

Singhal, A. (2012, May 16). *Introducing the knowledge graph: Things, not strings.* Google. https://blog.google/products/search/introducing-knowledge-graph-things-not/

Smith, M. (2021). Linked open data and aggregation infrastructure in the cultural heritage sector: A case study of SOCH, a linked data aggregator for Swedish open cultural heritage. In K. Golub & Y.-H. Liu (Eds.), *Information and knowledge organisation in digital humanities.* Taylor & Francis, Routledge. https://doi.org/10.4324/9781003131816

Topham, K., & Huff, N. (2021, November 1). *The Marmaduke problem: Comics, linked data, and community-led authority control* [Lightning talk]. Digital Library Federation Forum 2021. https://www.youtube.com/watch?v=Rcg3_KS0vAE

Wallis, R., Isaac, A., Charles, V., & Manguinhas, H. (2017). Recommendations for the application of Schema.org to aggregated cultural heritage metadata to increase relevance and visibility to search engines: The case of Europeana. *The Code4Lib Journal, 36.* https://journal.code4lib.org/articles/12330

Wearn, S. (2021). Reality check. Changing the metadata ecosystem. *Technicalities, 41*(5), 1, 5–7.

Yoshimura, K. S. (2018). Analysis of 2018 international linked data survey for implementers. *Code4Lib Journal, 42.* https://journal.code4lib.org/articles/13867

Zepheira. (n.d.). *BIBFRAME Lite + supporting vocabularies.* BIBFRAME Vocabulary Navigator. Retrieved November 29, 2021, from http://bibfra.me/

5 User Searching in Digital Repositories

Oksana L. Zavalina and Mary Burke

Content and Audiences of Digital Repositories

To discuss user search behavior in digital repositories meaningfully, one must start by understanding the audiences that the repositories are intended to serve: the geographic regions the users are expected to come from, the domains of knowledge the users represent, and so on. To offer easy access to the rich pools of digital content (especially the valuable, rare, and unique materials digitized over the years to enable broader access to them), large-scale digital repositories aggregate hundreds of separate digital collections and function as portals to these collections and the individual items they contain. Some repositories aggregate content at the levels of a continent, country, state, or region (e.g., Europeana, Digital Public Library of America, Gateway to Oklahoma History, and Digital Library of the Middle East). While many of these digital repositories are created for the general public, others serve more specific audiences, such as educators, students, and scholars across disciplines and domains like the sciences or history, and provide solutions to learning and teaching on a digital platform (Mardis et al., 2012). Their development is often supported by federal funding. For example, in the United States, the Institute of Museum and Library Services (IMLS) awarded National Leadership Grants and/or Library Services and Technology Act grants to over 1,700 digitization projects of various scales between 1998 and 2015 to support the digitization of valuable information resources.[1] Furthermore, the National Science Foundation (NSF) funded over 300 science, technology, engineering, and mathematics (STEM) digital collections through its National STEM Education Distributed Learning program[2] (Skog et al., 2009).

Cultural heritage materials of historical and educational value, particularly resources about local and national history, were prioritized in mass digitization, especially in its early stages in the 1990s and 2000s. Therefore, many digital repositories were created for users in the history domain. In the United States, some of these repositories function at the state level (e.g., The Portal to Texas History)[3] or at the regional level (e.g., Mountain West Digital Library).[4] Several were created at the federal level. The American Memory[5] was a well-known federal-level digital library in the U.S. history domain until it was disassembled as a separate entity. It was created by the U.S. Library of Congress, in cooperation with other cultural

DOI: 10.4324/9781003216438-7

heritage institutions in the mid-1990s with financial support from the IMLS, and aggregated the most carefully selected and highest quality information resources (Arms, 1996). Its collections were "migrated to new presentations" as part of the Library of Congress Digital Collections[6] in February 2018. Similarly, IMLS funded the creation of the Opening History[7] digital repository that was a spin-off from the IMLS Digital Collections and Content (IMLS DCC)[8] portal to all digital collections supported by IMLS that existed from 2003 to 2015. The purpose of Opening History was to further develop the strongest content area within IMLS DCC – U.S. history – and improve discoverability. Opening History's primary user group was broadly defined as history researchers, including both academic and non-academic history scholars; teachers and students at all education levels; genealogists and citizen historians; and others (Palmer et al., 2010). Opening History functioned as a separate entity from October 2008 to July 2012 and aggregated over 1,500 digital collections and more than a million items. In August 2012, Opening History was absorbed by its parent digital library, IMLS DCC, and later, after the end of the IMLS funding period, both were absorbed by the Digital Public Library of America,[9] which launched in 2013.

STEM is another important domain served by large-scale digital repositories. Among other contributions, digital repositories have become major players in STEM education (Mardis et al., 2012). The National Science Digital Library (NSDL), launched in 2000, is a notable example. It caters to administrators, educators, general public, learners, parents/guardians, professionals/practitioners, and researchers. NSDL was accessible at http://nsdl.org for 15 years, and after the end of the NSF funding period, it became accessible (with somewhat altered functionality) through the Open Educational Resources (OER) Commons at https://nsdl.oercommons.org/. With an increasing demand for access to high-quality STEM education resources for teachers and learners, NSDL served as a starting point to locate and retrieve these discipline-specific resources in a variety of formats for different learning levels (McIlvain, 2010; Perrault, 2010; Quinones, 2010; Toomey, 2010). NSDL aggregates online educational resources from a wide variety of providers. Most of these resources are free, based on OER access. The resources are organized by educational level (from pre-kindergarten to higher education, including informal education and professional development education) and grouped by resource type (assessment materials, audio/visual, instructional material, reference material, and others). The NSDL not only serves as a repository for resources but also provides useful services and tools for professional development of educators and for network collaboration among NSDL audiences (Brisco, 2010; McIlvain, 2010).

Irrespective of the domain, digital repositories aim to improve user experiences and facilitate the discoverability of items. To achieve this, digital repository services must adjust to the evolving expectations, needs, and information-seeking behavior patterns of user groups in the online environment (e.g., Horava, 2010; Lavoie et al., 2007; Verheul et al., 2010). The following sections provide an overview of research findings on user expectations and user search behavior and review other relevant literature on how users interact with information in digital repositories and the factors that affect these interactions.

User Expectations

From the very inception of digital repositories, user expectations have been, and continue to be, shaped by experiences with other widely used information technology tools. According to Bawden and Vilar (2006), before social media began greatly impacting the lives of information users, these expectations were shaped by their experiences with major search engines such as Google, sites such as Amazon and eBay, and the popularity of computer games. More broadly, changes in Western society, such as faster development, the perceived need for immediate gratification, and a more information-rich environment, have influenced users' expectations. They noted the emergence of the "satisficing" approach to finding information that is when the user is satisfied with "good enough" results that reach the minimum acceptability threshold by meeting only some of the search criteria. Bawden and Vilar (2006) therefore concluded that users typically expect more from digital libraries than from conventional library services. For example, these new expectations, which users did not have toward traditional brick-and-mortar libraries, include ease of use through a single interface, availability of materials in multiple formats (text, images, sound), immediate gratification (high response speeds), comprehensiveness of search results (high recall), and accessibility of papers and books in full-text. However, users' expectations of digital library services are often higher than what a digital library can deliver (Bawden & Vilar, 2006). Some user studies reveal that users view these services, particularly those of academic libraries (Matusiak, 2012), as being not useful or not easy to use. To combat this perception, it is important for all libraries to understand the methods used by their users to search and then attempt to facilitate those methods (Rather & Ganaie, 2019).

The term *domain knowledge*, first coined in 1991, refers to the user's level of knowledge both on a specific topic that they are looking for information on and the broader subject domain or discipline that topic falls within (Allen, 1991). Both the level of domain knowledge and a specific domain that a user represents were found to affect user expectations toward a digital repository and the patterns of user interactions with that repository. For example, Marchionini et al. (1993) found that domain experts focus on the answers to their search questions and have clear expectations for both the answer and the context in which it would appear. Furthermore, Palmer's (2005) study demonstrated that scientists' searches are usually aimed at specific questions or problems they face when conducting an experiment or writing results or checking the accuracy of available information. Digital library user expectations, including "collection expectation" – an expectation that certain kinds of resources and information would be found in library or academic sources and not through search engines – differ by user domain and level of expertise (Bawden & Vilar, 2006).

In addition to domain knowledge, user experiences and success in information discovery are influenced by *system knowledge*: users' technical skills and general understanding of how the information system behind the search bar functions (Borgman, 1996) and their knowledge of which sources to search and how their searches should be ordered (Markey, 2007b). Borgman (1986) pointed out that failure to incorporate sufficient understanding of users' searching behavior, knowledge, and skills in database design makes them difficult to use.

By observing how users interact with the existing interface, researchers can understand their information-seeking behavior and ask clarifying questions. For example, Green and Lampron (2017) sought to understand the experience of various users of Emblematica Online[10] and the challenges they faced. Furthermore, interacting with actual users may also help practitioners understand users' goals in different scenarios, and thus guide interface and metadata decisions and support outreach efforts (Achieng, 2016; Reilly & Thompson, 2014). These studies may focus on user interactions with a specific digital repository (e.g., Green & Lampron, 2017; Willis & McIntosh, 2019) or seek to describe the behavior of a certain group or demographic, such as art history students (Kamposiori, 2012; Kröber, 2021; Münster et al., 2018) or young children (Druin et al., 2001, 2007; Hutchinson et al., 2005. User studies can also help practitioners understand and cater to the needs of underserved user groups (e.g., blind users in Xie et al.'s 2015 study).

While some user studies aim to assess the usability of repositories overall (e.g., Dong, 2019; Jabeen et al., 2017; Kous et al., 2020; Liang et al., 2020), others target one aspect of a digital library. For example, Burns et al. (2019) surveyed student users for input on the best terminology to describe resources (e.g., *e-book* vs. *digitized book*). Studies also examine users' opinions and preferences on existing services. For example, Agosti et al. (2007) found that 81 percent of respondents who used The European Library expressed a preference for advanced search. User studies may also include potential users of a digital repository, either one that already exists or one that is being developed. For example, Wu et al. (2012) explored users' expectations of multilingual searching capabilities. Al-Smadi et al. (2016) reported the needs of users of language archives – digital repositories archiving and providing access to language data – in northeast India. They found that without a stable Internet connection, users were unable to access the digital repository. Thus, user studies conducted with the potential users of a digital repository help practitioners understand their expectations, as well as the barriers they face in accessing the repository.

User Interactions With Digital Repositories

Searching and browsing are the two major types of interactions between users and discovery and access systems such as library catalogs, databases, search engines, or digital libraries (Wilson, 2000). This section discusses these interactions in the context of digital repositories and highlights relevant research from before the emergence of digital repositories.

Searching is expressed through queries, which are sets of one or more characters (organized in words, phrases, etc.) combined with other syntax used as commands for the information system to locate potentially relevant content indexed therein. According to Jansen and Rieh (2010), the query is a key theoretical construct in the fields of both information retrieval research and information searching behavior research. The following is a simple example of a search query for "digital repositories" in Microsoft Bing, one of the major search engines: www.bing.com/search?q=digital+repositories.

User studies focused on query analysis have long been conducted, and their findings regarding pre-digital era libraries provide a useful historical perspective. A few library catalog user studies conducted from the 1930s to the early 1970s were summarized by Krikelas (1972). The studies compared how traditional library card catalogs were searched and how library patrons used the cards' different bibliographic description elements (fields). For example, at the time of the studies, users heavily consulted author, title, subject headings, call number, and date of publication, while place of publication, publisher, edition, and content note tended to be consulted less often, and size, series note, and illustration statement were of even less interest. In the early 1980s, when end-users received direct access to online library catalogs, they initially expressed much greater satisfaction with online catalogs than with traditional library card catalogs, which was largely explained as being due to the new ways of interaction (including keyword searching) that became available then (Bates, 1989; Larson, 1991; Matthews et al., 1983).

Allen (1991) found that information-seeking behavior (i.e., selection of search strategy and tactics) and the outcomes of the search depend, to a large extent, on a searcher's domain knowledge. Numerous other studies confirmed this observation (reviewed by Xie & Matusiak, 2016). For example, studies show that when a user's domain knowledge is low, higher numbers of searches per session are required because of the user's inability to choose appropriate terms initially; more domain-knowledgeable users make fewer changes to their searches (Hembrooke et al., 2005; Wildemuth, 2004). Subsequent sections of this chapter, focusing on search query construction and utilization of system features, will include a discussion of the effect of domain knowledge on these user searching behaviors.

Browsing is another significant way in which users interact with an information system, including a digital repository (Wilson, 2000). Various options for browsing exist: browsing based on when the item was added to the digital repository, author/contributor names, terms representing types of materials and subjects, geographic browsing – either hierarchical or using an interactive map – and more (some of these are shown in Figures 5.1 and 5.2). Browsing is not a mutually exclusive alternative to searching when interacting with a digital repository; rather, users tend to engage in both kinds of interactions, sometimes starting with one and continuing with another. The choice of the initial interaction type depends on the context. For example, a participant in a 2009 digital repository user study explained:

> If I am looking for something specific, I search. A lot of times I browse because I am looking for things that might be helpful. I might do just a general search and then just look at everything or look at what looks interesting and take a look deeper.
>
> (Zavalina, 2010, pp. 115–116)

Both browsing and searching can be studied on their own (at the level of individual search or browse queries) or at the level of a session – a sequence of moves the user engages in while interacting with a digital repository in one sitting. Session-level studies of user interactions provide a richer picture of user behavior. For example, Phillips et al. (2019) explored user interactions within a digital repository in the UNT Libraries' Digital Collections and found that users were accessing items of multiple types and originating from multiple disciplines within one session.

Domain knowledge levels have been found to affect browsing as well. A large-scale user study commissioned by the British Library published in 2008 found that the main characteristics of researchers (users with higher domain knowledge) tend to include the following: horizontal information-seeking (a form of skimming activity, where researchers view just one or two pages from the list of search or browse results in a digital repository and then "bounce" out); extended navigation (researchers spend as much time finding their way around the repository as actually viewing results); horizontal "power browsing" through titles, content pages, and abstracts; squirreling behavior, where researchers save information – particularly free content – in the form of downloads for later use but rarely revisit it; and spending little time on evaluating information (Information Behaviour of the Researcher of the Future, 2008, p. 10; Williams & Rowlands, 2007).

The specific domain the users represent also affects interactions with the digital repository. Both students and scholars in the Humanities and Social Sciences domains have been found to actively use timeline and chronological browsing, and interactive map browsing, and have also been found to express the need for search limits by date (Harum, 2008, personal communication; Wu & Chen, 2007). However, user studies demonstrated that digital library users within the same domains were found to prefer searching to browsing. Some explained this to be because of the lack of call number browsing capabilities in a digital library environment (Buchanan et al., 2005; Wu & Chen, 2007).

Developers of digital repositories must remember that user interactions with digital repositories and discoverability also depend on the tools used to access the resources. For example, Khait et al. (2021) used a multilingual survey of underrepresented language communities around the world with the goal to establish best practices for archiving language data. Preliminary results from nine language community participants indicate that these users rarely search for language materials directly in the digital repositories that provide access to these materials but mainly access these through social media platforms. The authors therefore conclude that, rather than focusing on educating the users about navigating – searching and browsing – "complex archiving environments" such as digital repositories, it would be more beneficial to invest resources into making materials available via the platforms the users are already comfortable navigating. As an example of a possible development in this area, they suggest "designing language archive chat bot interfaces for popular messengers to search and deliver the data" (p. 4).

Although Khait et al. (2021) specifically examined user expectations for digital repositories providing access to language materials, it is logical to assume that this trend of exploring information of interest through third parties (most prominently,

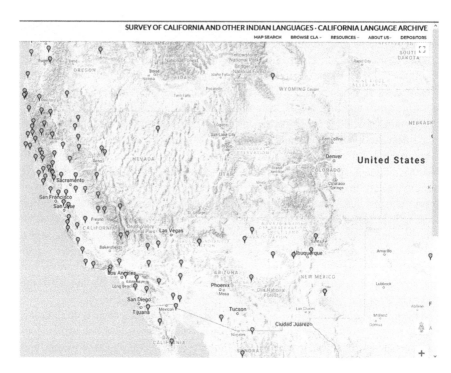

Figure 5.1 Example of geographic browsing

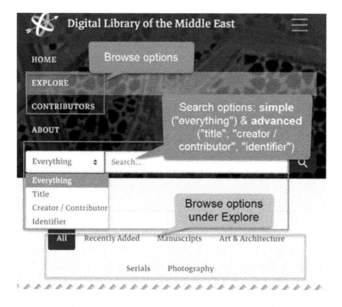

Figure 5.2 Example of browsing and searching options supported in a digital repository

through social media platforms) rather than through digital repositories directly applies to a much broader user community and to various kinds of digital repositories. This emphasizes the importance of high-quality and interoperable metadata that supports linked data using URIs and the thorough representation of relationships among information resources and other entities. Such metadata would be the most functional for the discovery of digital repository content in the broader online environment.

Keyword Search Constructions

Analysis of keyword search construction and formulation is conducted through a range of qualitative and quantitative methods. Transaction logs recorded through servers of information retrieval systems provide a wealth of data for analyzing various patterns of user information-seeking as expressed through queries. Transaction log analysis (also referred to as search log analysis) – "the study of electronically recorded interactions between online information retrieval systems and the persons who search for the information found in those systems" (Peters, 1993) – is one of the methods used for researching user behavior in various information systems, including digital repositories. Information systems of various kinds, including digital content management applications used in digital repositories, allow the recording of transaction logs. Additionally, it is easy to set up a Google Analytics account for any website, including that of a digital repository, and obtain transaction log data through this service. Both Google Analytics and other transaction log data are used in the analysis of user interactions with digital repositories.

   A few studies, starting with studies focused on searching using web search engines, have examined the quantitative parameters of user interaction sessions (session length, the number of queries per session, percentage of sessions in which users modify their initial search queries), and specifically search queries – query length (measured in the number of terms, characters, etc.), frequency (the number of times the same search query appears in the dataset), and so on. For example, Jansen et al. (2004) found that users modified initial search queries in 48 percent of sessions, with an average of 32 percent of sessions including three or more search queries. Query lengths were measured as the number of terms per query, ranging from 1.9 in video searching to 4.0 in image searching. Markey (2007a) reviewed findings from studies of user searching in online catalogs, web search engines, and digital repositories, such as the New Zealand Digital Library, and reported search query lengths ranging from 1.9 words in the 1999 log data from the Excite web search engine to 10.3 in a 2004 analysis of a Norwegian-based web search engine called Fast. Furthermore, they reported query length ranging between 1.3 in a 1994 online catalog study and 7.8 in a 2002 study of the web search engine Excite. Moulaison's (2008) analysis of user queries in a college online catalog revealed that the most common query lengths were two terms (36.5 percent of searches) and three terms (25.5 percent). Zavalina and Vassilieva (2014) observed lower average search query lengths than those summarized by Markey (2007a); however, the query lengths – 2.36 in Opening History and 2.66 in NSDL digital repositories – were very close to those previously observed in the New Zealand Digital Library – between 2.2 and 2.6 words per query (Jones et al., 2000). Studies also found that users tend to utilize more terms in keyword search queries as their level of domain knowledge increases (Zhang et al., 2005; Hee Kim & Ho Kim, 2008).

The qualitative characteristics of the terms used in keyword search queries have also been examined. Recent work explores how search queries are influenced by current events. For example, researchers observed searches relating to popular culture (e.g., "game of thrones"; "twilight") in the Edmonton Public Library BiblioCommons database (Oliphant & Shiri, 2017; Shiri & Oliphant, 2017). In the 1990s and 2000s, several studies categorized web search queries into topical categories by applying qualitative research methods (Bates, 1996; Beitzel et al., 2007; Jansen et al., 2007; Koshman et al., 2006; Spink & Jansen, 2004). In the early 2010s, Zavalina and Vassilieva (2012) compared both quantitative and qualitative patterns of user searching for items and collections in a digital aggregation that provided a collection-level search (infrequently available elsewhere) in addition to the more ubiquitous item-level search. They qualitatively sorted user searches into categories that were partly derived from the Functional Requirements for Bibliographic Records' (IFLA, 2008) set of entities and found five categories of user searches that had not been observed in earlier research: *object, corporate body, work, ethnic group,* and *class of persons.* Another study by Zavalina (2014) used transaction log analysis to compare user searching in a state-level digital repository that aggregates content from the state of Texas (Portal to Texas History) and a federal-level digital aggregation, Opening History. It revealed significant differences in the distribution of most search categories in user queries: *person* and *family* terms occurred more frequently in the state-level digital repository while *object* terms occurred in the federal-level digital repository.

Studies have investigated the ways in which representatives of a specific domain or discipline searched for information. For example, Bates (1996) developed a search term taxonomy of users from the humanities fields. Bates found that the most common types of query terms appearing in the searches of humanities scholars (e.g., historians) include individuals' names, geographical names, chronological terms, and discipline terms (concepts within the field). Furthermore, user search queries in different types of digital repositories aimed at different user communities were examined and compared. Several studies analyzed transaction logs of domain-specific large-scale digital libraries, such as the NSDL, American Memory, and Opening History, or domain-independent large-scale digital libraries, such as the IMLS Digital Collections and Content Collection Registry or The European Library (e.g., Khoo et al., 2008; Pan, 2003; Verberne et al., 2010). Some studies have also examined the content of user search queries (Zavalina, 2007; Zavalina, 2011; Zavalina & Vassilieva, 2014). For example, a study of user searching in two representative large-scale digital libraries designed for different domains and user populations – Opening History and the NSDL – found that it differed substantially between the two libraries (Zavalina & Vassilieva, 2014). The search queries of NSDL users varied more widely in length, and, on average, were longer and occurred more frequently than those of users of the Opening History digital repository. Search queries of Opening History users varied more widely in frequency and contained more search categories than those of NSDL users. In addition, the frequency of occurrence of some term types in user search queries indicated noticeable differences between the two digital repositories, which might be explained by the focus of each of the repositories. For example, *concept* and *object* search categories occurred significantly more often in NSDL users' queries, while *place, person, corporate body, ethnic group, event,* and *class of persons* occurred significantly more often in Opening History users' search queries. On the basis of these data, Zavalina and Vassilieva (2014) concluded that geographical and personal names, identified earlier as major search kinds by Bates' (1996) search term taxonomy of humanities users, retained their prevalence, while *object* searches had also gained recent prominence. Furthermore, the study's unexpected finding was the low frequency of *event* searching in a US history-focused Opening History digital repository.

Domain knowledge was found to influence keyword search query construction. For example, domain experts incorporate more unique terms (e.g., Hee Kim & Ho Kim, 2008; Zhang et al., 2005). As students acquire more domain knowledge on their research topic, they start to use wider and more specific vocabulary in their subject search (Vakkari et al., 2003). Furthermore, domain differences for keyword search query construction were also observed. For example, studies of web searching discovered that humanities scholars most often include personal and geographic names and chronological and discipline terms in their search queries. Other studies have shown that water quality researchers frequently use topical, geographical, and format or genre search terms and occasionally use chemical formulas, dates, names, and URLs. Medical researchers' prevailing search query types include laboratory/test results, diseases/syndromes, body parts/organs, pharmacological substances, or diagnostic procedures (Bates, 1996; Natarajan et al., 2010; Nowick & Mering, 2003; Wu & Chen, 2007). User bases for domain-independent information systems aimed at a broad user audience tend to include more novice users than experts, while the audience of domain-specific information systems (e.g., those focusing on history and science) normally includes a higher proportion of experts (Zavalina & Vassilieva, 2014).

System Features and Their Utilization

Digital repository developers make decisions regarding system features beyond a basic keyword search. This includes decisions on whether to include features like browsing-supporting tools such as interactive maps, or multilingual searching that allows users to switch the language of the search interface. Another important system feature is advanced search – *fielded advanced search*, in which the user can enter search terms into specific search fields, or *faceted advanced search*, in which the user can narrow search results by selecting a specific facet. Both types rely on database indexes created using specific metadata fields in records representing separately searchable resources. Practitioners developing, implementing, and seeking to improve their digital repositories need to make informed decisions regarding the facets that should be enabled for users to limit search results, the metadata fields available for fielded advanced search, and so on. Another advanced search option utilized in some information systems is Boolean searching, which allows users to combine search terms and/or query multiple fields of a meta-data record using Boolean logic operators AND, OR, and NOT. Along with these logic operators, web search engines also allow plus (+) and minus (−) operators (Markey, 2007a). Some advanced search options also enable the use of controlled vocabularies such as thesauri, classification systems, lists of subject headings and names, and so on when constructing a search query.

The number of options included in advanced search and browse functionalities varies across digital repositories and is based on an understanding of the repository's actual and/or potential user needs, and on the richness of the metadata that represents resources collected in the digital repository. For example, in 2010, the NSDL offered "well-defined" search, browse, and help instruments, which included keyword searching, browsing collections by subject area, combining search by broad subject area and audience, and limiting searches to new collections (Perrault, 2010; Toomey, 2010). At the time of writing this chapter, NSDL's faceted advanced search options allow limiting keyword search results by terms organized into nine categories: subject area, educational use, material type, member activity, content source, primary user, education level, media format, and accessibility.[11] Figure 5.2 shows the relatively small selection of advanced search options – title, contributor/author, and identifier – available in the recently created international digital repository providing access to cultural heritage materials to a broad audience: the Digital Library of the Middle East. By contrast, Figure 5.3 shows an example of an extensive selection of advanced search options available in another digital repository of datasets aimed at experts in multiple scientific domains: Dataverse.

Studies of user search behavior within various discovery systems found that users have a preference for simple keyword searches rather than any advanced search (Curl, 1995; Fidel, 1992; Hildreth, 1997; Moulaison, 2008; Muddamalle, 1998; Spurgin & Wildemuth, 2009; Zavalina & Vassilieva, 2014). However, an interesting observation of a comparative analysis of user searching in state-level and federal-level digital aggregations in the United States was that users initiated an advanced search almost twice as often (in 24.96 percent of queries) in the Portal to Texas History state repository than in the Opening History federal repository (Zavalina, 2014). Moreover, some user studies show an upward trend in the use of faceted searches in online catalogs (e.g., Niu & Hemminger, 2015). Overall, the frequency of advanced searching was observed to be high in more recent studies (e.g., Zavalina & Vassilieva, 2014) compared to the findings of previous studies of user searching on the web or in online databases (Nicholas et al., 2009; Spink & Jansen, 2004). This may indicate a higher proportion of domain expert users in large-scale digital repositories, as previous analyses suggest that the occurrence of selecting the advanced search options increases with an increase in a user's domain knowledge (e.g., Wildemuth, 2004).

Figure 5.3 Example of advanced search options in the Dataverse digital repository

Studies show that more domain-knowledgeable users utilize advanced search options more and conduct more complex searches by combining multiple search criteria in a query (e.g., Hee Kim & Ho Kim, 2008; Hembrooke et al., 2005; Wildemuth, 2004; Zhang et al., 2005). Humanities researchers with high domain knowledge were found to use a variety of search types and to experience differ- ent levels of success in different types of advanced search; known author-title search was the most successful, while success in more uncertain types of searches such as a conceptual/discipline term search heavily depended on the level of the searcher's domain knowledge and experience in using a particular digital library. Subject classifications were almost never used by academic searchers because the scholars' conceptual models usually differed from those represented in the classification scheme (Buchanan et al., 2005).

System features allow users to set search limits that filter search results. Moulaison (2008) analyzed user queries in a college online catalog and found a "much higher than anticipated" level of use of these search limits (p. 235). In 10 percent of keyword searches, users applied search limits, including date of publication, type of material, and location of material in the library. The author concluded that the number of search limits applied by users in their searches can be utilized to measure search complexity and document query sophistication (Moulaison, 2008). Zavalina and Vassilieva (2014) observed that NSDL users utilized advanced search capabilities more often than Opening History users. They therefore suggested that this trend might be due to differences in system design between the two digital aggregations, as NSDL offers more search limit options than Opening History does.

Boolean searching capabilities and various advanced searching options have been enabled in library databases for several decades, starting with online library catalogs and early computerized article databases such as DIALOG. Several studies have analyzed patterns of user searching utilizing Boolean operators and controlled vocabulary in online catalogs. Boolean searching options provided in the online catalogs in the 1980s and 1990s were found to be ineffective, not only because most library users – even highly educated ones – experienced difficulties with Boolean logic concepts but also because the execution order of Boolean commands was not standardized across different online catalogs (Borgman, 1996). Moreover, research from the early 1990s found that performance was improved in systems that did not require the use of Boolean operators for complex queries (Allen, 1991).

Jansen et al.'s (2004) transaction log analysis study compared the Boolean searching rates for different types of materials and observed a wide range: Boolean queries occurred in between one percent of search queries for video resources and 28 percent of image searches. Markey's (2007a) review of findings of user searching studies included data on the levels of use of advanced search approaches, including Boolean search, and demonstrated that overall, less than 20 percent of searches used Boolean operators. The review found that the plus (+) and minus (−) operators were used most often, and the NOT operator was used the least (less than 2 percent of searches). Zavalina and Vassilieva (2014) suggest that developers of digital repositories with a STEM focus might benefit their users by prioritizing faceted search options and search result limits, as well as by documenting metadata records on the *concepts* the resources are about, their genres, formats, and so on in metadata records. At the same time, user searching data suggests that developers of cultural heritage digital libraries that focus on local history would meet their users' needs better by paying more attention to representing relevant *persons* and *places* in their metadata (Zavalina & Vassilieva, 2014). The high frequency of *place* searching observed by Zavalina and Vassilieva (2014) also suggests that user experience and discoverability in digital repositories can be improved by supplying an option to limit search results by geographical area.

Interface Design Effects on User Interactions With and Discoverability in Digital Repositories

Beyond search options and system features, studies show that the interface of a repository can also impact user experience (Zhang et al., 2013). For example, a user study of art history students emphasized the importance of how relationships between items were represented on the digital library website (Kröber, 2021). Interface design contributes to user searching strategies. This includes decisions made by repository developers about where the system features discussed earlier are located on the repository website or homepage, and how noticeable they are made with the help of fonts and colors. For example, upon finding that NSDL users engaged in advanced searches more often than Opening History users, Zavalina and Vassilieva (2014) concluded that this observation might at least partly be attributed to interface differences between the two digital repositories. While the NSDL interface offered some of its search limit options on the home page, all of the Opening History's search limit options were offered on a separate page deeper within the site. In a recent study, Alokluk and Al-Amri (2021) found that a complicated repository interface was a primary issue that users cited in interview and survey responses about their experiences with a university's digital library.

The settings selected by digital repository developers in interface design can also impact discoverability and user experiences in other ways. For example, in a recent dissertation investigating information organization in digital repositories in the Middle East, Aljalahmah (2021) pointed out another issue with user search in digital repositories as something they had experienced first hand in the process of collecting data by searching the metadata records databases on the websites of two institutions. The navigation was negatively impacted because the web pages frequently timed out, even when the user was still actively browsing the list of search results. In the case of Aljalahmah (2021), the time-outs, which happened every five minutes, took the user back to the main search page without preserving the last used search criteria. This time-out pattern persisted regardless of the device used for navigation or the internet browser utilized. Such a practice forces users to start the same search repeatedly, and, in most cases, demotivates users from continuing with their exploration. Aljalahmah (2021) points out that such usability issues can be a serious barrier to discovery in digital repositories.

Multilingual Access

For a digital repository to be relevant to its users' needs, its creators must consider the domain knowledge and backgrounds of the intended user groups, including the languages they speak and those they can effectively use for interacting with a digital repository. Such information is generally gathered through user studies. In this section, we review a current research area dealing with increasing the accessibility of digital language archives and multilingual resources.

Burke et al. (2021, 2022) interviewed language archive users and managers about how they interact with language archives. Findings from interviews and observations indicated that, for many users, the language element of metadata records and representations of the relationships between items (e.g., an audio recording and any textual transcriptions or translations) are top priorities in their interactions with language archives. Some users also noted that maps displaying the geographic area where the languages are spoken allowed them to find materials easily. Furthermore, though the exploratory study focused on academic end users, many noted that the needs of language community users must also be considered.

Al-Smadi et al. (2016) proposed the creation of different portals for different user groups of language archives (e.g., academic users and language community users), featuring different browsing tools based on users' preferences and a multilingual interface. Users interviewed by Burke et al. (2022) also noted that multilingual interfaces would enable more users to access digital language data. The Tibetan and Himalayan Library[12] interface, for example, can be viewed in Mandarin, English, and Tibetan. However, for fully multilingual access, metadata must also be translated. Currently, metadata in language archives is almost exclusively displayed in English. One exception is the Archive of Indigenous Languages of Latin America (AILLA),[13] which provides complete metadata records in both English and Spanish. AILLA also allows depositors to supply data values for some metadata elements (title, content description) in the Indigenous language of the collection (also called *target language*), although this is not required. Though other language archives do not explicitly include metadata fields for data values in the target language, Burke and Zavalina (2020) found that some depositors provided both English and target language data in the same instance, within the free-text description field. Similarly, some metadata records in the Computational Resource for South Asian Languages (CoRSAL)[14] digital repository include titles and keywords in the target language of the collection. Currently, some language archives are experimenting with employing members of relevant language communities to enrich existing metadata accompanying language materials (Burke, 2021; Harris et al., 2019), including by adding metadata in the target language.

Multilingual access in digital repositories with a broader focus was discussed by multiple authors. Stiller et al. (2013) reviewed how multilingual access was implemented in Europeana, with regard to its interface, multilingual information objects, metadata, and the corresponding challenges involved. Wu et al. (2012) found that 84 percent of participants wanted digital repositories to offer translation functions for discipline-specific terminology, and 74 percent wanted multilingual searching capabilities. Several major digital repositories provide this multilingual access, including options for selecting a language in which the search is to be conducted and in which the list of search results (and retrieved metadata records) is to be displayed. The European Library, International Children's Digital Library, World Digital Library, Digital Library of the Caribbean, and – most recently – the Digital Library of the Middle East all provide this functionality to their users. According to van Oudenaren (2019), although The World Digital Library website provided multilingual services where users could interface with and conduct searches in seven languages – Arabic, English, Chinese, French, Portuguese, Russian, and Spanish – the only "language of the interface that the user would see was keyed to his or her browser" which resulted in a lack of user awareness about the website being multilingual (p. 72). Such a practice can potentially limit discoverability for users that share the same computer with the standard system profile settings (such as, for example, at a public library or a computer lab) but speak different languages. Thus, it is recommended to make the availability of multilingual services clear on the home page of the digital repository.

Contribution of Controlled Vocabularies to Discoverability From the User Standpoint

Many digital repositories, continuing the practice of libraries, rely on controlled vocabularies for ensuring improved recall and precision in user searching and meaningful collocation of search results. Multiple fields in metadata records (e.g., Dublin Core subject, coverage, creator, contributor, type, and format) are normally populated with authorized/preferred forms of terms and names taken from standard controlled vocabularies, some of which are quite extensive and include thousands of choices. Digital repositories also often develop and implement local controlled vocabularies, such as short lists of broad subject categories based on the topical coverage of items in a repository, that support browsing and searching in a digital repository. One example of such a small-scale local controlled vocabulary for subject terms is shown in Figure 5.3.

The importance of controlled vocabularies for supporting discoverability has long been acknowledged and examined by practitioners and library and information science researchers. In particular, the role of controlled vocabularies for subject representation (i.e., representing what an information object is about) in information access has been researched and proven essential. For example, Gross and Taylor (2005) found that, in the absence of subject headings in a catalog record, over a third of available resources indexed by a database would not be discovered when a user performed a keyword search. In a follow-up study 10 years later, Gross et al. (2015) found that, even with the addition of tables of contents and summaries or abstracts in the catalog records, the absence of subject headings in records led to an average loss of 27 percent in discoverability. A user study conducted on Northwestern University Library's Eighteenth-Century Collections Online (ECCO) by Garrett (2007) revealed the importance of controlled-vocabulary subject headings (such as the Library of Congress Subject Headings, or LCSH) for access to historical materials in digital libraries. It also demonstrated the value added by subject headings even in the full-text environment of a digital repository. A study of another digital repository (Ma et al., 2009) asked users to rate the effectiveness of keywords and controlled-vocabulary terms for subject representation in a sample of the Internet Public Library metadata records and found that users perceive subject headings, rather than keywords, to be more effective in supporting information discovery.

Several transaction log analyses matched user search terms with terms in controlled vocabularies such as LCSH, Medical Subject Headings, and Art and Architecture Thesaurus and reproduced user queries in databases (e.g., Gault et al., 2002; Greenberg, 2001; Gross & Taylor, 2005; Nowick & Mering, 2003; Zavalina, 2007). These analyses found that the application of subject-controlled vocabularies greatly supports discovery regardless of the terms included in user search queries. The prevalence of subject searching among users of digital libraries analyzed by Zavalina and Vassilieva (2014) suggested the need to prioritize providing the subject-based advanced search option. Several studies found that interfaces could support subject-based searching by displaying hierarchical relationships between terms and items and facilitating the use of thesauri in searching (Gaona-García et al., 2014; Gaona-García et al., 2018; Koutsomitropoulos & Solomou, 2018; Shiri & Revie, 2005). Solomou and Koutsomitropoulos (2015) present an enhanced semantic searching system designed for DSpace which received positive feedback from users.

In addition to subject terms, controlled vocabularies are instrumental in consistently representing personal, corporate, and geographic names. Using name authority files such as the Library of Congress Name Authority File (LCNAF) and the Virtual International Authority File (VIAF) in metadata records ensures that names appear the same way throughout the repository. Thus, users searching for works by, for example, Edgar Allen Poe, would get search results that include any variants of the author's name as well (e.g., Poe, E. A. (Edgar Allan), 1809–1849).[15] Geographical searching and browsing are also supported by controlled vocabularies such as Geonames.[16]

Different repositories will require different types of controlled vocabularies depending on their focus and content. For example, language archives contain material in a variety of languages, including lesser-known languages, and those with multiple names (e.g., the language *Mizo* has also been called *Lushai* in the past). As such, these repositories rely heavily on controlled vocabularies of language names (ISO 639–3,[17] Glottocodes,[18] AUSTLANG)[19] for representing these names and their variants.[20] Genre authority control was also identified as a crucial missing component for language archive users, many of whom recalled seeking a particular type of language data (such as a list of words) but were hindered by the inconsistent usage of genre terms (e.g., "wordlist"; "word lists"; "wordlists") (Burke et al., 2021).

Key Take-Aways and Recommendations

This chapter has summarized user search behavior in digital repositories with a focus on content available in these repositories and the methods used to investigate user search behavior patterns (transaction log analysis, surveys, interviews, observations). It demonstrates that the common user study methods and tools used by practitioners to examine user searching in digital repositories include the following:

- Content analysis of system features and metadata records
- Transaction log analysis using Google Analytics and/or search log tools enabled by the digital content management system: CONTENTdm, Digital Commons, Fedora, Islandora, and so on
- Interviews/surveys of actual and potential users

Observations of users, a valuable method of obtaining data that is important for formative and summative quality evaluations of a digital repository service, are also occasionally utilized. Another user-centric method of understanding user search behavior that is worth considering is the card-sorting method. In this approach, users write terms on note cards and arrange them to demonstrate their understanding or conceptualization of the relationships between these terms (Hennig, 2001; Hutcherson, 2004). Findings from card sorting can then inform repository managers' decisions on representing hierarchies of terms to support subject browsing.

However, each method of data collection and analysis has its limitations. For example, transaction log analysis fails to capture users' underlying motivations. Content analysis does not address how the system is actually used. Interviews and surveys rely on a user's memory and ability to retell their digital repository interactions which negatively affects the accuracy of collected data. Furthermore, in the current pandemic environment, there are significant barriers to face-to-face interviews. Relying on online tools such as ZOOM may substitute these interactions, but this method also has limitations because it excludes potential respondents with insufficient access to infrastructure. User observations are time consuming and create artificial environments for interaction with the digital repository. They also prove to be more difficult in terms of recruiting participants because observation is the most obtrusive method of data collection. Therefore, mixed-methods studies enable researchers to utilize the advantages of each method while neutralizing their disadvantages.

Additional kinds of studies of user interactions with digital repositories that will provide richer data are needed. One example is session-level transaction log analysis that goes beyond the individual search query to include sequences of search queries, as well as other user interactions with digital libraries, such as browsing and viewing of metadata records. Another suggestion is a comparative analysis of traffic in digital repositories of different sizes and scopes, conducted at various time scales: daily, weekly, monthly, and yearly. Google Analytics is a low-barrier tool that can be used by anyone for collecting some of these data and would allow cross comparisons because of how ubiquitous it is. Both the Digital Library Federation Assessment Interest Group (2015) and Szajewski (2013) review the best practices for using Google Analytics for transaction log analyses.

Furthermore, in 2015, the Digital Library Federation Assessment Interest Group identified directions for future research based on gaps in user behavior literature, including large-scale user studies with representative sample sizes in naturalistic settings. It emphasized the importance of understanding users' underlying behaviors and motivations while searching. Though some recent studies have started addressing these gaps, continued work is needed.

As evidenced in the body of literature examined here, user search behavior changes over time. It is important for practitioners to be aware of these trends to meet their users' information needs most effectively. More studies examining digital repository users' perspectives are needed, especially as user experiences and expectations continue to be shaped by rapidly evolving information technologies and social media platforms. Though many existing user studies have been conducted over the last several years, the need for advanced search options in the user interface – including options that were not widespread in digital repositories at the time – has been strongly indicated across user surveys in the past and present. The influence of interface design on user searching and discoverability in digital repositories, which has not yet been sufficiently examined, also warrants further investigation.

To conclude, we offer the following recommendations for practitioners based on available literature regarding the methods and approaches to be used when investigating user searching in their own digital repositories:

- Regularly conducting user studies to track changes in user behavior that are influenced by environmental factors beyond the control of digital repository developers
- Conducting user studies before and after each change in interface design: formative and summative evaluations
- Utilizing a study approach that combines multiple data collection methods because this allows researchers to obtain answers to a variety of questions, examine digital repository user behavior from different perspectives, and obtain richer (more valid) results through triangulation, with the meaningful interpretation of findings. For example, if the Google Analytics report shows that users rarely utilize a certain search option, is this because it is irrelevant to users, or because it is not easy for users to find that particular search option on the repository website, or because the naming of this option is confusing for users? Conversations with actual repository users will help identify these reasons, and the results of such mixed-methods studies will inform changes that improve user experiences and discoverability of items. Mixed-methods user studies therefore need to include a combination of the following:

  - Transaction log analysis (quantitative and qualitative) using Google Analytics – while keeping its limitations in mind – and/or the search log tools enabled by the digital content management system used by the digital repository. Examine distributions of lengths, frequencies, structure, and types of user search queries, click patterns, query reformulation patterns, time users spend on the page, and so on
  - Think aloud protocol observations of actual and potential users in the process of interacting with the digital repository to identify any problems/issues that negatively affect discovery
  - Interviews and/or surveys of actual and potential users about satisfaction levels with regard to various system features, and their expectations and preferences for system features that support discoverability
  - Engagement of representatives of target user communities in evaluation and augmentation of metadata to better support overall discoverability and the more specific information needs of those user communities

Notes

1 The numbers are based on the IMLS Digital Collections and Content registry of digital collections supported by IMLS (https://web.archive.org/web/20150414080724/http://imlsdcc.grainger.uiuc.edu/).
2 https://beta.nsf.gov/funding/opportunities/national-stem-education-distributed-learning-nsdl
3 https://texashistory.unt.edu/
4 https://mwdl.org/
5 https://web.archive.org/web/20180202170632/http://memory.loc.gov/ammem/index.html
6 www.loc.gov/collections/
7 https://web.archive.org/web/20120211200344/http://imlsdcc.grainger.uiuc.edu/history
8 https://web.archive.org/web/20150414080724/http://imlsdcc.grainger.uiuc.edu/
9 https://dp.la/
10 http://emblematica.grainger.illinois.edu/
11 *NSDL Advanced Search*, accessed August 2, 2022, at https://nsdl.oercommons.org/advanced-search/
12 http://mms.thlib.org/
13 www.ailla.utexas.org/
14 https://digital.library.unt.edu/explore/collections/CORSAL/
15 https://id.loc.gov/authorities/names/n79029745.html
16 www.geonames.org/
17 https://iso639-3.sil.org/
18 https://glottolog.org/glottolog/language
19 https://collection.aiatsis.gov.au/austlang/about
20 See Matisoff (1996) and Morey et al. (2013) for further discussion of variation in language names.

References

Achieng, J. (2016). *An analysis of the usage of a digital repository in an academic institution* [Thesis]. University of Nairobi.

Agosti, M., Angelaki, G., Coppotelli, T., & Di Nunzio, G. M. (2007). Analysing HTTP logs of a European DL initiative to maximize usage and usability. In D. H. L. Goh, T. H. Cao, I. T. Sølvberg, & E. Rasmussen (Eds.), *Asian digital libraries. Looking back 10 years and forging new frontiers*. ICADL 2007. Lecture Notes in Computer Science, vol. 4822. Springer. https://doi.org/10.1007/978-3-540-77094-7_9

Aljalahmah, S. (2021). *The status of the organization of knowledge in cultural heritage institutions in Arabian Gulf countries* [Unpublished doctoral dissertation]. University of North Texas.

Allen, B. L. (1991). Cognitive research in information science: Implications for design. *Annual Review of Information Science and Technology*, *26*, 3–37.

Alokluk, J., & Al-Amri, A. (2021). Evaluation of a digital library: An experimental study. *Journal of Service Science and Management*, *14*, 96–114. http://doi.org/10.4236/jssm.2021.141007.

Al-Smadi, D., Barnes, S., Blair, M., Chong, M., Cole-Jett, R., Davis, A., Hardisty, S., Hooker, J., Jackson, C., Kennedy, T., Klein, J., LeMay, B., Medina, M., Saintonge, K., Vu, A., & Wasson, C. (2016). *Exploratory user research for CoRSAL: Report prepared for the computational resource for South Asian languages* [Unpublished manuscript]. University of North Texas Libraries.

Arms, C. R. (1996). Historical collections for the National Digital Library: Lessons and challenges at the Library of Congress: Part 1. *D-Lib Magazine*. www.dlib.org/dlib/april96/loc/04c-arms.html

Bates, M. J. (1989). Rethinking subject cataloging in the online environment. *Library Resources & Technical Services, 33*(4), 400.

Bates, M. J. (1996). The Getty end-user online searching project in the humanities: Report no. 6: Overview and conclusions. *College & Research Libraries, 57*(6), 514–523.

Bawden, D., & Vilar, P. (2006). Digital libraries: To meet or manage user expectations. *Aslib Proceedings, 58*(4), 346–354.

Beitzel, S. M., Jensen, E. C., & Chowdhury, A. (2007). Temporal analysis of a very large topically categorized web query log. *Journal of the American Society for Information Science and Technology, 58*(2), 166–178.

Borgman, C. L. (1986). Why are online catalogs hard to use? Lessons learned from information retrieval studies. *Journal of American Society for Information Science, 37*(6), 387–400.

Borgman, C. L. (1996). Why are online catalogs still hard to use? *Journal of American Society for Information Science, 47*(7), 493–503.

Brisco, S. (2010). The motherlode of STEM. *School Library Journal, 56*(2), 65–66.

Buchanan, G., Cunningham, S. J., Blandford, A., Rimmer, J., & Warwick, C. (2005). Information seeking by humanities scholars. *Proceedings of the European conference on digital libraries (ECDL2005)* (pp. 218–229). Springer Verlag.

Burke, M. (2021). Collaborating with language community members to enrich ethnographic descriptions in a language archive. In O. L. Zavalina & S. L. Chelliah (Eds.), *Proceedings of the international workshop on digital language archives: LangArc 2021*. IEEE. https://doi.org/10.12794/langarc1851172

Burke, M., Chelliah, S., Zavalina, O. L., & Phillips, M. E. (2022). User needs in language archives: Findings from interviews with language archive managers, depositors, and end-users. *Language Documentation & Conservation, 16*, 1–24. http://hdl.handle.net/10125/74669

Burke, M., & Zavalina, O. L. (2020). Descriptive richness of free-text metadata: A comparative analysis of three language archives. *Proceedings of the Association for Information Science and Technology, 57*, e429. https://doi.org/10.1002/pra2.429

Burke, M., Zavalina, O. L., Phillips, M. E., & Chelliah, S. (2021). Organization of knowledge and information in digital archives of language materials. *Journal of Library Metadata, 20*(4), 185–217.

Burns, D. S., Sundt, A., Pumphrey, D., & Thoms, B. (2019). What we talk about when we talk about digital libraries: UX approaches to labeling online special collections. *Weave: Journal of Library User Experience, 2*(1). https://doi.org/10.3998/weave.12535642.0002.102

Curl, M. W. (1995). Enhancing subject and keyword access to periodical abstracts and indexes: Possibilities and problems. *Cataloging & Classification Quarterly, 20*(4), 45–55.

Digital Library Federation Assessment Interest Group Analytics Working Group. (2015). *Best practices for Google analytics in digital libraries*. https://osf.io/th8av/download

Dong, H. (2019). *A task-oriented usability study of the Carolina Digital repository with casual users* [Master's thesis, UNC Chapel Hill]. Carolina Digital Repository. https://doi.org/10.17615/nps5-pm39

Druin, A., Bederson, B. B., Hourcade, J. P., Sherman, L., Revelle, G., Platner, M., & Weng, S. (2001). Designing a digital library for young children. *Proceedings of the 1st ACM/IEEE-CS joint conference on digital libraries* (pp. 398–405). IEEE.

Druin, A., Weeks, A., Massey, S., & Bederson, B. B. (2007). Children's interests and concerns when using the International Children's Digital Library: A four-country case study. *Proceedings of the 7th ACM/IEEE-CS joint conference on digital libraries* (pp. 167–176). IEEE.

Fidel, R. (1992). Who needs controlled vocabulary? *Special Libraries, 83*(Winter), 1–9. https://faculty.washington.edu/fidelr/RayaPubs/WhoNeedsControlledVocabulary.pdf

Gaona-García, P., Martín-Moncunill, D., Sánchez-Alonso, S., & Fermoso-García, A. (2014). A usability study of taxonomy visualisation user interfaces in digital repositories. *Online Information Review, 38*(2), 284–304. https://doi.org/10.1108/OIR-03-2013-0051

Gaona-García, P., Montenegro-Marin, C. E., Gaona-García, E., Gómez-Acosta, A., & Hassan-Montero, Y. (2018). Issues of visual search methods in digital repositories. *International Journal of Interactive Multimedia and Artificial Intelligence, 5*(3), 90. https://doi.org/10.9781/ijimai.2018.10.005

Garrett, J. (2007). Subject headings in full-text environments: The ECCO experiment. *College & Research Libraries, 68*(1), 69–81.

Gault, L., Shultz, M., & Davies, K. (2002). Variations in Medical Subject Headings (MeSH) mapping: From the natural language of patron terms to the controlled vocabulary of mapped lists. *Journal of the Medical Library Association, 90*(2), 173–180.

Green, H. E., & Lampron, P. (2017). User engagement with digital archives for research and teaching: A case study of Emblematica Online. *Libraries and the Academy, 17*(4), 759–775.

Greenberg, J. (2001). Automatic query expansion via lexical – semantic relationships. *Journal of the American Society for Information Science and Technology, 52*(5), 402–415.

Gross, T., & Taylor, A. (2005). What have we got to lose? The effect of controlled vocabulary on keyword searching results. *College and Research Libraries, 66*(3), 212–230.

Gross, T., Taylor, A., & Joudrey, D. (2015). Still a lot to lose: The role of controlled vocabulary in keyword searching. *Cataloging & Classification Quarterly, 53*(1), 1–39.

Harris, A., Gagau, S., Kell, J., Thieberger, N., & Ward, N. (2019). Making meaning of historical Papua New Guinea recordings: Collaborations of speaker communities and the archive. *International Journal of Digital Curation, 14*(1), 136–149.

Hee Kim, H., & Ho Kim, Y. (2008). Usability study of digital institutional repositories. *The Electronic Library, 26*(6), 863–881. http://doi.org/10.1108/02640470810921637

Hembrooke, H. A., Granka, L. A., & Gay, G. K. (2005). The effects of expertise and feedback on search term selection and subsequent learning. *Journal of the American Society for Information Science and Technology, 56*(8), 861–871.

Hennig, N. (2001). Card sorting usability tests of the MIT Libraries' web site: Categories from the user's point of view. In N. Campbell (Ed.), *Usability assessment of library-related web sites: Methods and case studies* (pp. 88–99). LITA, American Library Association.

Hildreth, C. R. (1997). The use and understanding of keyword searching in a university online catalog. *Information Technology & Libraries, 16*(June), 52–62.

Horava, T. (2010). Challenges and possibilities for collection management in a digital age. *Library Resources & Technical Services, 54*(3), 142–152.

Hutcherson, N. B. (2004). Library jargon: Student recognition of terms and concepts commonly used by librarians in the classroom. *College & Research Libraries, 65*(4), 349–354. https://doi.org/10.5860/crl.65.4.349

Hutchinson, H. B., Rose, A., Bederson, B. B., Weeks, A. C., & Druin, A. (2005). The International children's digital library: A case study in designing for a multilingual, multicultural, multigenerational audience. *Information Technology and Libraries*, *24*(1), 4–12. https://doi.org/10.6017/ital.v24i1.3358

IFLA (International Federation of Library Associations and Institutions). (2008). *Functional requirements for bibliographic records.* https://cdn.ifla.org/wp-content/uploads/2019/05/assets/cataloguing/frbr/frbr_2008.pdf

Information Behaviour of the Researcher of the Future. (2008). www.webarchive.org.uk/wayback/archive/20140613220103/www.jisc.ac.uk/media/documents/programmes/reppres/gg_final_keynote_11012008.pdf

Jabeen, M., Yuan, Q. Y., Yihan, Z., Jabeen, M., & Imran, M. (2017). Usability study of digital libraries: An analysis of user perception, satisfaction, challenges, and opportunities at university libraries of Nanjing, China. *Library Collections, Acquisitions, & Technical Services*, *40*(1–2), 58–69. http://doi.org/10.1080/14649055.2017.1331654

Jansen, B. J., & Rieh, S. Y. (2010). The seventeen theoretical constructs of information searching and information retrieval. *Journal of the American Society for Information Science and Technology*, *61*(8), 1517–1534.

Jansen, B. J., Spink, A., & Koshman, S. (2007). Web searcher interaction with the Dogpile.com metasearch engine. *Journal of the American Society for Information Science and Technology*, *58*(5), 744–755.

Jansen, B. J., Spink, A., & Pedersen, J. O. (2004). The effect of specialized multimedia collections on web searching. *Journal of Web Engineering*, *3*(3–4), 182–199.

Jones, S., Cunningham, S. J., McNab, R., & Boddie, S. (2000). A transaction log analysis of a digital library. *International Journal of Digital Libraries*, *3*(2), 152–169.

Kamposiori, C. (2012). Digital infrastructure for art historical research: Thinking about user needs. *Electronic Visualisation and the Arts (EVA 2012)*, 245–252. https://doi.org/10.14236/ewic/EVA2012.41

Khait, I., Lukschy, L., & Seyfeddinipur, M. (2021). Linguistic archives and language communities questionnaire: Establishing (re-)use criteria. In O. L. Zavalina & S. L. Chelliah (Eds.), *Proceedings of the 1st international workshop on digital language archives* (pp. 11–14). University of North Texas. https://doi.org/10.12794/langarc1851179

Khoo, M., Pagano, J., Washington, A. L., Recker, M., Palmer, B., & Donahue, R. A. (2008). Using web metrics to analyze digital libraries. *Proceedings of the 8th joint conference on digital libraries* (pp. 375–384). ACM, Pittsburgh.

Koshman, S., Spink, A., & Jansen, B. (2006). Web searching on the Vivisimo search engine. *Journal of the American Society for Information Science and Technology*, *57*(14), 1875–1887.

Kous, K., Pušnik, M., Heričko, M., & Polančič, G. (2020). Usability evaluation of a library website with different end user groups. *Journal of Librarianship and Information Science*, *52*(1), 75–90. https://doi.org/10.1177/0961000618773133

Koutsomitropoulos, D. A., & Solomou, G. D. (2018). A learning object ontology repository to support annotation and discovery of educational resources using semantic thesauri. *IFLA Journal*, *44*(1), 4–22. https://doi.org/10.1177/0340035217737559

Krikelas, J. (1972). Catalog use studies and their implications. *Advances in Librarianship*, *3*, 195–220.

Kröber, C. (2021). German art history students' use of digital repositories: An insight. *Proceedings of the 16th international conference, iConference 2021, lecture notes in computer science, vol. 12646* (pp. 176–192). Springer. https://doi.org/10.1007%2f978-3-030-71305-8_14

Larson, R. (1991). Between scylla and charybdis: Subject searching in online catalogs. *Advances in Librarianship*, *15*, 175–236.

Lavoie, B. J., Connaway, L. S., & O'Neill, E. T. (2007). Mapping WorldCat's digital landscape. *Library Resources & Technical Services, 51*(2), 106–115.

Liang, S., He, D., Wu, D., & Hu, H. (2020). Challenges and opportunities of ACM Digital Library: A preliminary survey on different users. In A. Sundqvist, G. Berget, J. Nolin, & K. Skjerdingstad (Eds.), *Sustainable digital communities. iConference 2020. lecture notes in computer science* (vol. 12051). Springer. https://doi-org.10.1007/978-3-030-43687-2_22

Ma, S., Lu, C., Lin, X., & Galloway, M. (2009). Evaluating the metadata quality of the IPL. *Proceedings of the American Society for Information Science and Technology, 49*, 1–17.

Marchionini, G., Dwiggins, S., Katz, A., & Lin, X. (1993). Information seeking in full-text end-user-oriented search systems: The roles of domain and search expertise. *Library and Information Science Research, 15*(1), 35–69.

Mardis, M. A., ElBasri, T., Norton, S. K., & Newsum, J. (2012). The digital lives of U.S. teachers: A research synthesis and trends to watch. *School Libraries Worldwide, 18*(1), 70–86.

Markey, K. (2007a). Twenty-five years of end-user searching, Part 1: Research findings. *Journal of the American Society for Information Science and Technology, 58*(8), 1071–1081.

Markey, K. (2007b, March 8). *Users and uses of bibliographic data* [Handout, Presentation]. Library of congress working group on the future of bibliographic control meeting, Mountain View, CA.

Matisoff, J. A. (1996). General introduction. In J. A. Matisoff, S. P. Baron, & J. B. Lowe (Eds.), *Languages and dialects of Tibeto-Burman* (pp. ix–xiv). Sino-Tibetan Etymological Dictionary and Thesaurus Project, Center for Southeast Asia Studies. University of California.

Matthews, J. A., Lawrence, G. S., & Ferguson, D. K. (Eds.). (1983). *Using online catalogs: A nationwide survey: A report of a study sponsored by the Council on Library Resources.* Neal-Schumann.

Matusiak, K. K. (2012). Perceptions of usability and usefulness of digital libraries. *International Journal of Humanities and Arts Computing, 6*(1–2), 133–147.

McIlvain, E. (2010). NSDL as a teacher empower point: Expanding capacity for classroom integration of digital resources. *Knowledge Quest, 39*(2), 54–63.

Morey, S., Post, M. W., & Friedman, V. A. (2013). The language codes of ISO 639: A premature, ultimately unobtainable, and possibly damaging standardization [Paper presentation] *Research, records and responsibility: Ten years of the pacific and regional archive for digital sources in endangered cultures.* University of Sydney. https://ses.library.usyd.edu.au/handle/2123/9838

Moulaison, H. L. (2008). OPAC queries at a medium-sized academic library: A transaction log analysis. *Library Resources & Technical Services, 52*(4), 230–237.

Muddamalle, M. R. (1998). Natural language versus controlled vocabulary in information retrieval: A case study in soil mechanics. *Journal of the American Society for Information Science, 49*(10), 881–887.

Münster, S., Kamposiori, C., Friedrichs, K., & Kröber, C. (2018). Image libraries and their scholarly use in the field of art and architectural history. *International Journal of Digital Libraries, 19*, 367–383. https://doi.org/10.1007/s00799-018-0250-1

Natarajan, K., Stein, D., Jain, S., & Elhadad, N. (2010). An analysis of clinical queries in an electronic health record search utility. *International Journal of Medical Informatics, 79*(7), 515–522.

Nicholas, D., Clark, D., Rowlands, I., & Jamali, H. R. (2009). Online use and information seeking behavior: Institutional and subject comparisons of UK researchers. *Journal of Information Science, 35*(6), 660–676.

Niu, X., & Hemminger, B. M. (2015). Analyzing the interaction patterns in a faceted search interface. *Journal of the Association for Information Science and Technology, 66*(11), 1140–1153.

Nowick, E. A., & Mering, M. (2003). Comparisons between Internet users' free-text queries and controlled vocabularies: A case study in water quality. *Technical Services Quarterly, 21*(2), 15–32.

Oliphant, T., & Shiri, A. (2017). The long tail of search and topical queries in public libraries. *Library Review, 66*(6/7), 430–441. https://doi.org/10.1108/LR-11-2016-0097

Palmer, C. L. (2005). Scholarly work and the shaping of digital access. *Journal of the American Society for Information Science and Technology, 56*(11), 1140–1153.

Palmer, C. L., Zavalina, O. L., & Fenlon, K. (2010). Beyond size and search: Building contextual mass in digital aggregations for scholarly use. *Proceedings of the Annual Meeting of the American Society for Information Science and Technology, 47*, 1–10.

Pan, B. (2003). *Capturing users' behavior in the National Science Digital Library (NSDL)* [Unpublished report]. Cornell University Human Computer Interaction Research Group. https://repository.arizona.edu/handle/10150/106332

Perrault, A. M. (2010). Making science learning available & accessible to all learners: Leveraging digital library resources. *Knowledge Quest, 39*(2), 64–68.

Peters, T. A. (1993). The history and development of transaction log analysis. *Library Hi Tech, 11*(2), 41–66.

Phillips, M. E., Andrews, P., & Krahmer, A. (2019). Understanding connections: Examining digital library and institutional repository use overlap. *Publications, 7*(2), 42. https://doi.org/10.3390/publications7020042

Quinones, D. (2010). Digital media (including video!): Resources for the STEM classroom and collection. *Knowledge Quest, 39*(2), 28–32.

Rather, M. K., & Ganaie, S. A. (2019). Information seeking models in the digital age. In D. B. A. M. Khosrow-Pour (Ed.), *Advanced methodologies and technologies in library science, information management, and scholarly inquiry* (pp. 279–294). IGI Global. https://doi.org/10.4018/978-1-5225-7659-4.ch022

Reilly, M., & Thompson, S. (2014). Understanding ultimate use data and its implication for digital library management: A case study. *Journal of Web Librarianship, 8*(2), 196–213. https://doi.org/10.1080/19322909.2014.901211

Shiri, A., & Oliphant, T. (2017). Temporal patterns of searching in a public library discovery system. *Canadian Journal of Information and Library Science, 41*(1), 1–17. www.muse.jhu.edu/article/666446

Shiri, A., & Revie, C. (2005). Usability and user perceptions of a thesaurus-enhanced search interface. *Journal of Documentation, 61*(5), 640–656. https://doi.org/10.1108/00220410510625840

Skog, J., McCourt, R. M., & Gorman, J. (2009). *The NSF scientific collections survey: A brief overview of findings*. National Science Foundation. https://digital.library.unt.edu/ark:/67531/metadc25978/

Solomou, G., & Koutsomitropoulos, D. (2015). Towards an evaluation of semantic searching in digital repositories: A DSpace case-study. *Program: Electronic Library and Information Systems, 49*(1), 63–90. https://doi.org/10.1108/PROG-07-2013-0037

Spink, A., & Jansen, B. J. (2004). A study of web search trends. *Webology, 1*(2), 4. www.webology.org/2004/v1n2/a4.html

Spurgin, K. M., & Wildemuth, B. M. (2009). Content analysis. In B. M. Wildemuth (Ed.), *Applications of social research methods to questions in information and library science.* (pp. 297–307). Libraries Unlimited.

Stiller, J., Gäde, M., & Petras, V. (2013). Multilingual access to digital libraries: The Europeana use case/Mehrsprachiger Zugang zu Digitalen Bibliotheken: Europeana/Accès multilingue aux bibliothèques numériques: Le cas d'Europeana. *Information – Wissenschaft & Praxis, 64*(2–3), 86–95. https://doi.org/10.1515/iwp-2013-0014

Szajewski, M. (2013). Using Google analytics data to expand discovery and use of digital archival content. *Practical Technology for Archives, 1.* https://practicaltechnologyforarchives.org/issue1_szajewski/

Toomey, D. (2010). The National Science Digital Library: STEM resources for the 21st-century learner. *School Library Monthly, 27*(2), 54–56.

Vakkari, P., Pennanen, M., & Serola, S. (2003). Changes of search terms and tactics while writing a research proposal: A longitudinal case study. *Information Processing and Management, 39*(3), 445–463.

van Oudenaren, J. (2019). The world digital library at the library of congress, 2005–2018 [Paper presentation]. *National digital library of India-UNESCO international symposium on engineering for digital library design (KEDL 2019).* http://kedl2019.ndl.gov.in/wp-content/uploads/2020/02/VanOudenaren_KEDL_Draft.pdf

Verberne, S., Hinne, M., van der Heijden, M., Hoenkamp, E., Kraaij, W., & van der Weide, T. (2010). How does the library searcher behave? A contrastive study of library search against ad-hoc search. *Proceedings of the conference on multilingual and multimodal information access evaluation.* www.cs.ru.nl/~mhinne/papers/2010_How_does_the_library_searcher_behave.pdf

Verheul, I., Tammaro, A. M., & Witt, S. (Eds.). (2010). *Digital library futures: Users perspectives and institutional strategies.* De Gruyter.

Wildemuth, B. W. (2004). The effects of domain knowledge on search tactic formulation. *Journal of the American Society for Information Science and Technology, 55*(3), 246–258. http://doi.org/10.1002/asi.10367

Williams, P., & Rowlands, I. (2007). *Information behaviour of the researcher of the future.* https://citeseerx.ist.psu.edu/viewdoc/download?doi=10.1.1.643.8970&rep=rep1&type=pdf

Willis, S., & McIntosh, M. (2019). What do the people want? A user study to establish cultural heritage scrapbook digitization practices. *Presented at the multidisciplinary information research symposium (MIRS).* https://digital.library.unt.edu/ark:/67531/metadc1506770/.

Wilson, T. D. (2000). Human information behavior. *Information Science, 3*(2), 49–55.

Wu, D., He, D., & Luo, P. (2012). Multilingual needs and expectations in digital libraries: A survey of academic users with different languages. *The Electronic Library, 30*(2), 182–197.

Wu, M., & Chen, S. (2007). Humanities graduate students' use behavior on full-text databases for ancient Chinese books. In D. H. L. Goh, T. H. Cao, I. T. Sølvberg, & E. Rasmussen (Eds.), *ICADL 2007, LNCS 4822* (pp. 141–149). Springer-Verlag.

Xie, I., Babu, R., Joo, S., & Fuller, P. (2015). Using digital libraries non-visually: Understanding the help-seeking situations of blind users. *Information Research, 20*(2), 1–23. www.informationr.net/ir/20-2/paper673.html

Xie, I., & Matusiak, K. (2016). User needs and search behaviors. In I. Xie & K. Matusiak (Eds.), *Discover digital libraries: Theory and practice* (pp. 231–253). Elsevier.

Zavalina, O. L. (2007). Collection-level user searches in federated digital resource environment. *Proceedings of the American Society for Information Science and Technology, 44*(1), 1–16.

Zavalina, O. L. (2010). *Collection-level subject access in aggregations of digital collections: Metadata application and use* [Doctoral dissertation, University of Illinois]. Illinois Library. www.ideals.illinois.edu/items/16676

Zavalina, O. L. (2011). Contextual metadata in digital aggregations: Application of collection-level subject metadata and its role in user interactions and information retrieval. *Journal of Library Metadata, 11*(3–4), 104–128.

Zavalina, O. L. (2014). Exploring the role of scale: Comparative analysis of digital library user searching. *Proceedings of the Association for Information Science and Technology, 51*(1), 1–4.

Zavalina, O. L., & Vassilieva, E. V. (2012). Longitudinal comparative analysis of item-level and collection-level user searching in a digital library. *Proceedings of the American Society for Information Science and Technology, 49*(1), 1–4.

Zavalina, O. L., & Vassilieva, E. V. (2014). Understanding the information needs of large-scale digital library users: Comparative analysis of user searching. *Library Resources and Technical Services, 58*(2), 84–99.

Zhang, T., Maron, D. J., & Charles, C. C. (2013). Usability evaluation of a research repository and collaboration web site. *Journal of Web Librarianship, 7*(1), 58–82. https://doi.org/10.1080/19322909.2013.739041

Zhang, X., Anghelescu, H. G. B., & Yuan, X. (2005). Domain knowledge, search behaviour, and search effectiveness of engineering and science students: An exploratory study. *Information Research, 10*(2), 1. http://informationr.net/ir/10-2/paper217.html

Part 2

Case Studies in Visibility and Discoverability Outside the Digital Repository

6 Discoverability Within the Library

Integrated Systems and Discovery Layers

JoLinda Thompson and Sara Hoover

Introduction

In the late 2000s, a new type of search platform became available to libraries. At the time, it was known as a web-scale discovery service, with Summon, from Serials Solutions, being the first such service to debut at the 2009 ALA Midwinter Conference (Breeding, 2009). *Web scale* referred to the large, centralized indexes of content deployed by discovery systems that were hosted on the cloud, where there is near limitless potential for growth. They proved to be a game changer in the world of library search and discovery, providing a one-box search that unites a library's electronic subscription content with local catalog holdings.

Academic libraries have embraced these services, which marry the centralized index of content with rich discovery layers and feature Google-like relevancy ranking and faceting or *clustering* that allows users to narrow down and access the content they want. Furthermore, users are also familiar with these interfaces through their extensive use of Google and other search engines, as well as shopping web interfaces, which use many of the same relevancy and faceting concepts (Figure 6.1).

Marshall Breeding's 2021 Systems Report notes that discovery services have played a diminishing role in the academic library marketplace because users prefer to start searches in Google Scholar or a more discipline-specific system like PubMed. Nonetheless, he still considers discovery systems that provide a single interface for searching the library's physical and electronic content essential for academic libraries. Discovery systems are now typically bundled with a contract for a library services platform, just as Online Public Access Catalogs (OPACs) were bundled with integrated library systems (Breeding, 2021).

The discovery service thus offers another avenue for the search and discovery of digital resource content. This chapter presents a literature review that explores the history of the integration of digital resources in library discovery services and the challenges encountered in the ingestion of common digital repository formats. Furthermore, it highlights the problems faced by libraries that have completed integration projects and provides some solutions for optimizing the discovery of this content for users. The literature review is followed by a case study that presents the loading of a collection of digital Doctor of Nursing Practice (DNP) projects

DOI: 10.4324/9781003216438-9

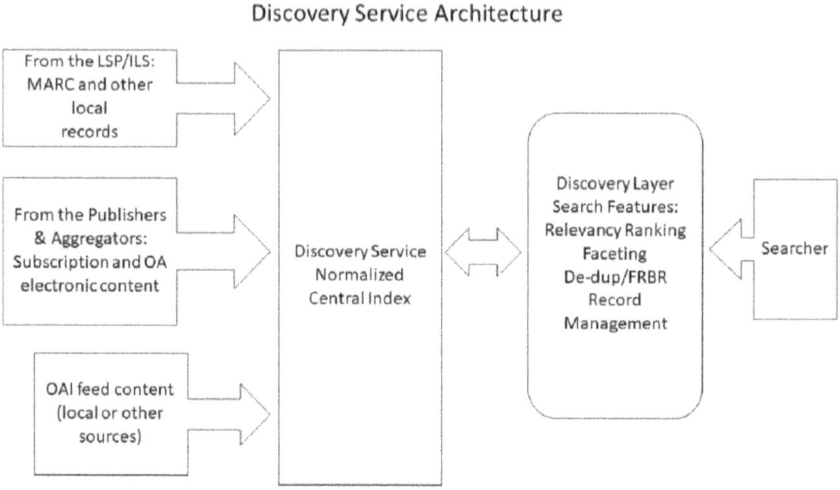

Discovery Service Architecture

Figure 6.1 Discovery service architecture

from the Digital Commons institutional repository (IR) platform into the Primo VE discovery service at Himmelfarb Health Sciences Library at The George Washington University (GW).

Literature Review

Before web-scale discovery services became common, IRs/digital archives and ILS and their associated OPACs were typically siloed. In 2009, when Summon debuted at ALA, Birrell et al. (2010) launched the Online Catalogue and Interoperability Study (OCRIS) which surveyed 85 higher education institutions in the UK with both an IR and a library OPAC. The survey provided insight into the state of integration and the relationships of these services within academic libraries before web-scale discovery began to be employed. At the time, only two percent of institutions reported interoperability between the IR and OPAC, with 15 percent planning future integration. Additionally, they found an 80 percent overlap in the types of materials in each, with abstracts, newspaper items, conference papers, and student coursework being unique only to the IR. The authors noted that "scoping distinctions and boundaries for IRs and OPACs are becoming increasingly blurred, with many IRs containing bibliographic data and OPACs containing links to full text" (Birrell et al., 2010, p. 385). They also maintained that duplications could lead to inefficiencies in cataloging and confusion among users about which system should be used under which conditions. Different subject schemas and authority control between IRs and OPACs impact semantic interoperability and could be disruptive to users' search experiences. The authors stated that "at present, complex, resource-intensive mapping exercises would be required in order to match terminologies to one another" (Birrell et al., 2010, p. 387). They concluded their study by arguing for the need to develop better policies for the scopes and uses of IRs and OPACs and a single scheme for describing item types and formats in particular.

Efforts to include IR data in library catalogs require multistep processes to convert records from Dublin Core (DC) or Encoded Archival Description (EAD) to MAchine Readable Cataloging (MARC) before loading. Wang (2012) described a project to bring DSpace ScHOLAR IR content from the Texas Tech School of Law to both the library's OASIS catalog and WorldCat to make the content more discoverable. The IR had 1,800 digital items at the time. Wang (2012) acquired a script from another unnamed university library to batch transfer the ScHOLAR DC records to MARC from XML. A programmer helped with the alterations needed for some mapping of DC to MARC elements for the local data. MarcEdit was used for further clean-up of the resulting MARC file before uploading it to the catalog. Note that MarcEdit now provides tools to do the entire conversion process without a separate script. To include the IR records in WorldCat, Wang used the OCLC Digital Collections Gateway, a self-service tool for uploading digital repository content. OCLC developed what is now called the WorldCat Digital Collections Gateway for its OCLC CONTENTdm digital collections platform but later expanded it for loading any Open Archives Initiative/Protocol for Metadata Harvesting (OAI-PMH) compliant archive materials to WorldCat. The service now remains free but requires institutional registration before use. Metadata mapping is configured in the OCLC tool before initial synchronization to load the data. Synchronization schedules can then be set up to harvest the metadata periodically. The ScHOLAR items in Wang's (2012) project were made searchable in WorldCat with a *downloadable archival materials* resource type and *view online* link that took the user to the record in ScHOLAR.

Discovery services like Summon, Primo, and EDS, with their central indexes, provide an avenue for bringing disparate content types together and include OAI-PMH integrations, like WorldCat's, to include local IR and archive content. Corrado (2018) discusses the ingestion process required for discovery services to incorporate OAI-PMH data in detail and compares it to other methods, like bulk export and import with a tool like MarcEdit. OAI-PMH is a simple protocol that uses HTTP and XML and can harvest any metadata in any schema that can be written in XML. However, the metadata needs to be available in unqualified DC to ensure interoperability. Unqualified DC is limited to the 15 DC Metadata Element Set elements: title, creator, subject, description, publisher, contributor, date, type, format, identifier, source, language, relation, coverage, and rights. If a repository is using a more advanced schema, some data elements may be lost.

Wesolek et al. (2015) described a 2015 project to include content from the local TigerPrints Digital Commons IR to Summon and the library catalog. The IR included a collection of Clemson patent records which used a metadata schema constructed from the standard Digital Commons template with the document type *patent* added. The entire TigerPrints IR contents were included in Summon using the OAI-PMH feed integration. At the time, the library maintained a Millennium OPAC, and they decided to include the patent material in the catalog.

> The library catalog enhances access by virtue of being one of any library's most authoritative and widely available resources. In addition, it is more famil-iar to many researchers than the institutional repository. The library catalog is also used by researchers worldwide, either directly or through WorldCat, and when the content it has cataloged is made openly available, such as through an institutional repository, those researchers may access it.
>
> (Wesolek et al., 2015, p. 226)

They used MarcEdit's OAI harvesting feature and XSLT stylesheets to convert IR records to brief MARC records that could be loaded to Millennium. The patent number was loaded to the 024 tag, which was indexed and searchable in the ILS as a standard number. An author heading was added for Clemson University via a Millennium load profile, and a genre heading was also added for *patent* to improve resource type metadata. Owing to the potential for content duplication in Summon from the direct OAI feed and the regular load of catalog records, the Clemson team opted to block the patent catalog records in favor of the OAI feed records "because the metadata in it is more extensive than that in the catalog" (Wesolek, 2015, p. 230). Similar concerns about the brevity of the catalog records led them to exclude the patent records in loads to their consortium union catalog.

Summon and Primo now share a common central index known as the Central Discovery Index (CDI). However, loading to the CDI with OAI feeds does not make these records part of the bibliographic record set that can be searched and managed in the library services platform/ILS. For example, a cataloger cannot find an individual record loaded by OAI and then edit or delete it using the Alma Meta-data Editor. Everything is done in a batch, with the OAI feed overwriting previous loads. For Primo, a normalization process determines if the imported records will be searchable in the local discovery service instance only or, if the library is part of a network, consortium wide. A library can take the next step of including the records as a collection in the Alma Community Zone where all customers can then activate it for inclusion in the CDI their users' search.

From 2013 to 2015, Ex Libris solicited IR open access (OA) content for inclu-sion in the Primo Central Index (PCI, the predecessor to the CDI) for all Primo libraries that purchased PCI content. At the time, 74 OA repositories were avail-able in Primo, and PCI customers could opt to enable as much of that content as they wanted for their users. Renaville (2016), from the University of Liege Library, explored this arrangement and examined how it could increase traffic to and awareness of these collections using a survey of PRIMO-DISCUSS-L listserv users. He found that a major roadblock to using this data was that not all of the OA collections were fully OA for all records, and libraries opted not to activate the collections so as to prevent users from being frustrated when they could not access the full text. Other libraries opted not to activate the collections so as to prevent *noise* from content considered irrelevant or out of scope. For example, several collections contained images or content specific to a particular institution. Renaville (2016) therefore suggested various improvements to the service, including providing fully OA content for linking and requiring content providers to supply quality metadata, which adhered to National Information Standards Organization (NISO) standards, and richer, more extended record formats. He also cited issues with resource-type assignments, with 29 percent of these records being assigned the nebulous *text resources* type.

Unlike abstracting and indexing databases or traditional OPACs that allow users to hone precision searches using subject headings to find the best content match, discovery services are built for keyword searching. Therefore, users are at the mercy of proprietary relevancy ranking algorithms to present the best results. EDS heavily weights subject headings and author-supplied keywords in rankings, while ProQuest's Primo and Summon rely more on term frequency and proximity. Summon also factors in citation counts while Primo considers the number of times a record has been accessed (Kumar, 2018). Renaville (2016) surveyed those harvesting or planning to harvest content about the methods they used (or planned to use) to feature and improve the retrieval of local IR content in Primo. The most popular response was the use of the boosting feature to boost local content in relevancy ranking (p. 4). Primo also allows boosting by resource type and date. Other methods used by Renaville's survey respondents to highlight and improve the findability of local content included customization of display labels and what facet types were made available in Primo.

Recent presentations highlight how OAI-PMH feeds continue to be common avenues for integrating IR contents to library discovery services. Xuan (2019) describes how the University of Manitoba incorporated LibGuides, Islandora, and DSpace content to Primo VE via the Alma OAI-PMH feed integration. The presentation outlines the normalization process in the Alma import profile setup, including job scheduling. Xuan notes that choosing the DC format enables the setup of the normalization rule to be quick and easy, but it does not allow for the removal of "unnecessary data". Magedanz and Dudley (2021) explore the normalization process further and note that normalization rules control how record data is displayed in Primo and how data, like resource type, can be added to records. They overview rule creation, the configuration of local resource types that provide clean faceting in Primo, and the setting up of local fields to add to the Primo record display when the field is not part of the standard DC set that is automatically mapped. They also discuss the setting up of linking parameters which determine what URL data is to be included in the Primo record for linking back to the IR or full-text source. Another important tip shared in the study is that users should be cautious about illegal characters in any incoming XML fields as these will break the import process and can frequently be difficult to track down due to vague and unhelpful error codes.

Beis et al. (2019) integrated the University of Dayton libraries' Archive-It collections to their UDiscover EDS instance to improve the discovery of these resources. Archive-It is a web archive service that University of Dayton libraries use to preserve institutional content on the web. They describe the process for OAI-PMH feed setup in EDS. The first step in the project was submitting an IR Database Questionnaire to EBSCO to determine harvesting schedules and mapping of DC elements. After the feed went live, they discovered that the source type icons in EDS were inaccurate, with all of them defaulting to academic journals. A publication type lookup table was then set up using a defined set of vocabulary for dc:type. Furthermore, some records were also missing key metadata, prompting the creation of local guidelines for elements required in records to maintain consistency and standardization. According to the guidelines, the required elements were "Collector", "Description", "Subject", "Title", "Type", and "URL".

The need for more complete OA content metadata in discovery services was addressed by Edmunds and Enriquez (2020). They highlight the 2018 revision of MARC fields 506 (Restrictions on Access Note) and 540 (Terms Governing Use and Reproduction Note) to accommodate data related to an item's OA status, while also noting that publishers who provide OA content are inconsistent in their use of these fields. Though Summon and Primo include a results filter for OA, its accuracy is unknown, as metadata to determine OA status at the record level is often lacking. Since IR and digital repository content are frequently OA as full text, the addition of metadata that will allow a discovery service to properly identify it as OA is an important consideration. Besides 506 and 540, the Penn State team also added subfields to MARC 856 URL tags to denote open status ($z "Open Access" and $7 0) to OA collection records in the library catalog.

Discovery Services at Himmelfarb

Himmelfarb Library serves the School of Medicine and Health Sciences, the School of Nursing (SON), and the Milken Institute School of Public Health at GW, a diverse population of 5,000+ undergraduate and graduate students, faculty, and staff with a wide range of information needs to support clinical and research activities. The library was an early adopter of discovery services, initially implementing a tailored version of EDS as Health Information @ Himmelfarb in 2013 (Thompson et al., 2013). EDS integrated Himmelfarb's subscription content and the library's catalog data; however, due to limitations of the catalog integration, Himmelfarb continued to offer a separate, traditional OPAC. Catalog records were updated weekly in EDS via file transfer protocol (FTP), which led to a substantial lag time between changes in the integrated library service and the discovery service. Health Information @ Himmelfarb had robust usage, with a growth of 75 percent in searches and full-text downloads between its implementation in 2013 and 2016. Meanwhile, OPAC usage reduced substantially (Thompson et al., 2018).

In 2018, the library joined the Washington Research Library Consortium (WRLC) and migrated with other consortium members to Ex Libris' LSP Alma and its discovery service, Primo. WRLC was an early adopter of Primo VE, which better integrates with Alma for both administrative functions and bibliographic data management. Bibliographic records appear and are updated in Primo VE within 15 minutes of creation or changes in Alma. Primo also offers all the requesting and library account functions (placing holds, renewing materials, etc.) that were lacking in EDS/Health Information @ Himmelfarb.

Primo VE also included consortium collections. This includes both centrally purchased subscription content and the bibliographic records of all member

libraries. At Himmelfarb, the default search scope for Primo is Himmelfarb catalog records and subscription content. Users can choose to change the default to
search the full consortium catalog and subscription content, and a consortium-level
resource-sharing service allows users to request monographs from other member
libraries, which are delivered via a courier service.

Digital Repository Services at Himmelfarb

In the 1990s, Himmelfarb Library started systematically compiling lists of faculty
publications by the department and providing them to administrators upon request. A
MUMPS database was used to enter and store citations and generate the lists. These lists
were also presented as static HTML pages housed on the library website. The reference
department solicited materials from departments and faculty, ran systematic database
searches to retrieve faculty publications, input data, and maintained the database.

In 2008, the Himmelfarb Library cataloging department was asked to experi-
mentally contribute content to the GW IR, ALADIN Research Commons, a DSpace
instance hosted by the WRLC. A Himmelfarb Health Sciences Library sub-commu-
nity was created within the ALADIN Research Commons. However, ultimately, this
platform did not provide the features necessary to enable easy systematic archiving.
The system also failed to meet the desired goal of exchanging learning objects and
teaching resources among health sciences faculty, students, and staff. After evaluating alternatives, it was recommended that bepress' Digital Commons be purchased.
Digital Commons was selected for its hosting platform, design, and customization
services, ability to store a wide range of formats, analytics suite, and high visibility
of records in Google and Google Scholar. Digital Commons was implemented as
the Health Sciences Research Commons (HSRC) in 2012.

Since 2012, HSRC has grown to include over 43,000 full-text items that have been
downloaded over 930,000 times at over 23,000 institutions in 225 countries. Items
in the IR cover over 360 disciplines and include a broad range of content types such
as conference posters, publications, policy briefs, instructional guides, presentation
citations, dissertations, and others. IR items are divided into topical collections for
GW Research Days, the Himmelfarb Health Sciences Library, the Milken Institute
School of Public Health, the School of Medicine and Health Sciences, the SON,
and others. Each major collection is subdivided into topical areas – the SON Collection, for example, is divided into smaller collections, including ones for Nursing
Faculty Posters and Presentations, Nursing Faculty Publications, Nursing Student
Publications, Nursing Student Posters and Presentations, and DNP Projects. The
ability to archive items in small, discipline- and department-specific collections has
the advantage of allowing viewers to see the scholarly output of a specific group.
HSRC's goal, like that of many IRs, is to both allow research tracking and provide a
forum for increasing the visibility of OA institution-specific content.

DNP Projects

In 2016, faculty from the GW SON approached Himmelfarb Library. They were
looking for a permanent archive to support their accreditation process. Their

accreditation guidelines required that DNP projects be stored in a permanent digital archive to enable historical research on nursing topics. Working with the SON faculty, the library developed a process for accepting student submissions of their DNP projects, along with several supplemental forms that the faculty deemed necessary: GW Institutional Review Board (IRB) approval form (or waiver, if the student's research did not require the IRB approval), HIPAA waiver, and written permission from the student's workplace to reuse and publish their data in the OA HSRC archive. This project brought together several librarians and faculty with varying areas of expertise, and it forced them to consider other important issues before archiving (patient privacy, use of hospital or workplace data, the IRB approval). HSRC began hosting these projects with the graduating class of 2018; they have since become some of the most frequently viewed and downloaded objects on the site, with over 93,000 downloads for items in the collection. Projects from this collection are easily viewable via the HSRC website, which is indexed by search engines such as Google Scholar. However, Himmelfarb librarians were also interested in exploring what it might mean to integrate this content into the library's discovery system.

Initial Primo/HSRC Integration

Shortly after the initial release of Primo VE in the summer of 2018, an OAI-PMH feed was established between HSRC and Primo. This is a standard feature in Alma/Primo, allowing any OAI-PMH-compliant archive content to be loaded to Primo and included in Primo's Central Index. The records were loaded to the PCI (now CDI) with a weekly scheduled job and became indexed and searchable in Primo.

This type of loading of IR content to discovery service is common in libraries with Alma and Primo, and the feature is available in other discovery services. Presentations describing the process at other libraries were discussed in the literature review. While it was convenient to load HSRC records in this way, Himmelfarb's Discovery Task Force decided to turn the OAI-PMH feed off after initial evaluation. Reference librarians were discontented that it often brought gray literature like posters and conference papers to the top of search results, pushing books or peer-reviewed articles further down the results list. Furthermore, much of the scholarly journal article content was already included in Primo from other sources, thus creating duplicate records. Since, with the feed, it was either all the IR content or none, the feed was turned off until a more selective method could be found. Based on this experience, we decided to explore similar projects from other libraries that looked at integrating IR content into a discovery system.

Case Study: Background

Based on the projects we explored from other institutions, our aim was to devise a project that allowed us to integrate specific IR content into our discovery system. As previously discussed, we concluded that the OAI-PMH feed did not meet our institutional needs with regard to making the desired IR content, which was not already represented in CDI, discoverable in Primo VE. Instead, our goal was to find a strategy for including specific IR collections with unique full-text content that would be valuable for our users and to increase awareness of these collections and HSRC without adding duplicative content to Primo. We ultimately elected to explore available options for integrating our DNP project collection directly into our instances of Alma and Primo VE.

The DNP collection was particularly well suited to this project for several reasons. First, the collection includes approximately 100 records, which seemed both small enough to contain a manageable amount of metadata but still large enough to generate substantive results. Furthermore, because this collection does not include content published elsewhere, we could avoid adding duplicate content to our discovery service. In addition to the collection's advantageous size, the lifecycle of the added records was also an asset. DNP projects are collected and digitally archived at the end of the spring semester each year; therefore, in theory, we would only need to make annual collection updates and additions. Lastly, practice scholarship is a unique type of content that could likely benefit from being included in an academic library discovery system. Nursing practice scholarship could address practice gaps to improve patient safety and quality of healthcare (Kesten et al., 2021). However, such research sometimes goes unpublished in traditional venues due to the demanding nature of the field. Therefore, the DNP collection in our IR was an ideal candidate for a project that aimed to increase avenues of content dissemination and explore interoperability between discovery systems and other library systems.

Selecting an Import Profile: Repository Type Versus Digital Import

What are the alternatives to the OAI-PMH feed for users considering the integration of specific IR collections into their discovery systems? In working with Ex Libris customer support, we ultimately identified two import profiles that would allow us to integrate content from our IR in a way that would make it discoverable in Primo. The first option was loading the data as external records directly into the discovery layer via the Discovery Import Profile. This Ex Libris Import Profile would allow us to load DC or MARC 21 Bibliographic records directly into the Primo CDI. From the perspective of our institutional needs, this option had numerous disadvantages. First, external discovery-level records could not be edited manually in Alma. Instead, any record changes would require a full-batch delete and upload annually when new records were archived in our IR or whenever any other changes were required. Second, as part of a consortium, we did not want our health sciences-focused IR records displayed in another institution's instance of Primo from the onset of the project. However, we did not also want to preclude the option of sharing records with the full network in the future. Records added via the Discovery Import Profile would have required an additional configuration to be made available as part of the shared CDI content of the consortium. Thus, while we wanted to keep records in our Alma Institution Zone (IZ) to monitor internal usage for the project's initial stages, we likewise wanted the option to easily share these records more widely at a future date.

The second alternative to the OAI-PMH feed was the use of the Repository-type Import Profile which would allow us to add our IR collection content as internal MARC records in Alma. The Repository-type Import Profile can be used to bulk load bibliographic records and create a physical or electronic inventory based on the import profile configuration. From the perspective of our institutional needs, this method had several advantages. A Repository-type Import Profile would allow us to add and edit records as needed rather than having to batch delete and reload records each time we wanted to make a change. Moreover, the use of internal records allowed us to keep our records in our IZ, which was better suited to the needs of this project's pilot phase. However, records can easily be shared as a batch to the consortium Network Zone with an Alma job, provided that a MARC 035 system control number is included. MARC format also allows the potential loading of the collection records to WorldCat for even wider sharing. The preliminary use of the records in our local IZ alone would give us a better sense of its usage within our institution. It would also enhance interoperability by allowing us to easily make modifications as we explored integrating IR content into our discovery system. In setting up the import profile, we could also designate bepress as the originating system for our collection and import via an Excel spreadsheet. We ultimately set up our Repository-type Import Profile with the following parameters (Figure 6.2).

The Repository-type Import Profile also allowed us to specify parameters for the creation of electronic items. This setup was valuable because it allowed us to utilize the URL included in the record itself for the creation of electronic items (Figure 6.3).

The Repository-type Import Profile allowed us to build a local collection of records that we could easily edit and to which we could make additions when necessary.

Building Collection Records: Metadata Schemas and Mapping

After selecting the Repository-type Import Profile as the best methodology for integrating IR content to our LSP, we focused on the question of how content from our IR could be translated into records that could then be used by our discovery system. At present, the Digital Commons platform allows users to export content to Excel via a content inventory report, but not to any particular metadata schema. Therefore, we knew that we would need to map our IR content to a metadata schema supported by Alma, such as DC or MARC 21. Initially, we considered mapping IR content to DC since its schema is highly flexible and could potentially accommodate substantial amounts of data from the IR records. However, at present, Ex Libris only supports batch imports of DC records via the Digital Import Profile. Since the Repository-type Import Profile would not support a batch upload of DC records, we concluded that mapping IR content to the MARC 21 Bibliographic format would be our best option. While somewhat less flexible than DC, MARC 21 would nevertheless still allow the mapping of most of the data from the IR records to Alma. We explored the use of

Figure 6.2 Repository-type Import Profile details set up in Ex Libris Alma. September 21, 2021

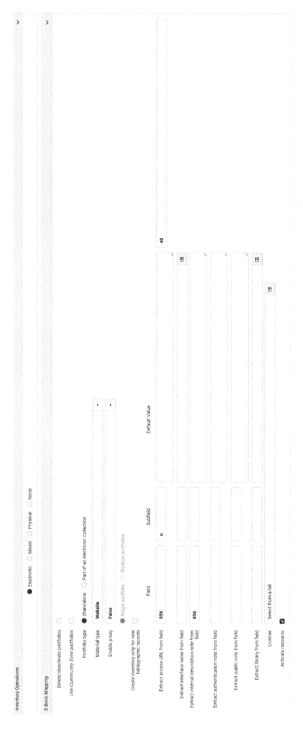

Figure 6.3 Repository-type Import Profile Inventory Information setup in Ex Libris Alma. September 21, 2021

MarcEdit to map IR content to MARC 21 but then rejected this method because it would require mapping to DC before conversion to MARC.

Before starting the conversion process, we elected to eliminate any of the DNP project collection items that had full-text embargos. Currently, several projects in the DNP collection have temporary full-text embargos as the project authors are exploring publishing options. Nonetheless, embargoed items currently comprise less than 10 percent of the total DNP collection. Additional items will be added to the catalog collection once the embargo period is complete and full text is available. We believed that IR items without full text were ill suited to inclusion in Primo since there were no alternative locations for obtaining the full-text materials.

In mapping IR content to the MARC 21 format, we created an XLSX file that included 30 fields. One advantage of the Repository-type Import Profile is that it allows you to designate information for MARC 21 second indicators and subfields as well as for the major numerical fields. We could therefore use common MARC 21 tags such as the 100 and 245 fields to provide title and author information, respectively, as well as tags such as the 264 to identify copyright and the 520 to include the project abstract. The 856 field proved to be particularly useful for creating the inventory portfolio. The 506 field was also especially useful for designating OA status and to ensure that records were included in retrieval in Primo searches limited to OA with the Availability facet. Furthermore, information from the Leader (LDR) field allowed us to designate the Dissertation resource type, which would enable the inclusion of similar resources in Primo faceted searches. We used the MARC 21 fields/indicators/subfields listed later to represent the data included in our Alma records (Table 6.1).

Table 6.1 MARC 21 fields, indicators, and subfields included in LSP records

1,001 $a (Personal name)	1,001 $e (Relator term)	24,500$a (Title)	24,500$c (Statement of responsibility)	264 4$c (Copyright notice)
264 1$a (Place of production)	264 1$b (Name of producer)	264 1$c (Date of production)	300$a (Physical description)	336$a (Content type term)
336$b (Content type code)	336$2 (Source)	337$a (Media type term)	337$2 (Source)	338$a (Carrier type term)
338$2 (Source)	502$a (Dissertation note)	502$b (Degree type)	502$c (Name of granting institution)	502$d (Year degree granted)
5,203 $a (Summary)	5,060 $a (Terms of governing access)	5,060 $f (Access restriction)	5,060 2 (Source of term)	590$a (Local note)
650 2$a (Topical term)	655 4$a (Genre)	830 0$a (Uniform title)	830 0$8 (Field link)	85,640$u (Electronic access)

Once the mapping process was complete, we tested loading by running several small-batch imports of two to three records to ensure that they were being mapped correctly and were importing without any errors. Once we confirmed that our batch import spreadsheet was set up correctly, we were able to run a job to import the remaining items.

System Limits: Subjects and Local Fields

One of the most complicated aspects of the project was the use of controlled vocabularies and the application of subject headings. Our IR utilizes keyword designations that are not necessarily mapped to any specific subject schema. Instead, the OA system relies on natural language keywords to support search engine optimization (SEO). Though Primo is similarly built for keyword search, the addition of traditional subject classification schemas like Library of Congress Subject Headings (LCSH) and National Library of Medicine Medical Subject Headings (MeSH) enhances subject retrieval. Furthermore, these terms appear and can be selected in the subject facet. As a health sciences library, our cataloging practices generally emphasize the use of MeSH over LCSH whenever possible; therefore, we concluded that applying MeSH to records that would be included in Alma and Primo would be advantageous. We elected to assign three MeSH terms to each entry in an effort to enhance the retrieval of these records.

However, the ensuing system limits when applying more than one subject heading to a batch upload were one of the difficulties we encountered. At present, Alma only supports the integration of a single 650 2$a field (MeSH Topical term) as part of the batch upload process; therefore, it was necessary to add the two additional MeSH terms to each entry manually. Another difficulty we encountered was the inability to designate a local 590$a field (Local catalog note), which we planned to utilize to create a special collection within Primo. Since the records we created are currently only included in our IZ, the inability to create a local designation was not problematic for the scope of our project. However, in the event that the records from this collection are shared to the consortium Network Zone, it would be necessary to manually change the 590 designation to a local field or to make batch changes via a normalization rule.

Results: Sample Records and Lessons Learned

We were ultimately able to generate 89 Alma bibliographic records for DNP projects via the Repository-type Import Profile, with content mapped from our IR to the MARC 21 format. Figure 6.4 contains a DNP record as displayed in our instance of Alma.

In addition to creating individual records, we could also create a DNP special collection within Primo (Figure 6.5). The special collection created an alternative location for viewing the full body of DNP projects, and it allows keyword searches

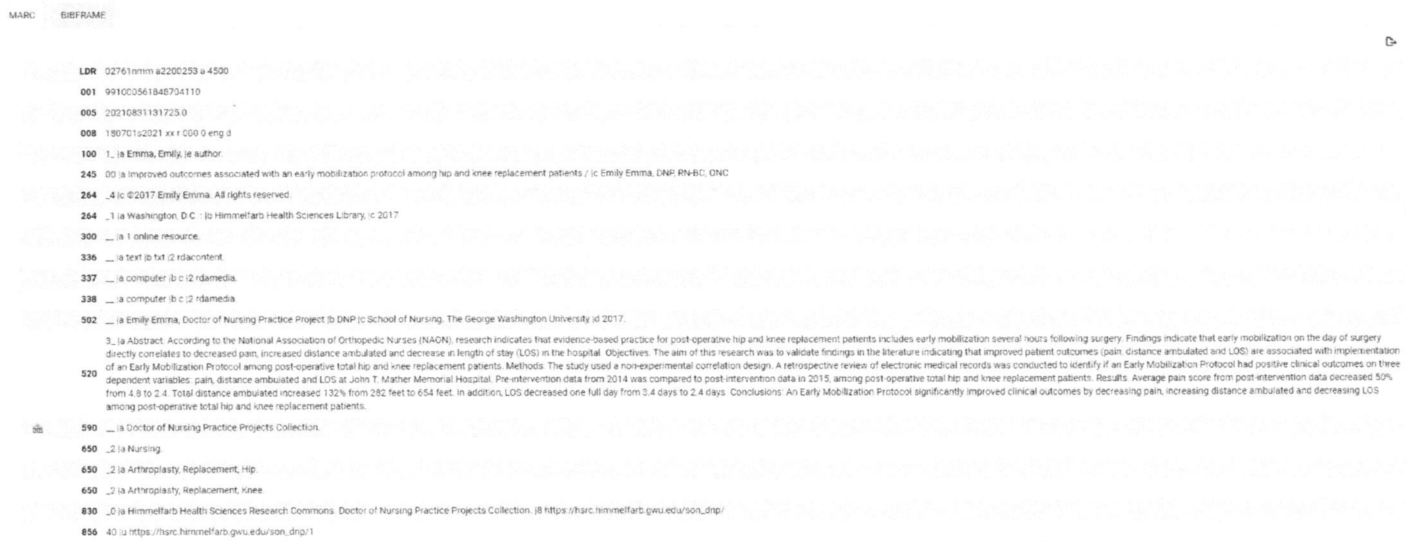

MARC   BIBFRAME

LDR   02761nmm a2200253 a 4500
001   9910C0561848754110
005   20210831131725.0
008   190701s2021 xx r000 0 eng d
100   1_ |a Emma, Emily, |e author
245   00 |a Improved outcomes associated with an early mobilization protocol among hip and knee replacement patients / |c Emily Emma, DNP RN-BC, ONC
264   _4 |c ©2017 Emily Emma. All rights reserved.
264   _1 |a Washington, D.C. : |b Himmelfarb Health Sciences Library, |c 2017
300   __ |a 1 online resource.
336   __ |a text |b txt |2 rdacontent
337   __ |a computer |b c |2 rdamedia
338   __ |a computer |b c |2 rdamedia
502   __ |a Emily Emma. Doctor of Nursing Practice Project |b DNP |c School of Nursing, The George Washington University |d 2017.
520   3_ |a Abstract. According to the National Association of Orthopedic Nurses (NAON), research indicates that evidence-based practice for post-operative hip and knee replacement patients includes early mobilization several hours following surgery. Findings indicate that early mobilization on the day of surgery directly correlates to decreased pain, increased distance ambulated and decrease in length of stay (LOS) in the literature indicating that improved patient outcomes; pain, distance ambulated and (LOS) are associated with implementation of an Early Mobilization Protocol among post-operative total hip and knee replacement patients. The aim of this research was to validate findings in the literature. Objectives: The study used a non-experimental correlation design. A retrospective review of electronic medical records was conducted to identify if an Early Mobilization Protocol had positive clinical outcomes on three dependent variables: pain, distance ambulated and LOS at John T. Maher Memorial Hospital. Pre-intervention data from 2014 was compared to post-intervention data in 2015, among post-operative total hip and knee replacement patients. Results: Average pain score from post-intervention data decreased 50%, from 4.8 to 2.4. Total distance ambulated increased 132% from 282 feet to 654 feet. In addition, LOS decreased one full day from 3.4 days to 2.4 days. Conclusions: An Early Mobilization Protocol significantly improved clinical outcomes by decreasing pain, increasing distance ambulated and decreasing LOS among post-operative total hip and knee replacement patients.
590   __ |a Doctor of Nursing Practice Projects Collection.
650   _2 |a Nursing.
650   _2 |a Arthroplasty, Replacement, Hip.
650   _0 |a Arthroplasty, Replacement, Knee.
830   _0 |a Himmelfarb Health Sciences Research Commons. Doctor of Nursing Practice Projects Collection. |8 https://hsrc.himmelfarb.gwu.edu/son_dnp/
856   40 |u https://hsrc.himmelfarb.gwu.edu/son_dnp/1

Figure 6.4 DNP project record in Ex Libris Alma. September 21, 2021

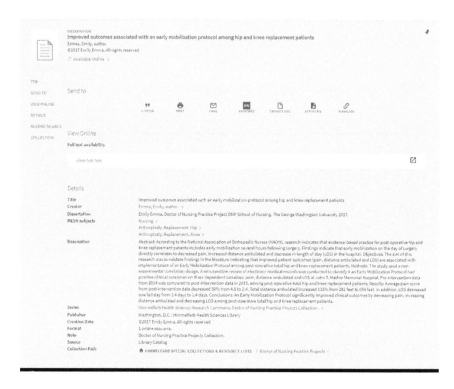

Figure 6.5 DNP project record in Ex Libris Primo VE. September 21, 2021

for items within the collection gallery view. In the full records view for collection items, a user can also easily navigate to other items in the collection via the *More from the Same Collection* feature at the bottom of the page (Figure 6.6).

Although the process of mapping IR content to the MARC 21 format was somewhat time consuming, we now have an effective model for mapping content from other IR collections into our discovery system. Therefore, the process is likely to take less time in the future. While there are still limitations with regard to the inclusion of multiple subject headings from traditional subject schemas, we are hopeful that future design modifications to Alma will eliminate this limitation. Going forward, we also plan to incorporate MeSH subjects as well as natural language subjects when creating IR records to enhance interoperability between systems.

Looking Forward: The Advantages of Interoperability

The process of adding a single collection from our IR into our library management and discovery systems ultimately had several benefits. Using the Repository-type Import Profile, rather than the OAI-PMH feed or the Discovery Import Profile, gave us greater control over which records were disseminated and enabled easier

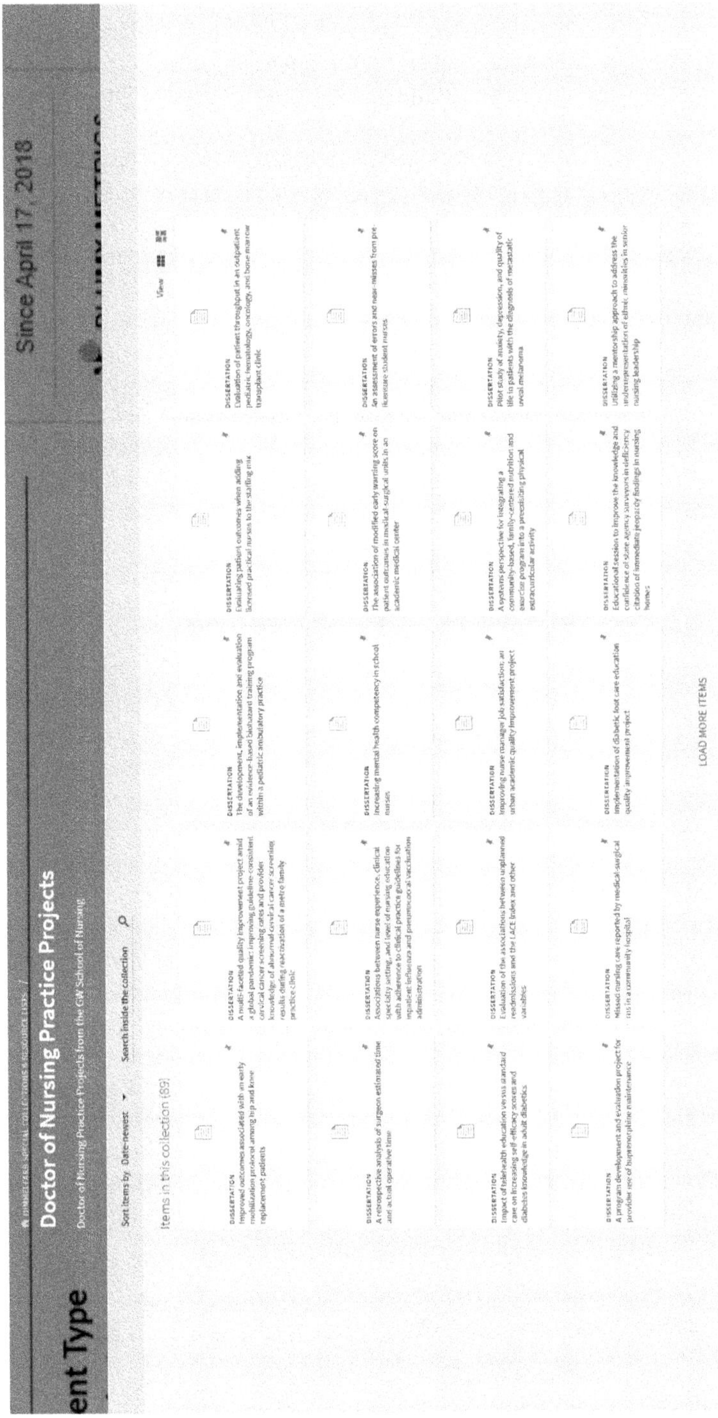

Figure 6.6 DNP project record in Ex Libris Primo VE Special Collection. September 21, 2021

record editing and addition options. For institutions wishing to incorporate non-traditional content into Alma, the Repository-type Import Profile offers an effective tool that allows batch imports rather than manual uploads. Perhaps, more importantly, this strategy also enhances the possibility of interoperability between systems.

In the short term, we will be monitoring the usage of the DNP project objects to observe whether their inclusion in the discovery service increases traffic to them in the HSRC. Alma Analytics allows monitoring of both the number of times the URLs in the Alma MARC records are used for linking to the IR records and the number of times the links are clicked in Primo specifically. If successful, other collections could similarly be included in Alma and Primo VE.

Ex Libris is developing an integrated suite of products that meet the research support and discovery needs of academic institutions. Esploro, described as a Research Information Management Solution, is an IR platform that includes *smart harvesting* and open application programming interfaces (APIs) that will enhance integration with other systems, likely including the Alma LSP and Ex Libris' discovery services. In the future, the transition from discovery service to IR or vice versa could therefore become seamless for researchers and students in libraries with these products. IR platforms like bepress' Digital Commons will need to be similarly open to compete and record metadata and will need to become more robust and standardized to enable these integrations.

Although the initial process of mapping metadata was time consuming, the highly structured nature of MARC data was ultimately an asset as it allowed us to easily translate content from one system to another. The amount of time that we utilized during the initial project setup was ultimately well spent because we now have the capacity to quickly translate data from other IR collections into formats that are usable in our library discovery service. For other libraries considering the undertaking of similar projects, we would advise starting with a relatively small collection (~50–100 records) and with a collection that shows similarity in metadata use across records. Our experience highlighted the value of defining desired metadata fields early on, but it also demonstrated the importance of being flexible when adding new tags as needed. Now that we have a process in place to integrate IR content into our library catalog, we hope to address the following questions in the future. What are the ultimate benefits of including OA content from an IR in a library catalog or discovery service? Is this a value-added strategy for improving readership? What role, if any, do academic libraries play with regard to improving readership for institution-specific content? Does including IR content in a discovery service increase usage of either? Future user experience studies focused on the dissemination of content across multiple platforms may help to flush out the advantages of working to meet users in different digital spaces.

Common Library Discovery Services

EBSCO Discovery Service (EDS)
Vendor: EBSCO Publishing

Initial release: 2010

EDS is sold with EBSCO's Folio library services platform (LSP) but can be integrated with other LSPs, integrated library systems (ILS), and link resolver products.

Primo and Primo VE
Vendor: Ex Libris/ProQuest
Initial release: 2007

Primo VE is sold with Ex Libris' Alma LSP and tightly integrated with Alma for administration, local library record management, and link resolving. Primo can be sold independently and integrated with other LSP, ILS, and link resolver products.

Summon
Vendor: ProQuest
Initial release: 2009

Summon is sold as an independent product and can be integrated with any of the common LSP, ILS, and link resolver products.

WorldCat Discovery Service
Vendor: OCLC
Initial release: 2007 (as WorldCat Local)

WorldCat Discovery Service is sold with WorldCat Management System (WMS) but can be integrated with other LSP, ILS, and link resolver products.

References

Beis, C. A., Harris, K. N., & Shreffler, S. L. (2019). Accessing web archives: Integrating an archive-it collection into EBSCO discovery service. *Journal of Web Librarianship*, *13*(3), 246–259. https://doi.org/10.1080/19322909.2019.1625844

Birrell, D., Dunsire, G., & Menzies, K. (2010). Match point: Duplication and the scholarly record: The online catalogue and repository interoperability study (OCRIS), and its findings on duplication and authority control in OPACs and IRs. *Cataloging & Classification Quarterly*, *48*(5), 377–402. https://doi.org/10.1080/01639371003738723

Breeding, M. (2009). Summon: A new search service from serials solutions. *Smart Libraries Newsletter*, *29*(3), 1–3.

Breeding, M. (2021). *2021 Library systems report*. American Libraries. https://americanlibrariesmagazine.org/2021/05/03/2021-library-systems-report/

Corrado, E. M. (2018). Discovery products and the open archives initiative protocol for metadata harvesting. *International Information & Library Review*, *50*(1), 47–53. http://doi.org/10.1080/10572317.2017.1422905

Edmunds, J., & Enriquez, A. (2020). Increasing visibility of open access materials in a library catalog: Case study at a large academic research library. *Journal of Library Metadata*, *20*(2–3), 127–154. https://doi.org/10.1080/19386389.2020.1821946

Kesten, K., Moran, K., Beebe, S. L., Conrad, D., Burson, R., Corrigan, C., Manderscheid, A., & Pohl, E. (2021). Practice scholarship engagement as reported by nurses holding a doctor of nursing practice degree. *Journal of the American Association of Nurse Practitioners, 34*(2), 298–309. https://doi.org/10.1097/JXX.0000000000000620

Kumar, V. (2018). Selecting an appropriate web-scale discovery service: A study of the big 4's. *DESIDOC Journal of Library & Information Technology, 38*(6), 396–402. https://doi.org/10.14429/djlit.38.6.12860

Magedanz, S., & Dudley, B. (2021, July 30). *PrimoVE: Discovery imports for the innocent, the eager, and the doomed* [Video]. ECAUG Conference. https://drive.google.com/file/d/1t3xqe6NvLZ16e1HyMDJHSP5Q1aADdStM/view

Renaville, F. (2016). Open access and discovery tools: How do Primo libraries manage green open access collections? In K. J. Varnum (Ed.), *Exploring discovery: The front door to your library's licensed and digitized content* (pp. 233–256). ALA Editions.

Thompson, J. L., Obrig, K. S., & Abate, L. E. (2013). Web-scale discovery in an academic health sciences library: Development and implementation of the EBSCO discovery service. *Medical Reference Services Quarterly, 32*(1), 26–41.

Thompson, J. L., Sullo, E., Abate, L. E., Heselden, M., & Lyons, K. (2018). Discovery assessment and improvement at an academic health sciences library: Health information @ Himmelfarb five years later. *Journal of Electronic Resources in Medical Libraries, 15*(1), 7–25. http://doi.org/10.1080/15424065.2018.1433093

Wang, F. (2012). Making IR content discoverable. *AALL Spectrum, 17*(1), 32–33. http://doi.org/10.31228/osf.io/d36mb

Wesolek, A., Comfort, J., & Bodenheimer, L. (2015). Collaborate to innovate: Expanding access to faculty patents through the institutional repository and the library catalog. *Collection Management, 40*(4), 219–235. https://doi.org/10.1080/01462679.2015.1093986

Xuan, W. (2019). *Making Primo VE a one stop search for users* [PowerPoint Slides]. IGeLU 2019, Singapore. https://igelu.org/wp-content/uploads/2019/09/primo_ve_one_stop_search.original.1566870204.pdf

7 Discoverability Beyond the Library
Wikipedia

Elizabeth Joan Kelly

Introduction

Digital repository managers looking to increase the visibility of their collections are working with nonprofits like the Wikimedia Foundation to boost awareness and contribute to public knowledge. By uploading digital surrogates to Wikimedia Commons, adding citations and links to Wikipedia articles, and sharing linked data via Wikidata, digital repository professionals can improve the visibility of their collections while simultaneously advancing the credibility of Wiki projects. Furthermore, making digital collection items available through Wiki projects also has the added benefit of increasing the reuse of these materials, both in other Wiki projects and on websites outside of the Wikisphere. The reuse of digital repository items is often considered to be more impactful than simple access to these same items via clicks or downloads; therefore, this is a much-desired effect among digital repository professionals. This chapter will provide an overview of successful digital repository Wiki projects, as well as the practical steps, tools, and considerations for this process.

Wikimedia Foundation Background

The Wikimedia Foundation, a nonprofit organization dedicated to free, public, open content, was created to fund the online open encyclopedia Wikipedia. The foundation now runs many other content and infrastructure projects, all free and equipped for public contribution. Three of the content projects most relevant to digital repository practitioners are Wikipedia, the free multi-language encyclopedia; Wikimedia Commons, the media repository for Wiki projects (including Wikipedia); and Wikidata, a structured data database containing items representing topics, concepts, and objects used by other Wiki projects ("Wikimedia Projects", n.d.).

Example Wiki Projects

Repositories have been uploading or adding references and links to their collections to Wiki projects in order to improve visibility since at least 2007. Marketing and public relations professionals outside of libraries, archives, and museums have

DOI: 10.4324/9781003216438-10

also long known that integrating their work with Wiki projects is an effective SEO strategy, with a 2012 United Kingdom study finding that popular search engines like Google frequently point to Wikipedia articles within the first page of search results (Silverwood Cope, 2012). Therefore, repositories without access to web developers and experts in SEO can utilize the popularity of Wiki projects to ensure that users easily find references to and items from their collections using search tools they are familiar with in their day-to-day lives.

The results are often quite impressive when digital repositories integrate their collections with Wiki projects as web traffic has been observed to be driven back to repositories, and even in-person visits for research using their physical collections have increased. There are many ways that repository staff can get involved with Wiki projects, from authoring new Wikipedia articles, to uploading digital surrogates to Wikimedia Commons, to sponsoring *edit-a-thons* that involve students in creating and/or editing existing Wikipedia articles. The following examples from academic and professional literature highlight some of the more successful efforts, and how that success was measured.

One of the primary ways that institutions determine the success of Wiki projects involving digital repositories is by considering web statistics and observing if page views of their collections increased after edits or uploads were made to Wiki projects, as well as whether traffic to their collections is coming from Wiki projects. For example, the University of Washington Libraries Digital Initiatives unit worked with students to add links of their digital collections to Wikipedia, resulting in an upward trend in referrals from Wikipedia to the institution's digital collections (Lally & Dunford, 2007). Later analysis showed that up to 15 percent of visitors to a Wikipedia article with links to the library's digital collections proceeded to click through to view the collection ("Collections are for use", 2009). Similarly, the University of North Texas received almost half of its referring traffic from Wikipedia after creating direct links from 700 articles to digital objects housed by their collections (Belden, 2008); the University of Las Vegas Nevada saw consistent traffic to their website and digital collections after linking them to Wikipedia articles (Griffis et al., 2007). After hiring their first Wikipedian-in-Residence, the National Archives' Daily Document received 12 million "*hits*" on Wikipedia, in contrast to several thousand *hits* on the National Archives website (Ferriero, 2011). A Ball State University project to add digital sheet music links to Wikipedia saw an increase of over 600 percent in page views for the individual items linked, and a tripling of page views for the entire digital collection (Szajewski, 2013). Finally, Texas Tech University saw an increase in digital collection traffic when links were added to Wikipedia; after adding just one digital image to a Wikipedia page, 22 percent of the traffic to this item in the institution's digital collection came from Wikipedia over the course of three years (Perrin et al., 2017). For an example of links added to the References and External Links section of a Wikipedia article, see Figure 7.1.

Institutions may also learn about user behavior by analyzing items from their repositories that other users have already linked or uploaded to Wiki projects. For example, an intern for Calisphere, part of the California Digital Library, added

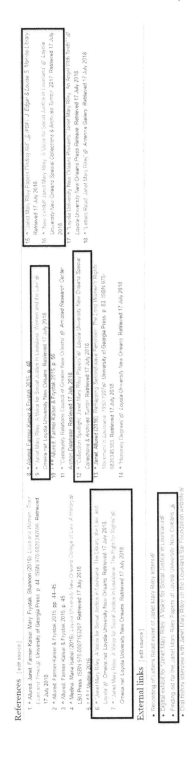

Figure 7.1 Screenshot of links to digital assets in the References and External Links section of the Wikipedia article for Janet Mary Riley (https://en.wikipedia.org/wiki/Janet_Mary_Riley)

digital collection links to Wikipedia. During this process, they also found existing links and Wikimedia Commons uploads from Calisphere, providing a glimpse of the resources Calisphere users had found most useful and had therefore wanted to share with open online communities (Zentall & Cloutier, 2008). Similarly, a study of Louisiana Digital Library usage on Wikipedia found 224 citations to the collection in Wikipedia articles, which were then analyzed to determine the topics that users gravitated toward the most (Kelly, 2018).

However, little research has been done about the effect of increasing access to digital collections through Wiki projects on reference requests. The University of Pittsburgh saw an increase in use of online finding aids and digital collections, and even email reference requests, after links to their digital assets were added to Wikipedia articles (Galloway & DellaCorte, 2014). While researchers in this study did not ask patrons who requested reference services through email about how they had discovered the collections, they did see a marked increase in email reference requests after they completed their Wiki edits, which could imply a correlation (Galloway & DellaCorte, 2014).

When it comes to uploading images to Wikimedia Commons, examples from other institutions can help ensure that the images reach the largest audience possible. The University of Houston initially focused on adding digital collection links to Wikipedia articles, until it realized that uploading images directly to Wikimedia Commons resulted in the proliferation of these images among Wikimedia projects and increased traffic to their website and digital resources. Thus, Wikimedia projects served as the top referring website to the university's digital collections (Elder et al., 2012). Similarly, an attempt to determine the overall impact of digital items from the Imperial War Museum Collections on Wikimedia Commons involved an analysis of image occurrences, page views for articles and media pages, and image size and position on the page. The study found that images were much more likely to be viewed on Wikipedia articles than directly in Wikimedia Commons (Morley, 2018).

Many of these projects involved large and/or well-known institutions whose collections are likely to have a broad appeal. In contrast, a case study in uploading digital cultural heritage objects from Loyola University New Orleans, a medium-sized liberal arts college, found that linking digital cultural heritage collections and items in Wikipedia articles did not result in increased traffic to the university's websites and digital libraries. However, the addition of images from the digital library collection to Wikimedia Commons led to increased reuse of these images; therefore, pursuing Wiki work for smaller institutions may still be beneficial (Kelly, 2019a; see Figure 7.2).

More recently, repositories have found success by contributing metadata to Wikidata, a structured data repository (see Figure 7.3). For example, what started as a Wikipedia edit-a-thon for articles about Canadian music and musicians expanded to include low-barrier linked open data creation through Wikidata. By incorporating Wikidata editing into the project, the organizing librarians ensured that articles edited in the more than 200 language variants of Wikipedia seamlessly linked together so that edits to one article were replicated across all (Allison-Cassin & Scott, 2018). The

Figure 7.2 Screenshot of Wikimedia Commons image from a digital repository. The Summary information includes a link to the digital repository; the File Usage on Commons and File Usage on Other Wikis sections show image reuse (https://commons.wikimedia.org/wiki/File:Janet_Mary_Riley_1946.tif)

Figure 7.3 Screenshot of a partial Wikidata item for the person Janet Mary Riley (www.wikidata.org/wiki/Q55725928)

Wicipobl project, from the National Library of Wales, used Europeana's Impact Playbook to plan and then assess the impact of 4,862 Welsh portraits that were uploaded to Wikimedia Commons. Corresponding metadata was then uploaded to Wikidata (Jason.nlw, 2019). A proof-of-concept interface combining Library of Congress collection items with information from Wikidata demonstrated the potential benefits of linking authority data with Wikidata as both open datasets complimented each other and allowed for robust searching across the Library of Congress image collections (Miller, 2019). Comparing the views for Smithsonian images on the Smithsonian website and on Wikipedia showed 1,000 times more views on Wikipedia, leading to efforts to increase the Smithsonian's presence on Wikipedia through edit-a-thons and contributing or enhancing data on Wikidata (Kapsalis, 2019). Furthermore, Vanderbilt University librarians developed *VanderBot*, scripts that read and write data about Vanderbilt faculty's scholarship to Wikidata in order to "enhance the online reputations of Vanderbilt's faculty and our overall status as a tier-one research university" and "advance the Jean and Alexander Heard Libraries' broader mission of contributing to the public good by promoting faculty scholarship and making it discoverable and accessible to researchers" ("Librarians work to broaden . . .", 2020).

Benefits of Participating in Wiki Projects for Digital Repositories

The advantages of initiatives to openly publish repository materials, especially digitized cultural heritage collections, include greater public awareness of collections, increased discoverability, opportunities for public participation in curation and enrichment, increased use of collections by teachers in the classroom, enhanced curation opportunities and use of text mining and visualization for researchers, improved understanding of cultural heritage by communities, and increased use of repository materials in new art (Terras, 2015). While repositories may already openly publish their collections, making those collections discoverable to users can still be a struggle. Taking advantage of popular platforms that users are familiar with, like Wikipedia, can therefore be a great advantage. A study found that 90 percent of faculty surveyed at research-intensive and liberal arts colleges and universities in the United States reported using Wikipedia once a month or more, and 65 percent reported using it once a week or more (Bauder & Emanuel, 2012). While this study did not differentiate between the use of Wikipedia for academic versus more informal research, Wikipedia is definitely a potential venue for reaching academic audiences.

In particular, engaging with Wikidata can be beneficial because it can link datasets. Wikidata contains thousands of external identifiers, including many that are familiar to library practitioners, such as the Virtual International Authority File (VIAF), Library of Congress Control Number (LCCN), and Social Networks and Archival Context (SNAC) ID. By uploading data to Wikidata and including a reference to just one of the included external identifiers, digital repository practitioners can ensure that their data is connected to other related data that may use a different external identifier, thus potentially enhancing the amount of information available about their collections and also increasing visibility (Lemus-Rojas & Pintscher, 2018). Outside of the immediate Wikidata environment, VIAF and the Library of Congress both harvest information from Wikidata and link back to it; thus, Wikidata acts as a data hub for many other repositories (Poulter & Sheppard, 2020). Moreover, because Wikidata includes fields for indicating digital records or surrogates, users can continue their research in digital repositories (Poulter, 2019). For example, the Wikidata entry for a research paper can include links to multiple versions of an article, such as a preprint, enabling easy discovery of open access versions of otherwise paywalled publications (Poulter & Sheppard, 2020; see Figure 7.4).

Contributing to Wiki projects can also improve and enhance the collection of information made available by repositories. Because Wiki projects are publicly editable, they aim to contain contributions of people from different languages and cultures. Lemus-Rojas and Pintscher (2018, p. 149) note,

> [t]his means that it accommodates multiple, even conflicting, data points about a topic, which eliminates the need for contributors to be in agreement with the contributed information. These contributions can then be qualified with additional information to specify, for example, where a certain belief is held. All of these qualifying statements can be supplemented with references. The references, in turn, provide users with information that indicates where the data is coming from – a valuable feature for deciding which data point to employ for their use case.

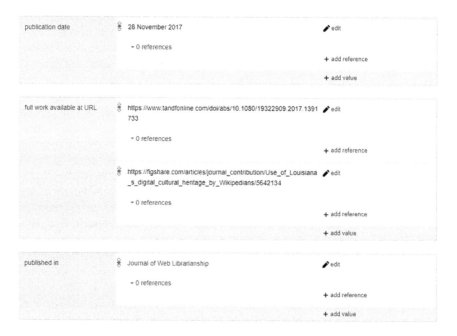

Figure 7.4 Screenshot of a Wikidata item for the scholarly article "Use of Louisiana's Digital Cultural Heritage by Wikipedians" showing links to the final published version of the article as well as a postprint in an open access repository (www.wikidata.org/wiki/Q58534448)

Wikidata's connections across the different language versions of Wikipedia also enhance the feasibility of increasing access to knowledge for non-English speakers (Allison-Cassin & Scott, 2018; Lemus-Rojas & Pintscher, 2018). The multilingual linking of names and identifiers in Wikidata means that users can research using terminology they are used to more easily and in their chosen language, without having to know thesaurus terms or controlled vocabulary (Poulter, 2019). Finally, the open nature of Wiki projects also introduces opportunities for public contributions to repositories; users can enhance metadata by identifying people or places in images that may only list their main subject and not all included entities or can translate titles and descriptions (Poulter, 2019).

Key Considerations for Digital Repositories Contributing to Wiki Projects

While there are many benefits to digital repositories engaging in Wiki projects, practitioners should consider several things before beginning to upload their collections, add citations, or contribute data.

Licensing

First, repositories should familiarize themselves with the open licensing requirements for the particular Wiki project that they are pursuing. For example, media uploaded to Wikimedia Commons must either be in the public domain or be designated with an open license by the rights holder ("Commons: Licensing", n.d.). Practitioners who contribute to Wikipedia should note that their text will be licensed to the public for reuse under Creative Commons Attribution-ShareAlike and GNU Free Documentation licenses ("Wikipedia: Copyrights", n.d.). Furthermore, Wikidata must be licensed under CC0, a Creative Commons license that is equal to a public domain declaration ("Wikidata: Licensing", n.d.).

Therefore, repository practitioners must ensure that any uploads or edits made to Wiki projects are within the confines of their licensing requirements. This may be particularly difficult with regard to uploading media to Wikimedia Commons, as repository staff are not always adequately trained in evaluating rights for their collections. An analysis of digital cultural heritage materials on Wikimedia Commons found that, while 90 percent of the uploaded media were correctly licensed, only 76 percent of those licenses corresponded to the license given to the media in its original repository. The observed inconsistencies in licensing stemmed from incorrect licensing in the original repository (Kelly, 2019b). However, uploading media to Wikimedia Commons actually creates a potential opportunity for crowdsourcing accurate rights statements:

> It is possible that the collaborative and peer-reviewed nature of [Wikimedia Commons] creates greater opportunities for evaluation and correction of rights statements compared to a cultural heritage institution in which library

practitioners may have limited training, support, and feedback in their rights and licensing assessment of digital objects.

(Kelly, 2019b, p. 14)

Reuse, Adaption, and Ethics

Uploading digital repository media to Wikimedia Commons may lead to them being reused to a greater extent. Reuse is defined as "active interaction with a digital object(s) that demonstrates an interest or value to an external user", including interactions such as transcription, modification, annotation, and curation, to name a few (Kenfield et al., 2022, p. 387). This contrasts with use, or "passive interaction with a digital object that indicates potential interest and/or value to an external user", which can include saving, downloading, and printing, among others (Kenfield et al., 2022). Reused digital repository objects show a greater level of engagement by users than used objects (Kenfield et al., 2022, p. 387). Digital object reuse is a qualitative measure that might be more useful to digital repository practitioners who wish to know what their users value rather than only focusing on quantitative measures such as clicks and downloads (Kenfield et al., 2022). The Wiki universe's wide popularity among different types of users in and of itself can lead to much greater awareness of digital repositories that have engaged in Wiki projects. But the ease and even automation of integration among Wiki projects, as well as the open licensing and repurposing of content outside of Wiki platforms, means that digital objects and metadata integrated into the Wikisphere may find new lives well outside of anything the digital repository practitioner might have imagined. This proliferation of access and reuse exposes digital repositories, and practitioners should therefore consider several factors regarding use and reuse when entering into a Wiki-related project.

Edits made to Wikipedia or Wikidata regarding repository collections, or newly created Wikipedia articles, may later be edited by other Wiki users and editors. Digital library stakeholders have expressed concern about digital content misuse and cultural appropriation (O'Gara et al., 2018). In addition, instances in which archives attempt to control the reuse of their online holdings by intentionally issuing restrictive or unclear rights statements have also been documented (Dryden, 2014).

Repository practitioners who contribute to Wiki projects must therefore prepare themselves for at least some lack of control over their collections. This lack of control begins as soon as collections are openly published, but the increase in traffic that may result from the popularity of Wiki projects may open collections up to a much wider audience than repository practitioners expect. An analysis of Wikimedia Commons images that have been reused on the *wider web* found very few instances of *misuse*, such as in the case of an image being used to represent something it was not (Kelly, 2019c). However, users can misrepresent repository items, or reuse them in instances that the practitioner may find offensive, such as the reuse of United States Southern Civil War collections to promote hate groups. Practitioners should therefore consider the potential impacts of making culturally sensitive materials more widely accessible via Wiki projects before beginning such an undertaking. This is particularly important with regard to protecting cultural heritage materials that might fall outside of copyright protections but whose access, permissions, and terms of use should be developed in conjunction with source communities (Kelly, 2019b). A number of resources relevant to this work are included in the "Useful tools and resources" section of this chapter.

Impact

Before beginning a Wiki project, repositories should identify the collections that might have the greatest impact. For example, a study found that users search for very different subjects across library catalogs, Google, and Wikipedia (Waller, 2011). Users were far more likely to search for pop culture topics in Wikipedia, while cultural practice searches were conducted similarly across all three platforms. Similarly, a study of how and where objects from the Louisiana Digital Library were cited on Wiki projects found that these objects were most referenced in Wikipedia articles about culture and the arts (Kelly, 2018).

Yet another study was conducted using Google's Reverse Image Lookup (RIL) tool to search 171 digital cultural heritage images from Wikimedia Commons and identify how and where they were reused across the internet. The study found 1,533 legitimate instances of reuse, with half of the results coming from Wiki projects – for example, an image uploaded to Wikimedia Commons was then used in Wikipedia articles. Images (especially photographs) of people were reused most often, and images of historical events, buildings, and locations were also reused frequently (Kelly, 2019c). Nearly half of the non-Wiki reuse instances were on social websites such as social media, blogs, discussion boards, and online journals (Kelly, 2019c).

Goal Setting

Before committing to a Wiki project involving their digital repository, practitioners should consider and document what their goals are and how the success of these goals will be measured. Outreach and discovery-enhancing efforts are likely to be somewhat time consuming, and practitioners should assess whether their efforts are worth the time and energy after a pilot or soft launch. For example, if the primary goal is to increase traffic to online repositories and websites, then web analytics will need to be monitored and assessed. On the other hand, if the goal is to increase research using objects and works in the repository, citation metrics and/or altmetrics will have to be collected. If the repository wishes to increase foot traffic or reference requests to their physical repository, researchers will need to be surveyed to discover how they found out about the repository's holdings. An initiative to support Wikimedia Commons contributions by GLAMR (Galleries, Libraries, Archives, Museums, and Repositories) institutions found that

> [d]onating media to Commons is a means to an end. GLAM organizations and the volunteers who work with them want to know the media they upload

is being used, and to be able to evaluate the impact of their donations against institutional goals.

(Research, 2018)

Best Practices, Tools, and Tips

How to Get Involved

Digital repository practitioners who are brand new to working with Wiki projects can begin getting involved in a variety of ways and can also consider some best practices.

Create an Account

First, create an account on the Wiki site of your choice. Wherever you originate your account, whether Wikipedia, Wikimedia Commons, or Wikidata, it will most likely transfer information across all Wiki platforms and other language versions. Wikipedia's Username Policy provides more information about rules and best practices ("Wikipedia: Username Policy", n.d.). Usernames should represent you as an individual, even if you are solely using the account to make edits as part of your institutional role. Some institutions document creating shared logins to keep track of edits made through a single account. This may also be useful for setting up *watchlists*, or lists of articles for which you can receive email notifications if an article has been edited. However, remember that creating such a shared account is in violation of Wikipedia's Username Policy, and accounts designated as *role accounts* or accounts shared by multiple people to represent an institution, office, or position could be blocked ("Wikipedia: Sockpuppetry", n.d.). It may also be advisable to add a conflict-of-interest statement to one's user page to indicate the institutional affiliation (Lemus-Rojas & Pintscher, 2018).

Training

All Wiki projects include copious amounts of training materials. New Wikipedia editors might review the *Wikipedia Help: Editing* guide to get started ("Help: Editing", n.d.). Familiarize yourself with the different editing environments: wikitext and VisualEditor. The *Introduction to Wikipedia* guide also walks you through the different editing options and best practices ("Help: Introduction", n.d.).

Each account has a sandbox space where you can test the writing and publishing process. There is also a *Talk* link that includes links to frequently asked questions, policies, and more. One of the most important things to remember is that, as a public good, it is important that you engage with Wiki projects with the best faith effort to contribute as much as you hope to gain from it. While your primary goal as a practitioner may be to improve the visibility of your collections, give equal thought to how you can improve access to knowledge with your Wiki work.

In Wikimedia Commons, take the *First Steps* tour ("Commons: First Steps", n.d.). For Wikidata, take the Wikidata tour to learn how to contribute your structured data ("Wikidata: Tours", n.d.).

Editing

After you have created your account and undergone some basic training, you can begin editing. There are several ways in which you can connect your collections with Wiki projects:

* Add citations to Wikipedia articles. For example, if an item in one of your collections provides further helpful information related to a Wikipedia article, include that information in the narrative of the article and reference your repository in the citation. Or, if an article already refers to an item in your repository, ensure that the citation includes a hyperlink.
* Many Wikipedia articles also have *External Links* sections which can be good places to include links to repositories.
* Author new Wikipedia articles for subjects that are included in your repository. But first make sure that your subject meets Wikipedia's Notability criteria ("Wikipedia: Notability", n.d.). Archival repositories can reuse biographical information from finding aids to create new Wikipedia articles about people or institutions whose papers they hold and make available online. Institutional and data repositories manage storage and online publication of academic work or datasets for notable researchers, and hence, such repositories can create Wikipedia articles for these researchers.
* Upload digital surrogates of your media collections to Wikimedia Commons. Ensure that you then link your media from Wikipedia articles; images are much more likely to be viewed on Wikipedia pages than directly in Wikimedia Commons (Elder et al., 2012). In addition, a study found that pages that included public domain images had 17–19 percent more visitors than pages that did not (Erickson et al., 2015).
* Label Wikimedia Commons images with as many relevant categories as possible. Doing so enables better discoverability and increases the chances of your images being found and reused (see Figures 7.5 and 7.6) (Elder et al., 2012).
* Create profiles for researchers whose collections you manage in Wikidata (Poulter & Sheppard, 2020), and then add identifiers for items from your collections to these profiles (Lemus-Rojas & Pintscher, 2018).
* Represent archival collections and their associated metadata in Wikidata (Lemus-Rojas & Pintscher, 2018).

The categories listed are hyperlinked to collections of additional media and related categories (see Figure 7.6) (https://commons.wikimedia.org/wiki/File:Tenth_annual_convention,_Catholic_Education_Association,_Loyola_University,_July_2,_1913,_New_Orleans_LCCN2007661758.tif).

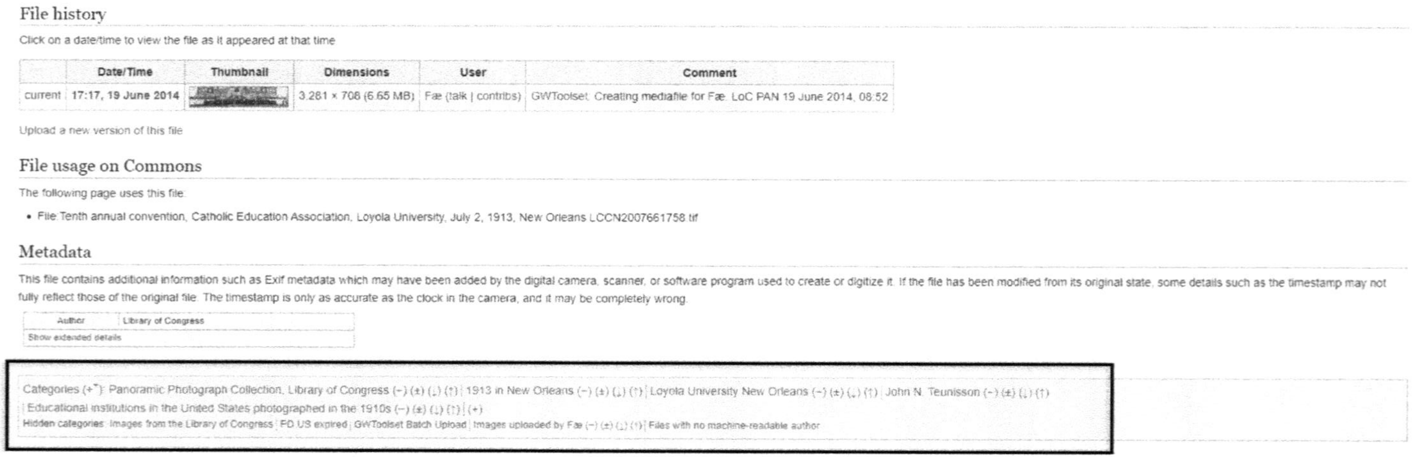

File history

Click on a date/time to view the file as it appeared at that time

Date/Time	Thumbnail	Dimensions	User	Comment
current 17:17, 19 June 2014		3,281 × 708 (6.65 MB)	Fæ (talk | contribs)	GWToolset: Creating mediafile for Fæ. LoC PAN 19 June 2014_08:52

Upload a new version of this file

File usage on Commons

The following page uses this file:

- File:Tenth annual convention, Catholic Education Association, Loyola University, July 2, 1913, New Orleans LCCN2007661758.tif

Metadata

This file contains additional information such as Exif metadata which may have been added by the digital camera, scanner, or software program used to create or digitize it. If the file has been modified from its original state, some details such as the timestamp may not fully reflect those of the original file. The timestamp is only as accurate as the clock in the camera, and it may be completely wrong.

Author | Library of Congress

Show extended details

Categories (++): Panoramic Photograph Collection, Library of Congress (−)(±)(↓)(↑) | 1913 in New Orleans (−)(±)(↓)(↑) | Loyola University New Orleans (−)(±)(↓)(↑) | John N. Teunisson (−)(±)(↓)(↑)
| Educational institutions in the United States photographed in the 1910s (−)(±)(↓)(↑) | (+)
| Files with no machine-readable author
Hidden categories: Images uploaded by Fæ (−)(±)(↓)(↑) | GWToolset Batch Upload | Images uploaded from the Library of Congress, FO (US excised), GWToolset Batch Upload

Figure 7.5 Screenshot of categories for a Library of Congress-uploaded image in Wikimedia Commons

Category:1913 in New Orleans

From Wikimedia Commons, the free media repository

English: 1913 in New Orleans
Svenska: 1913 i New Orleans

New Orleans in the 1910s: — · — · 1910 · 1911 · 1912 · **1913** · 1914 · 1915 · 1916 · 1917 · 1918 · 1919 · →

Subcategories

This category has the following 4 subcategories, out of 4 total.

*

▲ Built in New Orleans in 1913 (3 C, 5 F)

1

▲ 1913 maps of New Orleans (2 F)

B

▲ The New Orleans Bee 1913 (12 C)

N

▲ New Orleans Mardi Gras 1913 (1 C, 11 F)

Media in category "1913 in New Orleans"

Show all ▾ The following 22 files are in this category, out of 22 total.

BicycleMessengerNewO

Bobet Memorial Library

Chirs Reuter Seedman

Cotton Exchange New

DupreeCanalStreetStatio

Ernest J Bellocq invoice

Four Marx Bros Mr

French Opera

Figure 7.6 Screenshot of category: 1913 in New Orleans in Wikimedia Commons. The category was used for the image in Figure 7.5https://commons.wikimedia.org/wiki/Category:1913_in_New_Orleans)

Beyond Wiki Projects

Once you have added data to Wikidata, media to Wikimedia Commons, and edits to Wikipedia articles, you can potentially begin to link your work together. Some examples of sites that combine Wikidata and Wikipedia information include Inventaire, Reasonator, and Scholia (Lemus-Rojas & Pintscher, 2018) (Table 7.1).

Required Skills and Knowledge

Beyond knowledge of your collections and their licensing limitations, and a willingness to learn how Wiki projects work, little prior skills or knowledge are necessary to begin working on them. A familiarity with Markdown could be beneficial in editing Wikipedia, but it is not necessary as Wikipedia also provides a WYSIWYG editor. Some repository staff have created scripts and tools to aid in pulling items from their existing collections automatically into Wikimedia Commons or Wikidata; some coding expertise may be required to run such tools. Github[1] is an excellent resource for finding such scripts and tools.

Table 7.1 Tools that extend Wiki projects

Platform	Description	Features	URL
Inventaire	User book inventory and author biography project	Users can search for books and add them to their inventory. A book record includes links to other editions of a book, and a link to a map showing the locations of users who own the book. Inventaire can also be used to keep track of book lending and borrowing, and users can alert others if they are interested in selling their copy.	https://inventaire.io/
Reasonator	Discovery interface built off of Wikidata	Reasonator aggregates content from related Wikipedia articles, Wikimedia Commons media, and Wikidata into a single page with a *prettified* user interface. It works best for items about people, locations, and species.	https://reasonator. toolforge.org/
Scholia	Scholarly profiles derived from Wikidata	Similar to Reasonator, Scholia pulls information from Wikidata to create "visual scholarly profiles for topics, people, organizations, species, chemicals, etc." (Scholia, n.d.).	https://scholia. toolforge.org

Conclusion

Contributing digital objects and metadata to Wiki projects can be very beneficial to repositories hoping to increase the discoverability and reuse of their digital collections. While this chapter refers to excellent research and case studies that have helped determine best practices for working with digital repositories and Wikis, there is still room for growth in developing sound methodologies for different types of institutions with different missions and goals. Much of the digital repository/Wiki research centers around large, well-resourced institutions, and it is not yet clear whether the impact of these types of efforts is the same for smaller and more niche organizations. There is also very little research available about the effect of integrating digital repositories with Wiki projects on non-digital access to repositories – for example, do users find out about collections through Wiki projects and then visit repositories for research? Finally, information regarding the feasibility and *return on investment* for practitioners engaging in Wiki projects is primarily anecdotal at this time. More research into this area could potentially produce a tool that would allow practitioners to determine, based on their types of collections, staffing, access to technology, and skills and training, whether engaging in such projects would be adequately beneficial to justify the time and resources necessary for it.

Useful Tools and Resources

The following are additional training and informational resources that may be helpful as you begin a Wiki project.

GLAMWiki

GLAM/Resources/Tools
https://outreach.wikimedia.org/wiki/GLAM/Resources/Tools

Wikipedia

Adding Images to Wikipedia Articles Via Dpla
https://johndewees.com/2021/03/18/adding-images-to-wikipedia-articles-via-dpla/

Wikidata

Works in Progress Webinar: Introduction to Wikidata for Librarians
www.oclc.org/research/events/2018/06-12.html
Wikidata Editing with OpenRefine
www.wikidata.org/wiki/Wikidata:Tools/OpenRefine/Editing
Wikidata:WikiProject Linked Data for Production/Practical Wikidata for Librarians
www.wikidata.org/wiki/Wikidata:WikiProject_Linked_Data_for_Production/Practical_Wikidata_for_Librarians#Lists_of_resources
Creating and Editing Libraries in Wikidata
https://coffeecode.net/creating-and-editing-libraries-in-wikidata.html

Wikimedia Commons

Commons Uploads Tools
https://commons.wikimedia.org/wiki/Commons:Upload_tools
"How to upload images to Wikimedia Commons in bulk"
www.ed.ac.uk/information-services/help-consultancy/is-skills/wikimedia/
    wikimedia-commons/how-to-upload-images-to-wikimedia-commons-in-bulk
*Flickr2Commons: tool to automatically upload Flickr images to Wikimedia
    Commons*
https://flickr2commons.toolforge.org/

Ethics

Architecting Sustainable Futures. (n.d.). https://architectingsustainablefutures.
    org/ Documenting the Now. (n.d.). www.docnow.io/
Eschenfelder, K. R., & Caswell, M. (2010). Digital cultural collections in
    an age of reuse and remixes. *First Monday, 15*(11). https://doi.org/10.5210/
    fm.v15i11.3060
Historypin. (2018). *Moving beyond colonial models of digital memory* (based
    on planning grant LG-72-16-0113-16). Institute of Museum and Library
    Services. https://drive.google.com/file/d/1xJlN_oyOKm8iQc_yuz6dr
    EVNqGNGaDoD/view

Note

1   https://github.com/

References

Allison-Cassin, S., & Scott, D. (2018). Wikidata: A platform for your library's linked open
    data. *Code4Lib, 40*. https://journal.code4lib.org/articles/13424
Bauder, J., & Emanuel, J. (2012). Being where our faculty are: Emerging technology use
    and faculty information-seeking workflows. *Internet Reference Services Quarterly,
    17*(2), 65–82. https://doi.org/10.1080/10875301.2012.718316
Belden, D. (2008). Harnessing social networks to connect with audiences. *Internet Refer-
    ence Services Quarterly, 13*(1), 99–111. https://doi.org/10.1300/J136v13n01_06
Collections are for use, but is Wikipedia the outlet? (2009). *Library Journal, 134*(19),
    15–16.
Dryden, J. (2014). Just let it go? Controlling reuse of online holdings. *Archivari, 77*, 43–71.
    https://archivaria.ca/index.php/archivaria/article/view/13486
Elder, D., Westbrook, R. N., & Reilly, M. (2012). Wikipedia lover, not a hater: Harnessing
    Wikipedia to increase the discoverability of library resources. *Journal of Web Librarian-
    ship, 6*(1), 32–44. https://doi.org/10.1080/19322909.2012.641808
Erickson, K., Heald, P. J., Homberg, F., Kretschmer, M., & Mendis, D. (2015). *Copyright
    and the value of the public domain: An empirical assessment.* World Intellectual Property
    Organization. www.wipo.int/edocs/mdocs/mdocs/en/wipo_ip_econ_ge_1_15/wipo_ip_
    econ_ge_1_15_ref_erickson.pdf

Ferriero, D. S. (2011). On the growing relationship between the National Archives and Wikipedia. *Vital Speeches of the Day*, *77*(10), 367–369.

Galloway, E., & DellaCorte, C. (2014). Increasing the discoverability of digital collections using Wikipedia: The Pitt experience. *Pennsylvania Libraries: Research & Practice*, *2*(1), 84–96. https://doi.org/10.5195/palrap.2014.60

Griffis, P., Costello, K., Del Bosque, D., Lampert, C., & Stowers, E. (2007). Discovering places to serve patrons in the long tail. In L. Cohen (Ed.), *Library 2.0 initiatives in academic libraries* (pp. 1–15). Chicago: Association of College and Research Libraries.

Jason.nlw. (2019). *English: An impact report for the Wicipobl (WikiPeople) project delivered by the National Library of Wales*. https://commons.wikimedia.org/w/index.php?title=File:Wicipobl_Impact_Report.pdf&page=2

Kapsalis, E. (2019). Wikidata: Recruiting the crowd to power access to digital archives. *Journal of Radio & Audio Media*, *26*(1), 134–142. https://doi.org/10.1080/19376529.2019.1559520

Kelly, E. J. (2018). Use of Louisiana's digital cultural heritage by Wikipedians. *Journal of Web Librarianship*, *12*(2), 85–106. https://doi.org/10.1080/19322909.2017.1391733

Kelly, E. J. (2019a). Assessing impact of medium-sized institution digital cultural heritage on Wikimedia projects. *Journal of Contemporary Archival Studies*, *6*(25). https://elischolar.library.yale.edu/jcas/vol6/iss1/25

Kelly, E. J. (2019b). Digital cultural heritage and Wikimedia Commons licenses: Copyright or copywrong? *Journal of Copyright in Education & Librarianship*, *3*(3), 1–25. https://doi.org/10.17161/jcel.v3i3.9771

Kelly, E. J. (2019c). Reuse of Wikimedia Commons cultural heritage images on the wider web. *Evidence Based Library and Information Practice*, *14*(3), 28–51. https://doi.org/10.18438/eblip29575

Kenfield, A. S., Woolcott, L., Thompson, S., Kelly, E. J., Shiri, A., Muglia, C., Masood, K., Chapman, J., Jefferson, D., & Morales, M. E. (2022). Toward a definition of digital object reuse. *Digital Library Perspectives*, *38*(3), 378–394. https://doi.org/10.1108/DLP-06-2021-0044

Lally, A. M., & Dunford, C. E. (2007). Using Wikipedia to extend digital collections. *D-Lib Magazine*, *13*(⅚). www.dlib.org/dlib/may07/lally/05lally.html

Lemus-Rojas, M., & Pintscher, L. (2018). Wikidata and libraries: Facilitating open knowledge. In M. Proffitt (Ed.), *Leveraging Wikipedia: Connecting communities of knowledge* (pp. 143–158). Chicago, IL: ALA Editions.

Librarians work to broaden Vanderbilt's research reputation with Wikidata tools. (2020, August 10). *Vanderbilt University research news*. https://news.vanderbilt.edu/2020/08/10/librarians-work-to-broaden-vanderbilts-research-reputation-with-wikidata-tools/

Miller, M. (2019, May 22). Integrating Wikidata at the library of congress. *The Signal*. https://blogs.loc.gov/thesignal/2019/05/integrating-wikidata-at-the-library-of-congress/

Morley, J. (2018). Use and impact of cultural heritage images on Wikimedia Commons and Wikipedia. *Catching the Rain*. www.catchingtherain.com/portfolio/use-and-impact-of-cultural-heritage-images-on-wikimedia-commons-and-wikipedia

O'Gara, G. M., Woolcott, L., Joan Kelly, E., Muglia, C., Stein, A., & Thompson, S. (2018). Barriers and solutions to assessing digital library reuse: Preliminary findings. *Performance Measurement & Metrics*, *19*(3), 130–141. https://doi.org/10.1108/PMM-03-2018-0012

Perrin, J. M., Winkler, H., Daniel, K., Barba, S., & Yang, L. (2017). Know your crowd: A case study in digital collection marketing. *Reference Librarian*, *58*(3), 190–201. https://doi.org/10.1080/02763877.2016.1271758

Poulter, M. (2019, March 14). What Wikidata offers Oxford's GLAM digital strategy. *Bodleian Digital Library*. https://blogs.bodleian.ox.ac.uk/digital/2019/03/14/what-wikidata-offers-oxfords-glam-digital-strategy/

Poulter, M., & Sheppard, N. (2020). Wikimedia and universities: Contributing to the global commons in the age of disinformation. *Insights: The UKSG Journal*, *33*(14), 1–16.

Research: Supporting Commons contribution by GLAM institutions. (2018). Wikimedia Meta-Wiki. https://meta.wikimedia.org/wiki/Research:Supporting_Commons_contribution_by_GLAM_institutions

Scholia. (n.d.). *Scholia.* https://scholia.toolforge.org/

Silverwood Cope, S. (2012, February 8). Wikipedia: Page one of Google UK for 99% of searches. *The Pi Datametrics news and blog.* https://web.archive.org/web/20160313142831/www.pi-datametrics.com/wikipedia-page-one-of-google-uk-for-99-of-searches/

Szajewski, M. (2013). Using Wikipedia to enhance the visibility of digitized archival assets. *D-Lib Magazine*, *19*(3⁄4). https://doi.org/10.1045/march2013-szajewski

Terras, M. (2015). Opening access to collections: The making and using of open digitised cultural content. *Online Information Review*, *39*(5), 733–752. https://doi.org/10.1108/OIR-06-2015-0193

Waller, V. (2011). Searching where for what: A comparison of use of the library catalogue, Google and Wikipedia. *Library & Information Research*, *35*(110), 65–82.

Wikidata. (n.d.). *Wikidata: Licensing.* www.wikidata.org/wiki/Wikidata:Licensing

Wikidata. (n.d.). *Wikidata: Tours.* www.wikidata.org/wiki/Wikidata:Tours

Wikipedia. (n.d.). *Help: Editing.* https://en.wikipedia.org/wiki/Help:Editing

Wikipedia. (n.d.). *Help: Introduction.* https://en.wikipedia.org/wiki/Help:Introduction

Wikipedia. (n.d.). *Wikipedia: Copyrights.* https://en.wikipedia.org/wiki/Wikipedia:Copyrights

Wikipedia. (n.d.). *Wikipedia: Notability.* https://en.wikipedia.org/wiki/Wikipedia:Notability

Wikipedia. (n.d.). *Wikipedia: Sockpuppetry.* https://en.wikipedia.org/wiki/Wikipedia:Sockpuppetry#Role_accounts

Wikipedia. (n.d.). *Wikipedia: Username Policy.* https://en.wikipedia.org/wiki/Wikipedia:Username_policy

Wikimedia Commons. (n.d.). *Commons: First steps.* https://commons.wikimedia.org/wiki/Commons:First_steps

Wikimedia Commons. (n.d.). *Commons: Licensing.* https://commons.wikimedia.org/wiki/Commons:Licensing

Wikimedia Foundation. (n.d.). *Wikimedia projects.* https://wikimediafoundation.org/our-work/wikimedia-projects

Zentall, L., & Cloutier, C. (2008). The calisphere Wikipedia project: Lessons learned. *CSLA Journal*, *32*(1), 27–29.

8 Discoverability and Search Engine Visibility of Repository Platforms

Danping Dong and Chee Hsien Aaron Tay

Introduction

Scholarly institutional repositories (IRs) and data repositories established by higher education institutions or research institutes often have the major goal of managing, disseminating, and providing access to the research outputs produced by their researchers. The institution often highly prioritizes maximizing the visibility and readership of such scholarly content, and search engines are a crucial means to expose repository content to the academic community and a wider audience. This chapter includes a literature review on the discoverability of IRs and presents a case study comparing the discoverability and search engine visibility of two hosted repository solutions, Digital Commons and Figshare.

Literature Review

For the last decade or two, literature around IRs has focused more on measuring and often bemoaning the lower-than-expected deposit rates at IRs. Until lately, less attention had been given to measuring and improving the discoverability of collected IR content.

Early Studies on Discoverability of IR Content

In the 2010s, studies on discoverability focused on measuring "indexing ratios of IRs in Google Scholar" (Arlitsch & OBrien, 2012, p. 60) or, in other words, the percentage of IR content indexed in Google Scholar. At the time, Arlitsch and OBrien (2012) suggested two methods to determine indexing ratios in Google Scholar. The first method involved searching Google Scholar with the site command of the IR's domain and dividing the number of results by the total number of expected items in the IR that could be found in Google Scholar. This method yielded a shockingly low average of 30 percent. However, Google Scholar does not encourage this method because the site command only shows primary records from an IR. Arlitsch and OBrien's (2012) second method adopted a sampling approach to determine the indexing ratio of IRs by searching the title of each item in Google Scholar. Using this approach, they found three IRs with very

DOI: 10.4324/9781003216438-11

high indexing ratios (89–98 percent) while four others had major issues and were indexed at under 50 percent.

Although IR managers might not have expected their items to be highly ranked in the results, being listed in Google Scholar seems to be a fairly low barrier that was still not always met. Many IRs of the time had issues with being properly indexed in Google Scholar. Some of the significant known issues included the following:

- Many IRs support of Dublin Core instead of Google Scholar, which recommended Highwire Press, Eprints, Bepress, and Publishing Requirements for Industry Standard Metadata
- Lack of proper support (Open Archives Initiative Protocol for Metadata Harvesting [OAI-PMH] support was dropped) for standards such as sitemaps to inform Google Scholar of new records
- Poor navigation and a cross-linking structure that deterred Google Scholar bots from indexing the whole repository

However, over the years, members of the Google Scholar team, such as Anurag Acharya, as well as Monica Westin, who was the Google Scholar Partnerships Lead, have been communicating more with IR developers and managers, and are providing guidance on best practices, common pitfalls, and fixes for common indexing issues (Acharya, 2015; Westin, 2019, 2021). These efforts have helped improve the discoverability of IRs as measured by their indexing ratios. This is particularly true for popular, well-established IR systems like DSpace, Eprints, and Digital Commons which have worked with Google Scholar over the years to ensure reasonable out-of-the-box settings that have resolved many problems that would have previously resulted in low indexing ratios (COAR, 2018). Still, it is highly recommended to check for best practices with peers or the platform vendor when setting up an IR. It is also equally important to conduct periodic checks. Westin's (2021) recent talk could serve as a guide for beginners. Furthermore, the checklists for DSpace repositories (EIFL, 2021) and COAR Repository Toolkit (COAR, 2018) will also prove helpful.

Metrics for Measuring the Discoverability of IRs

To begin measuring the discoverability of IRs, reliable metrics are needed for comparison. Arlitsch and OBrien's 2015 paper and toolkit is important in the area of measuring discoverability in IRs. It provides a step-by-step guide on how libraries can measure and monitor the search engine optimization (SEO) of IRs. The guide advocated monitoring not just Google Analytics but also Google Webmaster Tools, now known as Google Search Console.

OBrien et al. (2016) note that there is a need to combine web analytics metrics from both page tagging analytics (e.g., Google Analytics) and log file analytics (e.g., build-in packages built into DSpace and Eprints). However, both methods have risks in terms of over- or under-counting metrics such as visits, downloads, and page views. While web analytics from page tagging are popular and typically easy to analyze, they can only capture HTML views or page loads. This is problematic because the major source of traffic to IR content is visits to the PDFs of resources directly via Google Scholar. In particular, they showed that relying solely on Google Analytics seriously under-counts file downloads when using page views as a proxy.

On the other hand, while log analysis can track all the content that users have interacted with, rather than only HTML, it has traditionally been more difficult to analyze (though improvements in technology have reduced this issue). More seriously, log analysis metrics are prone to over-counting because it is difficult to distinguish bots and web scrapers that hit the servers. Some estimate as much as 30–50 percent of log traffic comes from bots.

Therefore, it is clear that to get a complete picture of the analytics of IRs, we will need to use a hybrid system. One common and highly popular solution is leveraging the use of the free Google Analytics and Google Search Console tools together with an IR's logging features, though the use of Google products comes with privacy concerns.

In particular, Google Search Console is powerful as it allows the tracking of every page-click to the handle (aka URL) of every repository item that appears in the Google Search Engine Result Page. In other words, it "provides accurate non-HTML download counts executed directly from all Google search engine results pages (SERP)" (Arlitsch et al., 2020, p. 317), which avoids the issue of Google Analytics not capturing such downloads.

Standardizing Metrics Across Institutions – RAMP, IRUS-UK – and the Making Data Count Project

As IRs started to band together to compare notes, it was natural to consider whether the metrics collected across different repositories could be standardized for benchmarking purposes. For example, when comparing log analysis results, it would be beneficial to have the same procedure and lists of bots to be filtered to allow metrics collected around different repositories to be comparable. If repositories were using Google Analytics and/or Google Search Console, using the same parameters for comparison was beneficial.

There are two major approaches to benchmarking repository metrics. First, in 2017, the Repositories Analytics & Metrics Portal (RAMP) was launched by Michigan State University Library and partners such as OCLC Research and Association of Research Libraries, with Institute of Museum and Library Services research funding (Arlitsch et al., 2018; OBrien et al., 2017). RAMP (https://rampanalytics. org/) is a web service to collect, standardize, and analyze Google Search Console data from participating repositories with data aggregated in an Elasticsearch index. Each registered institution is given access to a set of dashboards on Kibana. At present, over 60 IRs from multiple countries are included.

Second, we have the Institutional Repository Usage Statistics UK (IRUS-UK) group run by JISC in the UK. While RAMP focuses on aggregating and standardizing Google Search Console data, IRUS-UK focuses on handling log data files and processing them into a standardized Counting Online Usage of Networked Electronic Resources (COUNTER) statistics (MacIntyre & Jones, 2016). Similar to RAMP, once registration into IRUS-UK is done and data is being sent, usage can be checked via the web portal, which provides various reports and visualizations at the institutional or item level. IRs like Eprints, Figshare, Pure, and DSpace have tracker code plugins and patches that can help submit data to IRUS-UK.

While standardized COUNTER statistics techniques can be easily applied to articles, IRs today also collect research data. Is there a COUNTER standard for research datasets?

This is where the Making Data Count project comes in, which introduced the COUNTER Code of Practice for Research Data in 2018. While research dataset usage can be defined easily as downloads or views (at the file or dataset level), the lack of standardized definitions means that the tracking and display of such statistics by repositories and stakeholders is, to some extent, arbitrary. As Lowenberg et al. (2019) put it, "Currently, to compare the downloads across datasets within a repository, or across repositories, would be comparing apples to oranges, as we do not know where these numbers are derived from, nor exactly what they apply to" (p. 30). A standard that is not adopted is not helpful. At the time of writing, uptake of the COUNTER Code of Practice for Research Data is promising. Data repositories, repository systems, and aggregator organizations who have adopted this include Figshare, Dryad, Zenodo, Dataverse, DataONE, and Caltech.

Google Dataset Search – the New Kid on the Block

While most repository managers are familiar with Google Scholar and Google, in 2018, Google added a new search engine exclusively for datasets, The Google Dataset Search, which quickly came out of beta in January 2020, and has since attracted considerable interest.

Without going into specific details, the Google Dataset Search bot crawls web-pages looking for Schema.org markup to index. This is also stated as a requirement for repositories to be listed on it. Similar to Google Scholar, a sitemap is not strictly required but is highly recommended.

Do most data repository systems support this? "A data citation roadmap for scholarly data repositories" report listed the following requirement as *recommended*: "The machine-readable metadata should use Schema.org markup in JSON-LD format" (Fenner et al., 2019, Table 8.1 Guidelines for Repositories). However, with the launch of Google Dataset Search, many data repository vendors such as Figshare, Mendeley Data, Zenodo, and Dryad support this so as to be listed in Google Dataset Search.

Because this development was relatively recent at the time of writing, there are limited guidelines (https://datasetsearch.research.google.com/help) and research on the discoverability of repository items in Google Dataset Search, although it is likely that many of the usual Google Scholar techniques work. Sampling datasets in Google Dataset Search may be a worthwhile exercise to ensure that most datasets are properly indexed and to use markup tools to verify the quality of metadata in the markup. The FAQ for Google Dataset Search offers more details by discussing the use of Markup Helper to create metadata and the Structured Data Testing Tool to verify if the metadata is correct. Unfortunately, while many data repositories, such as Figshare, Dryad, Dataverse, and Mendeley Data, support Schema.org,[1] many others may not. This is bad, particularly as there is increasing evidence that supporting Schema.org might increase discoverability.

What if you have a data repository but do not have the capability to add Schema.org to the landing pages? Are you completely invisible? Not quite. Chances are you registered your dataset with a DataCite DOI, and DataCite has done some work to ensure their entry is indexed in Google. As datacite.org states,

> If a data repository doesn't provide schema.org metadata via the dataset landing page, the next best option is the indexers that store metadata about the dataset. DataCite Search is such a place, and in early 2017 we started to embed schema.org metadata in DataCite Search pages for individual DOIs, and we generated a sitemaps file (or rather files) for the over 10 million DOIs we have.
>
> (Cousijn et al., 2018)

Unpaywall and Other Non-Google Channels

While Google, Google Scholar, and Google Dataset Search are the major sources of visitors, there might be a need to ensure that discoverability in other aggregators, indexes, and search engines is not neglected. Before doing so, the low-hanging fruit is to ensure that the repository is listed in registries of repositories whenever possible, as this is where aggregators generally start. At the time of writing, three major registries exist:

- OpenDOAR (https://v2.sherpa.ac.uk/opendoar/)
- Registry of Open Access Repositories (http://roar.eprints.org/)
- Registry of Research Data Repositories (www.re3data.org/)

Some sources worth checking for discoverability of content are as follows:

- CORE (https://core.ac.uk/)
- BASE (www.base-search.net/)
- OpenAIRE (www.openaire.eu/)
- Unpaywall (https://unpaywall.org/)
- OpenAlex (https://openalex.org/)

Other sources that the University of Liège Library used to optimize their repository to make it more discoverable (Bastin & Renaville, 2018) include the following:

- PubMed LinkOut
- Primo Central Index

- Summon
- EBSCO Discovery Service

Of the aforementioned sources, Unpaywall may be one of the most important non-Google sources to ensure the discoverability of repository content, as it has become the de facto source that most abstracting and indexing databases, search engines, and link resolvers use to link to open access (OA) journal articles. Some of the important consumers of Unpaywall data include the following:

- Web of Science
- Scopus
- Dimensions
- SFX
- 360Link
- Primo link resolver

Besides driving repository usage, Unpaywall is also an important source of OA data for research studies and university rankings, such as the Centrum voor Wetenschap en Technologische Studies Leiden Ranking. Given the ease of querying Unpaywall to check OA status, most research studies use Unpaywall data to determine the percentage of university output that is made OA. If such results are important, ensuring high discoverability of repository content with quality metadata in Unpaywall is also important.

If an IR is not yet indexed in Unpaywall, a request to be indexed (https://unpaywall.org/sources) can be submitted. Like Google Scholar, the Unpaywall bot may sometimes have issues while fully indexing repository content. According to the support page (https://support.unpaywall.org/support/solutions/articles/44001937113-how-are-documents-located-from-repository-records-), Unpaywall uses OAI-PMH to identify records and attempts to look for a URL leading to a record. Depending on the repository setup, the URL is often not the PDF but a landing html page, and from there, the Unpaywall bot will try to identify the direct link to the full text, typically a PDF or an html page. Unpaywall is often *smart* enough to identify the full-text link, although it is not 100 percent reliable.

Unpaywall also needs two pieces of metadata information that is sometimes hard to come by in typical repository setups:

- Version of full text
- Usage license

When testing your repository for discoverability in Unpaywall, consider doing the following:

1. Do an internal calculation on the percentage of repository records with full text.
2. Run the Unpaywall application programming interface (API) over your repository records (using DOIs as a priority followed by title) to calculate the same metric based on Unpaywall data.

3. Compare (1) and (2); if they are significantly different, your repository may have a problem with indexing by Unpaywall.

In particular, the percentage of (2) can be lower than (1) because it indicates that either the record itself is not indexed by Unpaywall or the metadata record is indexed but Unpaywall is unable to locate the full text. For better accuracy of OA status on Unpaywall, it is also important to check the field reflecting the OA status (some IRs use the license field) and to ensure that the field is properly captured by Unpaywall. Working with Unpaywall support to resolve any existing issues may be required.

Repository managers should also be familiar with the following Unpaywall support pages (https://support.unpaywall.org/support/solutions/folders/44000583618); a few important ones include the following:

*   Recommendation for IRs: Version reporting https://support.unpaywall.org/support/solutions/articles/44000826872-recommendation-for-irs-version-reporting
*   How are repository records matched to published articles? https://support.unpaywall.org/support/solutions/articles/44001937102-how-are-repository-records-matched-to-published-articles-
*   How are documents located from repository records? https://support.unpaywall.org/support/solutions/articles/44001937113-how-are-documents-located-from-repository-records-
*   Recommendation for IRs: License reporting https://support.unpaywall.org/support/solutions/articles/44002198169-recommendation-for-irs-license-reporting

Discoverability and SEO of Hosted Solutions

Chapter 2 discussed several features and functionalities affecting the discoverability of content from outside of the repository platform, including metadata management, support of harvesting standards and protocols, as well as SEO. Certain adjustments and improvements can be made to a repository to improve its discoverability (Macgregor, 2019). For tweaking and adjusting repository settings to improve discoverability, open-source solutions often offer more flexibility as changes can be made when needed. In comparison, it might be less straightforward, or sometimes not possible, to customize certain technical aspects of a proprietary hosted solution, hence the need to thoroughly investigate its discoverability and SEO before adoption. Whether to run an open-source or proprietary repository solution depends on the institutional context. Institutions that adopt an open-source solution often need to hire staff with the relevant technical expertise to implement and maintain the repository software, whereas institutions with proprietary solutions may often place more emphasis on day-to-day operations, growing content, and supporting faculty services, leaving the technical aspects to the vendor. For adopters of hosted and proprietary solutions, it is important to make sure that the right choice is made at the beginning.

There has been little prior research attempting to answer the question of whether repository platforms inherently differ in terms of their discoverability and SEO. Comparing existing repositories hosted on different platforms is not helpful; it will be neither a fair comparison nor statistically convincing as a post-hoc analysis that does not control for or isolate other factors that impact usage and discoverability, such as quality and age of the papers and subject disciplines.

The case study in the next section of this chapter outlines a method that uses a randomized controlled trial (RCT) to compare two hosted solutions, Digital Commons and Figshare. It attempts to examine whether these two platforms differ in their ability to attract downloads to hosted papers. It also explores patterns of paper indexing and visibility in Google Scholar. The method as well as the results may provide some useful information for institutions that are planning to adopt a hosted IR or are considering switching to another platform.

Case Study: Comparing Discoverability of Digital Commons and Figshare

We conducted an RCT to compare the downloads of two hosted IR solutions, Digital Commons and Figshare, and explored the patterns used for indexing their records in Google Scholar.

This case study is conducted using the IR and data repository of Singapore Management University (SMU), hosted on Digital Commons and Figshare, respectively. SMU has been running its IR, InK (https://ink.library.smu.edu.sg/), on Digital Commons since 2011. In April 2020, SMU started its Research Data Repository (RDR) (https://researchdata.smu.edu.sg/) with the hosted solution Figshare. While Figshare is more well-known as an RDR, some institutions also use Figshare as an all-in-one repository for mixed types of research outputs, including publications, for example, Carnegie Mellon University's KiltHub Repository (https://kilthub.cmu.edu/). While this is a possible direction for SMU to move toward in the future, we do not plan to rush migrating to a new repository and risk losing the existing advantages of Digital Commons, such as good discoverability, comprehensive statistics, and institutional users' familiarity and acceptance.

In 2021, we conducted an exploratory project to study the feasibility of using Figshare as an IR and to compare it with Digital Commons. One major objective of this project was to understand the discoverability and search engine visibility of the repository. Therefore, we decided to conduct an experiment to study whether the downloads of deposited papers will be impacted by the IR platform used.

Methodology

Hypothesis Development

The main purpose of this study was to explore whether any platform difference exists between Digital Commons and Figshare in attracting downloads to deposited academic publications. We planned to experiment with two random groups of full-text journal articles uploaded to both platforms around the same time. The usage and download statistics of both groups were tracked and monitored over seven months. We worked with the assumption that other factors affecting downloads, such as quality of the article and popularity of research topics, will be randomized among the two groups. Therefore, the difference in download counts can serve as a reasonable approximation of the platform discoverability difference between Digital Commons and Figshare.

We established the following hypothesis:

H0: There is no difference in average paper downloads between Figshare and Digital Commons.
H1: Average paper downloads differ between Figshare and Digital Commons.

The significance level was set to 0.05.

Setting Up Test Collections of Randomly Assigned Full-Text Records

To compare the platform discoverability of Digital Commons and Figshare, we decided to use download counts, which is a reasonable measure of usage resulting from web traffic driven to the repository. We set up two test collections with randomly selected journal articles on both platforms. The source of the articles was SMU's Current Research Information System (CRIS), which is used by our faculty to update their publications for reporting purposes. The disciplinary coverage of the articles thus included social sciences, business, computing, law, economy, and accountancy, contributed by faculty from the six schools of SMU.

A total of 96 journal article records with full-text PDFs were exported from CRIS. Half the records (48) were uploaded to InK, SMU's IR hosted on Digital Commons, and the other half to SMU RDR on Figshare. As seen in Figure 8.1, 79.3 percent of the articles were published recently in 2020 and 2021, which is expected as most faculty use CRIS to report on their latest academic publications.

For the rest of this chapter, Digital Commons will be used to refer to InK records, and Figshare will be used for records uploaded to RDR.

We also attempted to control for the assignment of articles by discipline, a factor known to affect usage metrics such as citations (Harzing, 2016; Marx &

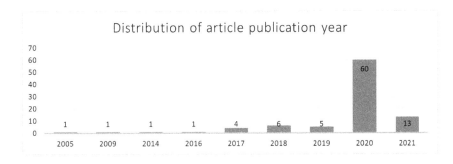

Figure 8.1 Distribution of article publication year in the sample (by count)

Bornmann, 2015). As mentioned earlier, the SMU schools associated with the records can serve as an approximation of the research areas of the articles, that is, social sciences, business, computing and information systems, law, economy, and accountancy. Within each research area, records were randomly divided by half and assigned to Digital Commons and Figshare.

Data Collection

The journal article metadata and full-text PDF were uploaded to both platforms toward the end of March 2021. Monthly download count statistics of each article from both platforms were collected from April to October 2021. The default download counts in Figshare include bots downloads, which are excluded in the statistics from Digital Commons. We therefore requested download counts excluding bots downloads from Figshare, who readily provided this information.

During the course of the study, a few records were removed because of issues such as duplication or author request. The final dataset as of December 2021 contained 45 valid records from Digital Commons and 47 from Figshare.

In June 2021, we discovered that records from Digital Commons were not properly indexed by Google Scholar, which might affect the discoverability of Figshare and our ability to perform a fair comparison between the two platforms. We approached Figshare support and were advised to fix issues with the field used for publication dates, which may have caused Google Scholar to ignore the Figshare records. After fixing the issue, we noted that the records appeared in Google Scholar around the end of July. To minimize the impact of this incident, we will analyze both the full dataset and a subset of the collected data from August 2021 onward.

In addition to testing the proposed hypothesis, we were also interested in exploring how records from our repositories were indexed in Google Scholar. In late September, we did a round of checking and data collection about Google Scholar indexing and added three additional fields to the dataset. We searched for each article by title and checked the following:

1) Whether the record is indexed in Google Scholar at all
2) If the record is in Google Scholar, whether our record is the only copy providing a unique PDF among the different versions of the same article after clicking "All n versions"
3) Whether our record is shown as the primary record in Google Scholar (see Figure 8.2)

Figure 8.2 Example of a primary record from Figshare on Google Scholar

Results

For this research, we used a two-sample t-test and a few other statistical tests, such as Levene's test, to assess our hypothesis and analyze the collected data. The analysis was conducted using Python in Jupyter Notebook, and the analysis can be reproduced with the raw data and code publicly shared on SMU RDR (Dong & Tay, 2022).

Hypothesis Testing

Some descriptive statistics are included for the 92 records in Table 8.1.

According to Table 8.1, the mean download count of Digital Commons is 51 and that of Figshare is 64. We used Levene's test to assess the equality of variances.

LeveneResult(statistic=0.3513837444070336, pvalue=0.5548174249693081)

The resulting p-value = 0.55 implies that the variances between the two groups are not significant. We then used a two-sided standard independent two-sample t-test that assumes equal variance to test our null hypothesis that there is no difference in average paper downloads between Figshare and Digital Commons. The result of the t-test is included in the following:

Ttest_indResult(statistic=-0.5260135324877442,pvalue=0.600172599662083)

The p-value is 0.596 and greater than the specified significance level of 0.05. Therefore, we failed to reject H1, which leads to the conclusion that there is no statistically significant difference in the download counts between the two platforms.

Additional Analysis Related to Google Scholar

We conducted further analysis on the data collected about Google Scholar to explore and gain insights on the discoverability of records in search engines and to observe if there are any patterns and relationships between how records are indexed and the associated downloads. The analysis and results are presented in the following, providing some answers and insights to the three questions raised earlier.

Table 8.1 Descriptive statistics of Digital Commons versus Figshare downloads

Name of IR	Count	Mean	Std	Min	25%	50%	75%	Max
InK (Digital Commons)	45.0	51.311111	78.227472	1.0	8.0	23.0	47.0	354.0
RDR (Figshare)	47.0	64.021277	142.855885	0.0	6.0	26.0	59.0	934.0

1) Compare download counts for records indexed versus not indexed by Google Scholar

All 45 Digital Commons records are indexed by Google Scholar, reaching a 100 percent indexing rate. However, we noticed that 20 percent (n = 9) of the Digital Commons records do not appear with a [PDF] icon next to the record, even though full-text PDFs are available in the repository. These nine records neither provide a unique PDF nor are they the primary records. There are alternate OA copies on Google Scholar; one has to click the "All n versions" button, and the Digital Commons record is usually not prominent on that page.

On the other hand, 68 percent of the 47 Figshare records are indexed by Google Scholar as of September 2021. The records that do not show up on Google Scholar can still be found in Google, which means that the download traffic observed for these articles might be mainly from Google. There are no obvious patterns observed in these non-indexed articles. Almost all of them can be found in Google Scholar with alternative sources of metadata or full text. There is no clear reason why our Figshare full-text records are picked up by Google but not by Google Scholar.

As there is no statistically significant difference between download counts of Digital Commons and Figshare, we do not differentiate by platform when comparing downloads between indexed and non-indexed records. Due to the Google Scholar indexing issue for Figshare records described earlier in this chapter, we decided to only include data from August to October 2021 for a fair comparison. Similar to the earlier analysis, we used Levene's test for equality of variance and t-test for comparing downloads. We also performed the Mann–Whitney U-test as the sample size of non-indexed records was relatively small (n = 16). The results are presented in the following:

LeveneResult(statistic=0.4149103399346608, pvalue=0.521125917434428)
Ttest_indResult(statistic=0.5681030671982966, pvalue=0.5713796493618881)
MannwhitneyuResult(statistic=581.5, pvalue=0.9704388586933024)

Based on the results, there is no observed difference in the variance of indexed v non-indexed records. Both the t-test and Mann–Whitney U-test show that there is no statistically significant difference in the download counts of indexed versus non-indexed records in Google Scholar. This is a surprising result that we will discuss later in this chapter.

2) Compare records that provide a unique PDF in Google Scholar versus those that do not

Another question explored was whether a record that provides the only full-text PDF in Google Scholar is correlated with higher downloads. As seen in Table 8.2, there are a total of 77 records indexed by Google Scholar, and 44.2 percent (n = 34) of the records provide the only full-text PDF in Google Scholar. In addition, 88.2 percent (n = 30) of them did appear as primary records, which is somewhat expected because Google Scholar is likely to prioritize the ranking of such records in the algorithm.

We conducted Levene's test and found that the variances between the two groups are not equal. Subsequently, we used a one-sided t-test to test the

Table 8.2 Descriptive statistics of download counts for records with and without a unique PDF

Unique PDF	Count	Mean	Std	Min	25%	50%	75%	Max
False	43.0	31.4	47.8	0.0	6.00	16.0	35.50	257.0
True	34.0	98.8	173.5	4.0	16.75	40.0	90.75	934.0

Table 8.3 Descriptive statistics for download counts of primary versus non-primary records

Primary Record	Count	Mean	Std	Min	25%	50%	75%	Max
FALSE	22.0	12.1	11.4	0.0	4.00	7.5	21.25	42.0
TRUE	52.0	82.5	146.6	1.0	13.75	37.5	79.50	934.0
not sure	3.0	51.7	15.0	36.0	44.50	53.0	59.50	66.0

hypothesis that records with unique PDFs are correlated with higher downloads. The results confirmed our hypothesis with a p-value less than 0.05. The mean download count of records with unique PDFs (98.8/article) is 2.15 times higher compared to records with non-unique PDFs (31.4/article).

LeveneResult(statistic=4.595255876125392, pvalue=0.03530232522808095)
Ttest_indResult(statistic=2.2001087678993465, pvalue=0.01706324
7719817036)

From the results, it can be inferred that IR records that provide a unique PDF in Google Scholar are positively correlated with a higher number of downloads compared to records with full-text PDFs that were already available elsewhere.

3) Compare primary versus non-primary records in Google Scholar

We also speculated that when we have records that show up as primary records in Google Scholar, these records should be able to get more downloads compared to non-primary records, since the primary records get more exposure and visibility when searching. Therefore, we compared the download counts of these two groups, and the descriptive statistics are listed in Table 8.3. Three records were excluded from the analysis due to inaccurate primary links, owing to a technical issue from Figshare during the course of the study.

As seen from Table 8.3, the mean download count of primary records (n = 52) was 82.5 per article, which is 5.8 times higher compared to non-primary records (n = 22). We used Levene's test and a one-sided t-test to show that the two groups do not have equal variance and that the download count of primary records is higher than that of non-primary records. Test results are indicated in the following:

LeveneResult(statistic=4.083484886906183, pvalue=0.04702404022812365)
Ttest_indResult(statistic=3.437979553995462, pvalue=0.000577941
6388394055)

Discussion

1   *The Two Platforms Do Not Differ Significantly in Terms of Attracting Paper Downloads*

The main research question of this study is whether there is any platform-level difference in terms of exposing OA content and attracting downloads between Digital Commons and Figshare. Based on the results of the RCT study, the two platforms do not differ significantly in their ability to expose IR content and attract paper downloads.

As repository managers, it is important to assess platform discoverability when selecting a hosted IR solution. One of the major goals of IRs is often to increase the visibility and readership of an institution's research outputs to reach a wider audience; the number of paper downloads is an important indicator and metric to measure how successful an IR is in achieving this goal. Institutions that would like to start an IR or would like to move to another platform should thoroughly investigate platform discoverability and SEO by performing literature searches, investigating existing repositories, or if circumstances allow, conducting a pilot test or comparison study such as the one outlined in this paper.

Both platforms are satisfactory in terms of their discoverability and content usage. We have been using the Digital Commons platform as our IR for more than 10 years and are happy with the usage reaching a total of 5.9 million downloads (as of November 2021). Digital Commons is considered to be a mature hosted IR solution, having existed for 17 years, and is claimed to be optimized for indexing by Google, Google Scholar, and other major search engines. Figshare was launched in 2011 and is more well-known as an RDR focusing on non-publication outputs. In 2017, Figshare gradually added more IR functionality and started describing itself as an "all in one repository" (Hyndman, 2018). Interestingly, the downloads of journal article content type on Figshare are at a similar level with a more established platform such as Digital Commons, confirming Figshare's potential to serve as a decent publications repository in addition to being a data repository.

Nevertheless, some differences exist between the platforms pertaining to Google Scholar indexing. Digital Commons achieved a 100 percent indexing rate in our study, although some of the full-text records are not correctly indicated as such on the platform, and direct links to the PDFs are not shown to Google Scholar users. In comparison, the indexing ratio of Figshare is only 68 percent and is therefore lower than expected. Although this did not result in a significant difference in downloads in our experiment, there might be other downstream implications. It is reasonable to expect that researchers might be concerned if their papers do not appear on Google Scholar, which likely caters to a more academic audience who is more likely to cite these papers.

We speculate that the indexing ratio for Figshare records is lower because after the initial publication date issue with Google Scholar was fixed, the re-indexing of our Figshare repository was partial and incomplete. Given more time, some of the records might eventually appear on Google Scholar. If this is the case, our poor indexing ratio should be regarded with a pinch of salt. Further investigation, such as repeating the experiment with another batch upload of test records on Figshare, could be done to measure the indexing ratio again to rule out this possibility. It is also possible that some other reasons innate to the platform might have caused the relatively lower Google Scholar indexing ratio. Therefore, based on the results from this experiment so far, Digital Commons seems to be more consistent and reliable in terms of exposing its content to Google Scholar.

2   *Google Versus Google Scholar Referrals*

Based on our earlier analysis, Google Scholar indexed versus non-indexed records do not differ significantly in terms of the number of downloads. The result is also in agreement with our observation during the experiment itself. However, from April to July, there was a problem with Google Scholar indexing for Figshare records. Even though we excluded data from this period from the analysis, we observed that the downloads during that period do not seem to be affected much, if at all.

We also obtained the referral statistics provided by Digital Commons for all time and calculated the percentage of downloads contributed by Google.com and Google Scholar (see Table 8.4).

Table 8.4 shows that Google.com alone contributed to 61 percent of total download traffic for our InK repository, considerably higher than the download referrals from Google Scholar (26 percent). Both search engines under Google contributed to 88 percent of our entire site's traffic, clearly demonstrating the crucial impact of search engine traffic on the usage of IRs. In comparison, only 7 percent of the downloads occur on the IR site itself. This aligns with results from another study on Strathprints, the University of Strathclyde repository, which found that 56 percent of all referrals came from Google, followed by 26 percent from Google Scholar (Macgregor, 2020).

Although the results from our experiment seem to suggest that being indexed in Google Scholar is not a significant factor correlated with higher download counts, we should not underestimate the importance of Google Scholar for IRs. First, it could be argued that traffic that occurred in Google Scholar may have a higher

Table 8.4 Referral analysis of InK downloads since launch

	No. of Referred Downloads	*% of Contributed Downloads*
Google only	2845405	61%
Google Scholar only	1210470	26%
Google and Google Scholar	4055875	88%
InK	336782	7%
Total	4631336	

chance of leading to a future citation, as more academic research-related searches are likely to happen in Google Scholar than in Google. From the perspective of an IR manager, we should emphasize exposing our institution's content to the research community, and the fact that Google Scholar is a vital channel to achieve this goal. In addition, Google Scholar itself also contributed significantly to download traffic, as seen from InK's historical data for all our repository records.

Furthermore, repository managers should not assume proper indexing of all repository records by Google Scholar, especially when starting a new repository. Configuration of publication dates on our Figshare repository was an unexpected issue that resulted in a Google Scholar indexing problem. Repository managers should therefore take a special effort to check and track the indexing of records in Google Scholar.

3   Further Analysis of Unique and Primary Records

Our exploratory analysis earlier suggested that records providing a unique PDF, or records that display as the primary records, are both likely to receive higher downloads. It is reasonable that primary records are likely to get higher downloads since they are more prominent when people search in Google Scholar. It is also plausible that being the unique OA source for a paper increases the likelihood for a user to eventually download the article from the repository, compared to when the IR needs to compete with other OA services and repositories such as ResearchGate, SSRN, publishers, and Arxiv.org. Moreover, the fact that a record is the unique source of an OA full text in Google Scholar also means that it is highly possible that it is the only OA copy on Google as well. All these factors might have contributed to the higher downloads for unique or primary records.

We also speculate that being a unique OA source is linked to a higher likelihood of being indexed by Google Scholar as a primary record. Based on Table 8.5, 90.6 percent of the records containing a unique full text in Google Scholar are listed as the primary record, compared to 54.8 percent for non-unique OA copies. Among the three copies that were unique but non-primary, one was not a primary record at the time of checking (September 2021) but has become a primary record since November 2021. The primary records of the other two articles both point to the publisher's official landing page with the "[HTML]" icon and, in both cases, lead

Table 8.5 Matrix of Google Scholar unique OA copy against primary record

Primary Record	Unique OA Copy		
	FALSE	*TRUE*	*Total*
FALSE	19	3	22
TRUE	23	29	52
Total	**42**	**32**	**74**

to the publisher's OA version of that article. One of the articles was found to be published in a fully OA journal, while the other was a gold OA article published in a hybrid journal. It is possible that Google Scholar was able to identify these two articles as publisher OA content, thus prioritizing them as primary records. That also means that our IR record in this case does not provide a unique OA copy even though it is the only record with a "[PDF]" button in Google Scholar.

The exact requirements and mechanism of becoming a primary record are unclear since Google does not make its algorithms transparent. However, providing a unique OA full text is more in the control of a repository. Theoretically, if an IR undertakes greater conscious effort in collecting unique OA full text that is not available elsewhere, it might help to attract more traffic to the repository. Realistically, most IRs will likely collect full text – whether or not there are already OA copies elsewhere – but it is still worth noting when planning and strategizing the development and growth of an IR.

We also closely analyzed records that do not provide a unique PDF in Google Scholar from Digital Commons (n = 29) and Figshare (n = 14). Among the non-unique records in Digital Commons, 65.5 percent (n = 19) appear as the primary record in Google Scholar, while 28.6 percent (n = 4) of the non-unique records in Figshare became the primary record. While this observed pattern could be purely incidental and possibly unrelated to the platform's intrinsic characteristics, it is interesting to explore whether platforms may be optimized so that there is a higher chance of their records being indexed by Google Scholar as primary records.

Limitations of This Study

One limitation of this study is the Figshare indexing issue by Google Scholar that occurred from April to June 2021. This was an unexpected episode that may or may not have impacted the results of this study. It should not have much impact on the main research question studying the discoverability of these two platforms, as our focus was on overall downloads to deposited papers and not specifically those from Google Scholar. Download patterns do not seem to differ before and after fixing the issue, and Google Scholar indexing was not correlated with higher downloads based on our results. Nevertheless, we are not sure if this issue had any impact on the lower-than-expected indexing rate of Google Scholar in our exploratory analysis.

Conclusion

By conducting an RCT of papers deposited in Digital Commons and Figshare, we were able to perform a fair comparison of their relative discoverability in terms of downloads to deposited papers. We concluded that there is no evidence supporting a platform-level difference. However, further exploratory analysis revealed a notable difference in their Google Scholar indexing ratio, yet this did not seem to affect the overall download counts. Our results, which are supported by prior literature, suggest that overall downloads might be heavily influenced by Google rather than Google Scholar, though further study is needed for confirmation. Our exploratory findings also suggest that records that are unique in Google Scholar or those that are listed as primary records tend to be associated with more downloads on average. However, due to a lack of controls, these results are preliminary. Future research can focus on the following:

1) Why are certain items deposited in Figshare not indexed by Google Scholar?
2) Attempt to unravel the relative importance of downloads from Google versus Google Scholar through the use of Google Search Console, Google Analytics, and log analysis (OBrien et al., 2016), as well as the possible long-term impact on citations for items not indexed in Google Scholar.

Note

1   A list can be seen here: https://zenodo.org/record/1263942#.W5VPiOgzbD4

References

Acharya, A. (2015, June 10). *Indexing repositories: Pitfalls and best practices – Media collections online*. https://media.dlib.indiana.edu/media_objects/9z903008w

Arlitsch, K., Kahanda, I., OBrien, P., Shanks, J. D., & Wheeler, J. (2018). *Data-driven improvement to institutional repository discoverability and use*. https://scholarworks.montana.edu/xmlui/handle/1/15631

Arlitsch, K., & OBrien, P. (2012). Invisible institutional repositories: Addressing the low indexing ratios of IRs in Google Scholar. *Library Hi Tech*, *30*(1), 60–81.

Arlitsch, K., & OBrien, P. (2015). Introducing the "getting found" web analytics cookbook for monitoring search engine optimization of digital repositories. *Qualitative and Quantitative Methods in Libraries (QQML)*, *4*, 947–953.

Arlitsch, K., Wheeler, J., Pham, M. T. N., & Parulian, N. N. (2020). An analysis of use and performance data aggregated from 35 institutional repositories. *Online Information Review*, *45*(2), 316–335. https://doi.org/10.1108/OIR-08-2020-0328

Bastin, M., & Renaville, F. (2018). *Open access discovery: ULiège experience with aggregators and discovery tools providers. Be proactive and apply best practices (if you can . . .)*. https://orbi.uliege.be/handle/2268/221340

COAR. (2018). *COAR repository toolkit*. https://coartraining.gitbook.io/coar-repository-toolkit/

Cousijn, H., Cruse, T., & Lammey, R. (2018, September 5). Taking discoverability to the next level: Datasets with DataCite DOIs can now be found through Google Dataset Search. *DataCite Blog*. https://blog.datacite.org/taking-discoverability-to-the-next-level/

Dong, D., & Tay Chee Hsien, A. (2022). *Data and code for the case study comparing discoverability of Digital Commons and Figshare*. SMU Research Data Respository (RDR). https://doi.org/10.25440/smu.19121768

EIFL. (2021). *EIFL checklist: How to make your OA repository work really well (Version 5) | EIFL*. www.eifl.net/resources/eifl-checklist-how-make-your-oa-repository-work-really-well-version-5

Fenner, M., Crosas, M., Grethe, J. S., Kennedy, D., Hermjakob, H., Rocca-Serra, P., Durand, G., Berjon, R., Karcher, S., Martone, M., & Clark, T. (2019). A data citation roadmap for scholarly data repositories. *Scientific Data, 6*(1), 28. https://doi.org/10.1038/s41597-019-0031-8

Harzing, A.-W. (2016). *Citation analysis across disciplines: The impact of different data sources and citation metrics.* https://harzing.com/publications/white-papers/citation-analysis-across-disciplines

Hyndman, A. (2018, December 11). *New funding information on Figshare items.* https://figshare.com/blog/New_funding_information_on_Figshare_items/446

Lowenberg, D., Chodacki, J., Fenner, M., Kemp, J., & Jones, M. B. (2019). *Open data metrics: Lighting the fire (Version 1)* [Computer software]. Zenodo. https://doi.org/10.5281/zenodo.3525349

Macgregor, G. (2019). Improving the discoverability and web impact of open repositories: Techniques and evaluation. *Code4Lib Journal, 43*, Article 43. https://journal.code4lib.org/articles/14180

Macgregor, G. (2020). Enhancing content discovery of open repositories: An analytics-based evaluation of repository optimizations. *Publications, 8*(1), 8. https://doi.org/10.3390/publications8010008

MacIntyre, R., & Jones, H. (2016). IRUS-UK: Improving understanding of the value and impact of institutional repositories. *The Serials Librarian, 70*(1–4), 100–105. https://doi.org/10.1080/0361526X.2016.1148423

Marx, W., & Bornmann, L. (2015). On the causes of subject-specific citation rates in Web of Science. *Scientometrics, 102*(2), 1823–1827. https://doi.org/10.1007/s11192-014-1499-9

OBrien, P., Arlitsch, K., Mixter, J., Wheeler, J., & Sterman, L. B. (2017). RAMP – the repository analytics and metrics portal: A prototype web service that accurately counts item downloads from institutional repositories. *Library Hi Tech, 35*(1), 144–158. https://doi.org/10.1108/LHT-11-2016-0122

OBrien, P., Arlitsch, K., Sterman, L., Mixter, J., Wheeler, J., & Borda, S. (2016). Under-counting file downloads from institutional repositories. *Journal of Library Administration, 56*(7), 854–874. https://doi.org/10.1080/01930826.2016.1216224

Westin, M. (2019, December). DSpace and Google Scholar webinar for Ghana. *EIFL.* https://www.eifl.net/resources/webinars-dspace-and-google-scholar

Westin, M. (2021, January 27). *Google Scholar indexing for repositories: Best practices and fixes for common indexing problems.* www.youtube.com/watch?v=C-miRaROsaE

Conclusion

Ensuring the intersection of system design and user behavior in the discovery process is an integral concern that all current and aspiring digital repository practitioners and designers should be cognizant about. At this intersection lies a more comprehensive understanding of the barriers that prevent discovery, as well as the means for overcoming them. In pursuit of this understanding, the chapters in this book have outlined the systemic elements of repositories, the functionality of metadata, the expectations and patterns of searchers, and the use cases that demonstrate these principles in action.

This book began with an examination of how digital repositories operate, from both a system and a metadata perspective. It examined common repository platforms used by libraries and outlined the similarities and differences in their system designs and functionalities. Then, it explored the metadata schemas used in these platforms, and how systems index and store information. Together, these two perspectives provide a broad overview of the ways in which digital repositories are structured and the key components of how they operate in order to build a baseline understanding of repositories for current and future practitioners. This approach included an exploration of linked data, including what it is, how it is created, and its impact on the discoverability of digital material. Later chapters in this book investigated what research on user search patterns has determined and how repository practitioners can use that information.

After providing this baseline understanding of repository systems, metadata, user groups, and discoverability within the repository, the last three chapters employed case studies to critically examine digital content discoverability and how it functions on platforms outside of the original repository. The chapters thus determined if exposure outside of a digital repository, including from the library discovery layer to integrating with Wikipedia and finally to the performance of a repository in browser searches, can have a broader impact.

A takeaway from this book for current and aspiring digital repository practitioners is the idea that the elements that allow for discovery can be examined through the lenses of systems, structure, search behavior, and space. In the following, we provide a detailed discussion of each of these key components.

DOI: 10.4324/9781003216438-12

Systems

Systems, at their core, are a series of functions and connections. Digital repository systems house and provide access to digital objects at the same time, enabling those objects to exist while providing the mechanisms for their search process to unfold.

George Macgregor's chapter "Digital Repositories and Discoverability: Definitions and Typology" examined digital repository systems. He defined a digital repository as a platform that houses digital objects, provides for the discovery of those objects through interoperable technology and standards, and manages digital content over time to promote persistence and preservation. He argues that "*discoverability* is a measure of the extent to which information systems or technologies purporting to be discoverable . . . are technically optimized to ensure it" (p. 13). Therefore, discoverability does not refer only to the tools and mechanics of how digital objects are found but also to the organization and ranking of information so that it is more *intuitive* to users. Macgregor examines the routes of discoverability, including natively within a repository and through local discovery systems, search engines, aggregators, linked data, and social networking services. He categorizes the types of repositories into instructional repositories, subject-based and preprint repositories, data repositories, mega-repositories, trusted digital repositories, learning objects repositories, and aggregating repositories. With this categorization, Macgregor proposes a typology of repositories that considers five characteristics: volume or size of the repository, object complexity, content heterogeneity, metadata curation, and governance.

Sharon Farnel, in her chapter "Understanding Repository Functionality and Structure", takes us further into an examination of the systemic nature of discovery. Farnel focuses on common repository platforms used in Galleries, Libraries, Archives, and Museums (GLAMR) institutions: DSpace, EPrints, Digital Commons, Samvera, CONTENTdm, Omeka, Mukurtu, and Dataverse. She examines repository features, including open-source capabilities, support for multiple object types, customization of metadata, availability of multilingual versions, and Open Archives Initiative Protocol for Metadata Harvesting (OAI-PMH) compliance, for each of the platforms. She notes that metadata within the repository is critical to discoverability, and variables for ensuring metadata effectiveness include tailoring and standardization, use of controlled vocabularies, and the extent of metadata description and customization. She observes that knowledge organization and the interconnectedness of objects (navigation) facilitate discoverability, and she discusses how each of the major repositories develops its navigation. The external components that impact discoverability include aggregations (facilitated by metadata interoperability) and the visibility of metadata to search engines. Perhaps most helpful of all, Farnel outlines the discoverability features (both internal and external) for each of the major systems, including the provision of key metadata schema, support for controlled vocabularies, use of persistent identifiers, organization of digital objects, navigation, search functionality (including sorting and display), multilingual capacities, and support for external harvesting or connection to other systems. This overview allows us to get a sense of the capacity and benefits of each system, and the challenges they present.

Structure

As mentioned in Chapters 1 and 2, metadata is one of the primary functions of all digital repository systems. To co-opt an architectural phrase, "form follows function"; therefore, the manner in which systems are designed relies heavily on their underlying metadata structures. Features such as facets or advanced search, even the structure of the design displayed to the user, are predicated on the structure of a repository's metadata schema(s).

In her chapter "Understanding the Role of Metadata in a Digital Repository", Jenn Riley categorizes the types of metadata standards, including conceptual models, structure standards, content standards, controlled vocabularies authority files, classification schemes, and markup language. She outlines the history of metadata in GLAMR institutions, using bibliographic description as an origin point, and shows the evolution of cataloging in response to structural changes in the physical carrier of the metadata record. Once metadata merges in a digital format, the limitations shift from what the physical carrier can handle to how systems and aggregators can communicate with one another or simple system interoperability. The next significant evolution in metadata was then less about a single record and more about breaking that record into discrete parts and assigning unique identifiers to both the descriptive elements and the relational elements, leading metadata structure to shift again and to now focus on connections and relationships between data points. Riley demonstrates how structured metadata can be used in a discovery system in search features such as facets, controlled vocabularies, algorithms and indexing, multi-language searching, and translation. One of the key points Riley made was to outline how, similar to system design, all metadata and structured information carries the potential for bias, overt or not. From the language used to record metadata to the capacity of the system to represent languages and scripts, emerging awareness about this bias is redirecting some of the efforts of metadata creators to examine the foundations of metadata structures and practices, thus moving practitioners "toward critical access to knowledge rather than simply discovery of items" (p. 63).

As an example of the potential to harness metadata in new and robust ways, Anna Neatrour and Teresa K. Hebron discuss the benefits of linked open data in their chapter "Understanding Linked Data and the Potential for Enhanced Discoverability". They note that linked data essentially means building relationships between data points. The purposes of linked data include interoperability, defining relationships that are flexible and open to communities outside of a Western-centric perspective, staving off obsolescence, facilitating aggregation of information, and ultimately making content more discoverable by increasing its access points. The authors also outline practical ways to engage with linked data, which include developing or reviewing policies, outlining clear metadata profiles and data models, finding appropriate controlled vocabulary sources, examining copyright issues, conducting environmental scans, and assessing staffing needs or availability. While noting that no single tool can be right for everyone working in linked data, the authors introduce potential tools that practitioners can consider, along with their strengths, and some examples of linked data projects in production.

Search Behavior

Understanding the intent driving digital repository users' search for material is important because not only does it inform collection development and digitization decisions, but it also inspires the ways in which standards are crafted by the professional community and how metadata is delivered in individual repositories. Therefore, every practitioner should aim to get to know users and how they search for, interact with, and interpret metadata and repository design.

In a central chapter of this book, "User Searching in Digital Repositories", Oksana Zavalina and Mary Burke outline user search behavior in exquisite detail. The central theme of their research shows that domain knowledge impacts search behavior and should inform both the design of repository system features and metadata construction. They begin by noting that the content and scope of digital repositories are geared toward specific audiences, from cultural heritage repositories that focus on primary source historical material to science repositories and open access repositories that contain educational material. Furthermore, users' expectations are shaped by their interactions with other online entities (such as search engines and social media); therefore, they expect more from the online sections of the library (digital repositories) than they do from traditional services. Observational studies are thus critical for helping practitioners to understand their audiences and design repository systems that better meet their users' needs.

Zavalina and Burke also define and articulate the research around searching and browsing in traditional library discovery systems, as well as the impacts of domain knowledge on search behavior. They note how searching and browsing behavior differs for digital repositories, observing that recent research has leaned away from "educating the users about navigating" (p. 93) repositories and has moved toward exposing digital repository resources through platforms and places where users already reside, such as social media platforms. They remark that it may be "more beneficial to invest resources into making materials available via the platforms the users are already comfortable navigating" (p. 93).

They briefly discuss how keyword searching can be studied and provide an overview of studies showing variations in average keyword length, with the primary takeaway being that an increase in domain knowledge tends to increase the number of terms in search queries. Similarly, domain knowledge also impacts the types or categories of search terms, with higher domain knowledge leading to more specific terms, and also increasing the likelihood of and methods for using facets, advanced searches, and other system features – a trend that practitioners should consider as they craft metadata and design search functions for their respective repositories. While there are substantive differences in audience needs and preferences, practitioners conducting research on audience engagement should also take into account flaws or design elements of system features that may also impact results.

For example, both Farnel and Riley noted that multilingual access is a major component of both systems and metadata structures. Zavalina and Burke also examine the need for a multilingual database to improve overall discovery, navigation, and metadata. This can be potentially achieved by expanding the browsing tools available in a repository or creating portals specific to a language. However, ensuring that all aspects of a repository – its system, metadata and structure, and available navigation – are consistently, appropriately, and authentically represented in that language remains a challenge. As Riley noted, this difficulty arises because some metadata structures are skewed toward an English- or Western-centric perspective. Here, it is useful to remind ourselves that Neatrour and Hebron provide some small hope that linked data can mitigate part of this multilingual interoperability with its capacity to break hierarchical metadata structures into discrete pieces that can be re-associated or re-connected differently based on the values and perceptions of different models. Similarly, Elizabeth Joan Kelly's examination of digital objects in Wikidata structures shows the potential to harness Wikidata's existing multilingual capacities. This also impacts how controlled vocabularies are crafted, structured, and presented in systems. Nonetheless, although controlled vocabularies remain an important access point for users, Zavalina and Burke note that some research has indicated that "conceptual models usually differed from those represented in the classification scheme" (p. 100).

Finally, Zavalina and Burke discuss the methods for conducting end-user studies, along with their associated benefits and limitations. They recommend a mixed-methods approach to utilize the strengths and minimize the pitfalls of each method. They also suggest that repository practitioners should consider conducting continual user studies to monitor and capture the changes and evolution of user search behavior.

Space

The spaces in which digital repository content resides outside of the repository can be thought of in at least two ways: as the location of the digital objects, such as copies available in aggregators or social media venues that link back to the original item in the repository, or as harvesting metadata about digital objects to facilitate their discovery. Regardless, considering space external to the repository is necessary to position digital object content in places frequented by potential users. To fully explore the opportunities presented by secondary and tertiary spaces, practitioners need to learn more about the digital ecosystem – how content can be aggregated, what elements are important for indexing, and the vagaries of ranking and algorithms. Maximizing the presence of a digital repository, and more specifically its digital objects, in spaces where users are more likely to find content may be just as critical to overall discovery as is the structure of data and development of intuitive systems.

Drawing upon the observation of Zavalina and Burke that user expectations are shaped by other online spaces and their idea that moving content into those spaces may increase its visibility and utilize the existing system functionality of those spaces, the case studies presented in Chapters 6–8 captured the idea of space. Each thus demonstrated a potential non-repository space where content could be discovered.

JoLinda Thompson and Sara Hoover, in their case study in the chapter "Discoverability Within the Library: Integrated Systems and Discovery Layers", explain the process and methods they used to integrate a specific collection from their institutional repository (IR) into their library's discovery layer. They provide an overview of integrations between repositories and discovery products to demonstrate some of the key challenges of the process, such as interoperability barriers, overlaps or duplication of resource records, differences in controlled vocabularies, record conversion difficulties, and normalization issues. They decided not to use interoperability features, such as the OAI-PMH harvest, in order to maintain granular control over the desired collection and the manner in which it was represented in the discovery system. Thompson and Hoover's details regarding the specific difficulties faced during this project, alongside their thought processes and ultimate conclusions, serve as an excellent template for current and future practitioners looking to implement a similar process.

In her chapter on "Discoverability Beyond the Library: Wikipedia", Elizabeth Joan Kelly explores the process of contributing repository content to Wiki spaces. She lists a range of institutions and repositories that tracked substantial improvements in traffic and online attention after including their digital content in Wikipedia and Wikidata. Practitioners can utilize Kelly's explanations and recommendations for key considerations in this process, including licensing, the ethics around reusing a digital object, an understanding of which types of digital objects would be most effective in spaces like Wikipedia versus those like social media platforms, and the importance of articulating the goal and supporting metrics used in the assessment phases. She also provides a quick and simple process for getting involved and familiar with Wikipedia and Wikidata, which are appropriate for a beginner, along with tools that any current or aspiring practitioner can use for their repository material.

Finally, in their research chapter on "Discoverability and Search Engine Visibility of Repository Platforms (Case Study)", Danping Dong and Chee Hsien Aaron Tay examine the performance of two repositories, Digital Commons and Figshare, in search engine discovery. They deliver an impressive outline of the discoverability and metric landscape of digital platforms, including where indexers get content from, the best metadata schemas to ensure exposure of IR data, and recommendations about where to register repositories. Their research found that both platforms performed equally as far as download counts were concerned but showed significant differences in indexing and display. Common issues affecting search engine discovery include non-prominent positioning of the primary record in cases where more than one open access copy was available and differences in indexing between Google and Google Scholar. Dong and Tay found a positive correlation between a digital object being the sole PDF provider in Google Scholar and the number of downloads that object received; furthermore, being listed as the primary record in Google Scholar correlated with higher downloads. Further, they noted that institutional repositories may be more likely to be indexed in Google than in Google Scholar. Since their experiment identified no major differences in downloads between the two repositories, Dong and Tay were encouraged by the performance of their repositories. However, they caution practitioners who are exploring the possibility of establishing an IR or who are switching to a new system to ensure that they assess repository discoverability or, at the very least, examine the available literature to determine what impacts may be likely on discoverability for their users.

As the authors in this book demonstrate, the four discovery elements – systems, structure, search behavior, and space – highlight known or traceable information about the environmental factors that influence digital repository users' discovery process. Echoing Zavalina and Burke's recommendation, we stress that continual assessment of digital repository discoverability and utility is an essential task for all digital repository practitioners. Without this assessment, all the labor that goes into creating and building a digital repository – selection, digitization, description, maintenance, and preservation – is essentially carried out in a bubble of the profession's perspectives instead of it being driven by the real needs of the communities we wish to benefit. It is our hope that both existing and emerging practitioners will take the ideas presented here and develop them further to expand the reach and impact of their own repositories.

Index

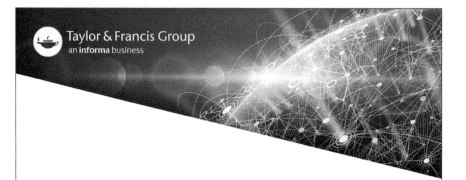

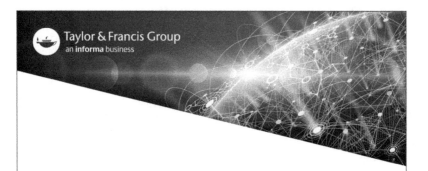